618 928588WIL 649.154 WIL

DATE DUE			

of related interest

Understanding Autism Spectrum Disorders
Frequently Asked Questions
Diane Yapko
ISBN 1 84310 756 2

Asperger's Syndrome
A Guide for Parents and Professionals
Tony Attwood
Foreword by Lorna Wing
ISBN 1 85302 577 1

Parenting a Child with Asperger Syndrome
200 Tips and Strategies
Brenda Boyd
ISBN 1 84310 137 8

Caring for a Child with Autism
A Practical Guide for Parents
Martine Ives and Nell Munro
ISBN 1 85302 996 3

Multicoloured Mayhem
Parenting the Many Shades of Adolescents and Children
with Autism, Asperger Syndrome and AD/HD
Jacqui Jackson
ISBN 1 84310 171 8

How to live with Autism and Asperger Syndrome

Practical Strategies for Parents and Professionals

Chris Williams and Barry Wright

Illustrated by Olive Young

Jessica Kingsley Publishers
London and Philadelphia

First published in 2004
by Jessica Kingsley Publishers
116 Pentonville Road
London N1 9JB, UK
and
400 Market Street, Suite 400
Philadelphia, PA 19106, USA

www.jkp.com

Reprinted twice in 2005

Library of Congress Cataloging in Publication Data

Williams, Chris, 1955-
    How to live with autism and asperger syndrome : practical strategies for parents and profession-
als / Chris Williams and Barry Wright ; illustrations by Olive Young.-- 1st American ed.
        p. cm.
    Includes bibliographical references and index.
    ISBN 1-84310-184-X (pbk.)
    1. Autism in children. 2. Asperger's syndrome. I. Wright, Barry. II. Young, Olive. III. Title.
RJ506.A9W485 2004
618.92'8588--dc22

                                                            2004010438

British Library Cataloguing in Publication Data
A CIP catalogue record for this book is available from the British Library

ISBN-13: 978 1 84310 184 0
ISBN-10: 1 84310 184 X

Printed and Bound in Great Britain by
Athenaeum Press, Gateshead, Tyne and Wear

Contents

List of figures and tables

Acknowledgements

We would like to thank many people for their help and support throughout the writing of this book. Thanks to Olive for her wonderful illustrations. Thanks to Gill Callaghan, Jenny Cook, Julie Wrigley-Howe and Anne McLaren for their reviews and helpful comments during the book's preparation. Thanks to all the children and young people we have worked with who have taught us so much and to their parents who encouraged us to write this book. Thanks to all our colleagues who supported us throughout this year. We would like to acknowledge Hilton Davis for his work on the Parent Advisor Model, which has influenced our approach to working with families. Most of all, thanks to our own families for their patience and encouragement and especially to Julia and Paul.

Authors' note

All of the case studies in this book are based around our clinical experience of working with children and young people with Autism Spectrum Disorders and their families. Names and personal details have been changed and transposed to protect confidentiality.

Preface

Parents of children with Autism Spectrum Disorders (ASD) often ask us to recommend books to help them to understand their children better and give them ideas about how best to encourage their development. Although there are hundreds of books, they tend to be either too difficult to read or rather basic. We consulted parents before, during and after writing this book in the hope of producing something that would fill this gap and be of value to as many families as possible. We aimed to make it easy to read and fill it with practical information about how to manage common problems in children with ASD. We have described up-to-date research knowledge in a common-sensical understandable way, to explain what strategies may be most helpful and why. There are separate chapters on feeding, soiling, sleeping, preoccupations, communication, tantrums and aggressive behaviour. Each chapter has several case examples describing different problems, why the child might be behaving in this way and how parents might deal with them.

The book is in three parts. Part 1 describes the behaviours that might alert parents to the possibility that their child has autism. It goes through the assessment process and explains the emotional impact of a diagnosis. Part 2 gives an overview of how researchers believe children with autism think and experience the world and hence why they tend to behave differently. This understanding is then used throughout part 3 of the book to help to make sense of the child's behaviour and plan strategies to deal with difficult behaviours but, more important, to encourage the child's development.

We have used the term 'Autism Spectrum Disorders' (ASD) throughout this book to include all children and young people with difficulties on the broader autism spectrum, including childhood autism, autistic disorder, atypical autism, Asperger syndrome, Asperger disorder and Pervasive Developmental Disorder Not Otherwise Specified (PDD-NOS). The difference between these diagnostic terms is described in Chapter 2, 'Assessment'. Where a specific diagnostic term is used – for example, Asperger syndrome or autism – we are referring to children with that particular condition.

This book by its nature tends to centre on the difficulties of children on the autism spectrum, but their strengths and abilities also need to be celebrated. They can experience great successes, be very skilled and knowledgeable in different ways, have lots of fun, bring joy into their families and be very much loved.

PART 1

Does My Child have Autism Spectrum Disorder?

First Worries

Parents are experts on their own children. No one knows your child as well as you do. If you suspect that there is something wrong, you may very well be right. The difficulty is often in working out what the problem might be, how serious it is and with whom to check out your worries. Many of us discuss these anxieties with family and friends in the first instance and then consult a health professional (such as a health visitor or doctor) if we are still concerned. Often we are reassured and, either quickly or gradually, the behaviours that were of concern to us disappear. Sometimes, however, the child's behaviour and parental worries remain. If this is the case you may need to consult a health professional again.

What is autism?

Autism Spectrum Disorder (ASD) is a developmental disorder that normally becomes evident in the first three years of a child's life. Current estimates are that ASD including all the spectrum diagnoses occurs in approximately two to seven per 1000 people. It is about one-tenth of this for the severe end of the autism spectrum. This varies depending on which research you read and also in which countries the research was carried out; it is also probably to do with the way the diagnosis is made and the criteria used. It is about three to four times more common in boys than in girls.

ASD affects communication, social interaction, imagination and behaviour. It is not something a child can catch. *Parents do not cause it.* It is a condition that carries on into adolescence and adulthood. However, all children with ASD will continue to make developmental progress and there is a great deal that can be done to help.

Important points to remember

- There is *no fixed pattern* for the way in which ASD shows itself.

- There is *no specific age* at which symptoms first appear.

- Symptoms usually become apparent gradually.

- Specific symptoms vary considerably. The vast majority of children will not have all of the symptoms listed.

- Symptoms vary with age. Some three-year-olds may repeat phrases they hear over and over again, but they may not repeat at all when they are seven.

- The severity of symptoms varies. For example, some children may avoid eye contact almost completely, while others may have only subtle difficulties.

- If your child has some of the symptoms, it does not automatically mean that he has ASD. Many of the behaviours associated with ASD can be due to other things; for example, avoiding eye contact can be due to anxiety; not interacting very well with other children may be due to shyness; delay in language development may be due to hearing difficulties caused by several ear infections.

- Bad parenting does not cause ASD.

Can ASD be detected at birth?

ASD is not a condition that can be detected at birth. Babies with ASD look just as beautiful as all other babies. There are no obvious characteristics and no blood tests to detect the condition.

What might be the symptoms in the first six months?

Again, there are no obvious symptoms. Some babies are very passive, others very restless – no different, in fact, from other babies, all of whom have their own personalities and characteristics. Most parents of children who are later diagnosed as having ASD comment that their babies seemed to be developing normally in the early months, although many parents develop fears that something is not right in the first year of life.

Some families describe very passive babies or distraught, inconsolable babies. These things can of course be due to many things, including temperament. Some describe babies who rarely look at their parentss faces or eyes, or who do little babbling or imitating of their parent's movements or sounds. These are signs to note and to talk about with a medical professional.

What might be the symptoms at six to twelve months?

Some children may be a little delayed in reaching their milestones, although others develop in the usual way. As a *very* rough measure, by the age of 12 months children can usually crawl or move about, stand with support, say single words such as 'momma' or 'dada' and use simple gestures such as waving 'bye bye'. If your child has not reached these milestones, he or she may develop these skills over the following few months. However, a health professional (such as a health visitor or doctor) may want to monitor your child's progress. This does *not* necessarily mean that your child has ASD but may signal other general developmental difficulties, speech and language delay or delay in physical development. As a general rule children should be babbling and using gestures by 12 months, and single words with meaning (other than momma and dada) should be present by 16 months.

What might be the symptoms at 18 months?

In general, first concerns are aroused when a child is aged about 17 months. This is relevant as this is the time that children receive their first vaccinations, and some parents may associate the two events. To date, no link has been found between the MMR vaccine and the cause of ASD and some researchers think that parents blame the vaccine because ASD often first shows itself at this age.

Children should be using two words together with meaning by the age of 24 months and failure to do this, or any loss of language in this period, is a reason for you to see a health professional (such as your health visitor or family doctor). Some children with ASD will have learnt skills which they then appear to lose. In particular, some children with ASD gain and subsequently appear to lose language skills.

There may be many reasons why a child shows some of the behaviours listed in the bax on the next page. If you are concerned, talk to a health professional (such as your health visitor or doctor). He or she will probably do some simple checks and either arrange to see you again over the coming months, or arrange for you take your son or daughter along to see a paediatrician. Paediatricians are doctors who specialise in the development of babies and

children. Chapter 2, 'Assessment', describes what may happen when you visit
the paediatrician.

Causes for concern at 18 months

Your child is:

- not making good eye contact with you.

- not responding readily to her name being called.

- showing very little interest in other people.

- seeming to be in 'a world of her own'.

- having delayed language development. Children are usually able
  to use ten words or more at this age.

- losing language. Some children stop using words they had used
  before and do not learn new words.

- not using gestures such as pointing to indicate she wants
  something.

- taking an adult's hand and putting it on things that she wants
  opened, rather than gesturing, pointing and using eye contact
  and language.

- not appearing to understand your gestures such as pointing.

- not playing pretend games (for example, playing pretend
  teatime).

- seeming to be fascinated by parts of toys, rather than playing
  with them as intended – for example, constantly spinning the
  wheels of a toy car rather than running it along the floor.

- spending long periods of time lining things up, and becoming
  much more distressed than you might expect when someone
  moves them.

- making unusual movements such as walking on tiptoes all of the
  time or flapping her hands excessively.

- insisting on carrying around items in twos, one in each hand,
  often the same shape and colour.

What might be the symptoms at three to five years?

It will be very clear by the age of three years, with some children, that there is something wrong. In more severe cases of autism, for example, the child may be very much in a world of his own most of the time, and may seem to treat people as if they were objects. He may be unable to use or understand language, seem fascinated by household items rather than toys, and spend long periods of time rocking or flapping his hands. Others may have much more subtle symptoms that only gradually become more evident. Sometimes, difficulties become clearer at nursery or play group.

Causes for concern at three to five years

Your child is:

- not making good eye contact with you or other people.

- not very interested in other people.

- playing on her own rather than showing interest in playing with other children.

- showing an unusual reaction to distress in others, for instance ignoring them or laughing.

- standing out as behaving differently at playgroup; for example, she may continue to wander around the room when the other children are sitting down at story time.

- using language that may seem different from that of the other children at nursery. For example, she may:
    - have very little language
    - have a great deal of language (but this may be very repetitive or verbose)
    - repeat phrases from films, videos or TV programmes
    - copy phrases she has just heard (this is often called 'echolalia')
    - have difficulty understanding.

- having little or no interest in pretend play or being puzzled by the imaginative play of other children.

- not interested in joining in group games such as 'Ring a ring o' roses' or may be insistent on playing it in a particular way.

- very preoccupied with particular games or toys (i.e. playing with the same thing every day for many hours at a time) and becomes extremely upset if prevented from continuing.

- preoccupied with unusual things for a young child, such as lamp posts, grids, potato peelers, maps, road signs, traffic lights, logos.

- insisting on things being the same – for example ornaments being in exactly the same position.

- showing a liking for routine – for example having to go into a particular room and sit on a particular chair before doing anything else.

- making unusual movements such as spinning round or rocking repeatedly

- making unusual hand or finger movements such as flapping his hands or moving his fingers in front of his eyes.

- fascinated by patterns or movement in everyday objects such as lining up books or cars and moving her hand back and forth repeatedly, watching the patterns she makes.

- very sensitive to noise, e.g. often putting his hands over his ears or becoming very upset at the sound of loud noises which do not seem to upset other people.

- very sensitive to smells, e.g. very often smelling food before eating it or sniffing clothes or people repeatedly.

- very sensitive to touch, e.g. stroking items for long periods of time or hating the feel of certain fabrics to the point of distress.

Many of these behaviours can be seen in children who are developing in a healthy way. However, in that case they usually stop after a few days or weeks. You should see your doctor if you are worried.

What might be the symptoms at six to eleven years?

All children are different. They often develop different skills at different times. They all have their own personalities. Some are very outgoing, others very shy. Some find the transition to school very difficult and take some time to settle, others settle almost immediately. However, after the first term at school,

Causes for concern at six to eleven years

Your child is:

- making poor eye contact with people.

- unlikely to use readily gestures such as pointing, beckoning, waving or a making a 'shhh' gesture with their finger to mean 'be quiet'.

- without close friends of the same age.

- not showing the teacher their drawings or work unless asked to.

- finding it much harder to share than other children.

- not very good at taking turns, and likes to be first all of the time.

- apparently unconcerned about other children's feelings.

- saying the same thing over and over again.

- not pursuing or enjoying pretend play with other children.

- not easy to converse with about something you want to talk about.

- you may feel, talking 'at' you and not really concerned whether you are interested or bored with the topic she is talking about.

- fascinated by a topic which takes up large amounts of time and may seem slightly unusual, for example learning the capacity of all of the football grounds in the league.

- talking in a way that may be slightly unusual: for example, in a very loud, expressionless tone or with a different accent – say, an English child with English parents talking with an American accent.

- wanting to play with the same things and nothing else for very long periods of time.

- flapping her hands or making odd movements when upset or excited.

experienced primary school teachers are usually very good at noticing if a child's behaviour is out of the ordinary compared with others of the same age. If you have concerns about your child's development, you may find their observations helpful. Some children with ASD will have more subtle difficul-

ties (such as those experienced with mild Asperger syndrome) and they may have escaped the notice of those around them until they are older and social skills are required more. As a child becomes older adults and peers are less tolerant of wide variations in social behaviour than they are when the child is in infancy. Social difficulties begin to stick out more as the child grows.

What might be the symptoms at 12 to 17 years?

In most cases, problems on the autism spectrum are detected before a young person reaches adolescence. ASD does not suddenly develop at this age. If your adolescent has been developing normally and there is a sudden and dramatic change in his behaviour, it is unlikely that ASD is the cause. Adolescence is a time of change and it is not unusual for young people to seek independence. This often causes conflict in families and, although a difficult time for parents, it is a normal developmental process. If you are very concerned, however, you should see your doctor as other problems or illnesses may arise in adolescence.

Sometimes parents may have suspected for some time that their child is a little different. They may have noticed some of the behaviours outlined above, but have explained them away by saying that the child is shy or introverted in nature – particularly if one of the parents or relatives is similar in personality. This may be the most likely explanation. If, however, you can look back and recognise several of the behaviours described above and notice continued problems in the following areas you should consider further assessment.

Causes for concern at 12 to 17 years
Your child is:

- making poor eye contact.
- making flat or unusual facial expressions.
- having difficulty making and keeping friends.
- manifesting a poor understanding of the needs of others in conversation.
- having difficulty guessing how others are thinking or feeling (and so regularly misjudging what to say or do in social or emotional situations).
- exhibiting socially inappropriate behaviour.
- showing an obsessive need for routine.
- showing a tendency to be very literal.
- displaying compulsive behaviours.

Remember that many of the behaviours described here can have other explanations. If you are concerned seek the advice of your doctor.

Summary

- Autism Spectrum Disorder (ASD) is a developmental disorder that normally becomes evident in the first three years of a child's life.
- ASD is not something a child can catch. It is not caused by parents.

- ASD is a condition that carries on into adolescence and adulthood, although all children will continue to make developmental progress.

- Symptoms vary in content and severity and by age.

- Children with ASD can have a range of temperaments and IQs.

- This chapter explains some of the more common difficulties apparent at different ages, but it is not exhaustive. If you are concerned you should see your doctor.

Chapter 2

Assessment

Chapter 1, 'First Worries', outlines some of the signs of ASD at different ages. If you think that several of these symptoms apply to your child you should go to see your health visitor or doctor. He or she will be able to help you to decide whether a more detailed assessment would be helpful, and may be able to reassure you that all is well or may give you some specific advice. If he or she is uncertain you will be referred to a specialist or a specialist service. This could be one of the following:

- a paediatrician (a specialist children's doctor)

- a child clinical psychologist (a psychologist specialising in children's development)

- a child psychiatrist (a psychiatrist specialising in children's development who is also a doctor)

- a speech therapist for a language and communication assessment (a therapist specialising in children's communication skills)

- a child development team (a group of different therapists who might all be involved in the assessment on the day you visit the hospital).

There are many different systems for the assessment of children. They vary depending on where you live and what is available. Waiting times for an appointment also vary.

What will happen when we get to see the specialists?

Again, this will vary, but some of the following scenarios are likely.

With you

The specialists will talk with you about your worries about your child. They will take you through the life of your child, asking you about your pregnancy and your child's birth, temperament, developmental milestones, sleeping and feeding, medical history, behaviour and interactions with other people and children.

They will ask about other members of your family and may draw a family tree.

With your child

- *Playing!* Most of the assessment with a young child is play. Children nearly always have a great time and are completely unaware that the purpose behind the play is assessment.

- *Talking.* With older children and adolescents, there may be some informal chatting with the therapist and some age-appropriate games and tests.

- *Hearing test.*

- *Blood tests.* ASD cannot be detected by blood tests. Occasionally blood tests are taken to rule out other genetic conditions such as Fragile X. (Fragile X syndrome is extremely rare. It is an inherited cause of learning disability.)

At the end of the first appointment

Occasionally, the specialists may be able to tell you straight away if they think your child has difficulties on the autism spectrum. More often this is not the case.

More assessment may be necessary. This might include some of the following:

- observing your child at nursery, school or home

- if your child is under five, attending a number of sessions in a group with other children where therapists will be able to help with his needs and continue to assess him

- the therapist talking with the teacher about any concerns

- referral to another specialist such as a speech therapist, child psychologist or child psychiatrist (sometimes there is a team assessment with several people assessing your child)

- a developmental or cognitive assessment of the child. (Again this is mostly play or games or puzzles which most children enjoy.) The purpose of this is to check whether there are any particular areas in development where the child has strengths or difficulties. It is important to remember, however, that cognitive assessments or IQ tests are often not very reliable indicators of young children's abilities, particularly for children with ASD when they don't want to cooperate

- more detailed discussion with you.

How long will it take before I get to know if it is an Autism Spectrum Disorder?

This will vary depending on the child. If the child's difficulties are at the severe end of the autism spectrum a diagnosis may be made very quickly. More often, it may be several weeks or months before the assessment is complete.

The specialists may need to see you and your child in different settings. They may need to see changes in development over a period of time.

ASD can be difficult to diagnose. This is because some of the behaviours and difficulties can be associated with other problems. For example, a child may not be responding to other people because of a hearing impairment. There may be delay in several areas of his development, such as walking, talking and understanding, which makes it difficult for the specialists to be sure about whether his behaviour is more like that of a much younger child (indicating an overall developmental delay) or whether the main problem is ASD. Some children are temperamentally rather shy and take a while to feel comfortable in the company of other children or adults. Occasionally other things, such as severe anxiety or traumatic life experiences, can lead to a child having some behaviours that look like ASD.

Although the assessment process may be long and frustrating, it is important that the right diagnosis is made.

Some of the assessments used in diagnosis

- Autism Diagnostic Interview – Revised (ADI-R). An interview with parents that takes around three hours.

- Autism Diagnostic Observation Schedule – Generic (ADOS-G). A play assessment with young children (or a structured informal chat with older children) that takes about one hour.

- Diagnostic Interview for Social and Communication Disorders (DISCO). An interview with parents that takes about three hours or more.

- Children's Autism Rating Scale (CARS). This is an assessment of the child's behaviour.

- Checklist for Autism in Toddlers (CHAT). For children aged 18 months. This is a brief screening (ten minutes) to check for things such as pretend play, pointing to show interest and joint attention.

- Developmental assessments such as the Wechsler Intelligence Scale for Children – Revised (WISC-R). An assessment with the child using various tests.

How is a diagnosis on the autism spectrum made?

The specialists will be using their wide theoretical knowledge about the nature of ASD. There are hundreds of books about ASD. The majority are long and complex. Although they are widely read by specialists, many parents complain that they haven't the time to read or make sense of the theories. We have, therefore, tried to summarise the main theories using everyday language in Part 2, 'How do Children with Autism Spectrum Disorders View the World?'. Our experience of working with families shows that this under-standing helps parents to understand more about diagnosis and about how best to help their children once they are diagnosed.

In additional to their theoretical knowledge, the specialists will concen-trate on the specific factors included below in order to make a diagnosis. They need to be sure that:

- the child or young person has the cluster of core problems associated with ASD

- the core problems are clear in all settings: at home and at school or nursery

- the core problems are sufficient in severity and

- there are no other explanations for the difficulties.

The cluster of core problems

There are three core areas of impairment in children with ASD. For a diagnosis of ASD, the child will experience significant problems in all three areas, which are:

1. social

2. communication

3. repetitive and unusual behaviour.

Each of these areas warrants detailed assessment.

Some symptoms in the *social* area are associated with something called Mindblindness, (see Chapter 4). If you don't understand that someone else has different thoughts and a different point of view, you are likely to have problems with:

- eye contact

- the use of gestures and facial expressions in communication

- playing with others and making friendships
- sharing and turn-taking
- understanding the emotions of others and being compassionate (for example, when people are upset)
- sharing excitement and pleasure with others.

Language and *communication* difficulties and impaired development of imagination are also core features and include:

- delay in language development with few attempts to compensate by using gestures
- for those children who have developed language
  - problems initiating and sustaining conversation
  - problems with abstract language and a tendency to take things literally
  - unusual, odd or repetitive use of language: for example, one teacher, in trying to encourage a boy with Asperger syndrome to start his maths by saying, 'Just get down to it Tom', was surprised to find him lying on the floor with his book!
- delay in acquisition of flexible imagination skills, e.g. it may take a long time for the child to understand the concept of pretend and to be able to extend pretend play.

Some of the problems with *repetitive and unusual behaviours* relate to problems understanding the gist of situations (see Chapter 5), problems with the development of imagination and a need to seek refuge from the stress of the social world. These include:

- preoccupations of an intense nature
- preoccupations with very unusual things
- preoccupations of a sensory nature or preoccupations with patterns, detail or the movement of objects
- mannerisms and repetitive odd movements
- intense routines or compulsions and problems dealing with change of routine.

Many of these problems are part of the standard diagnostic criteria that specialists look for as part of the assessment. These are usually either:

- criteria from the American Psychiatric Association – the *Diagnostic and Statistical Manual of Mental Disorders,* Fourth Edition (DSM-IV) (1994) or,

- criteria from the World Health Organisation – *International Statistical Classification of Diseases and Related Health Problems,* Tenth Edition (ICD-10) (1992).

If the specialists find that there are significant problems with language or repetitive behaviours but not with social functioning, a diagnosis of ASD may not be appropriate. This does not mean to say that your child does not have needs that require attention, just that a different diagnosis or explanation is appropriate and that your child should be treated accordingly. For example, if the child exhibits lots of repetitive behaviours – such as lining toys up in particular way, insisting that he will only drink out of a certain coloured cup or that he has to count up to ten before he can enter a room – but has good social, language and communication skills, then the possibility that he has Obsessive Compulsive Disorder may be explored. Similarly some children have problems with language but have healthy social development and no repetitive behaviours – this may be a Specific Language Impairment.

Core problems in all settings

If a child has ASD, his behaviours are clear in *all* settings: ASD is not something that happens just at school or just at home, for example. The behaviours may be worse in some settings than in others but careful assessment will help to make this clear.

Severity

The specialists will pay particular attention to the severity of each of the symptoms. A diagnosis of ASD is likely to be made if there are several symptoms in the core cluster that are judged to be severe. Less severe symptoms can make diagnosis more difficult and it may take a longer period of time. The specialists will assess this by comparing the behaviour of normally developing children of the same age or ability with the behaviour of the child being assessed.

Other explanations

Assessing professionals will want to make sure that some of the child's behaviours that look like ASD are not being caused by other problems. These include hearing problems, behavioural problems, developmental delay, speech and language impairment and certain types of brain damage. Problems such as dyspraxia (when the nerves and muscles work normally but coordinating complex movements is difficult) and dyslexia (where there are specific reading and spelling problems) are not on the autism spectrum although they may be found alongside ASD in some people. Children with ASD may of course also have some or all of the above difficulties. Some children may have some of these difficulties but not ASD! For example, some children with speech delay are also delayed in their social development and show some repetitive behaviours. However, as their language skills improve, their social skills develop, their behaviour becomes less repetitive and ASD is no longer considered. The job of the specialists is to ensure that a correct diagnosis is made. If there are any uncertainties, they will discuss this with you and possibly delay making a diagnosis.

Diagnosis

what is the difference between autism, Asperger syndrome, atypical autism and high functioning autism?

There is a lot of confusion about the labels used to describe ASD. Although ASD describes a set of behaviours, these behaviours vary from person to person in the severity of symptoms and the combination of symptoms.

While children with autism may be more likely to have low intelligence, some can be very intelligent. Similarly, the temperament of children with ASD may differ radically. Some are very placid while some may be very strong willed. Thus, children with the same diagnosis will be different.

Another confusion is that when doctors use one of the two internationally recognised diagnostic criteria they will use different words to describe diagnoses.

Table 2.1 shows the different use of words for the same broad symptoms.

Table 2.1 DSM-IV and ICD-10 diagnostic classifications used to describe the same broad symptoms	
ICD-10	*DSM-IV*
Childhood autism	Autistic disorder
Asperger syndrome	Asperger disorder
Atypical autism	Pervasive Developmental Disorder Not Otherwise Specified (PDD-NOS)

Autism Spectrum Disorder

The term 'Autism Spectrum Disorder' (ASD) is not a single diagnosis. It refers to any one of the above diagnoses: autism, Asperger syndrome, Pervasive Developmental Disorder Not Otherwise Specified, etc. It is a catch-all phrase to include all the diagnoses on the spectrum.

Autism (childhood autism or autistic disorder)

Children and young people given this diagnosis will have shown impairments in social interaction, communication and imaginative play before the age of three years as well as stereotyped behaviours, interests and activities.

Asperger syndrome or Asperger disorder

Children and young people given this diagnosis will have shown impairments in social interactions and restricted interests and activities, with no significant general delay in language, and fall in the average or above average range of intelligence.

Atypical autism or Pervasive Developmental Disorder – Not Otherwise Specified

This diagnosis may be made when a child does not meet the full criteria for a diagnosis of autism or Asperger syndrome, but there is a severe and pervasive impairment in the areas affected by ASD.

Other terms sometimes used

HIGH FUNCTIONING AUTISM

This term is sometimes given to indicate that the young person has the same difficulties as those described as having autism but that he or she has an average or above average level of intelligence.

SEMANTIC PRAGMATIC DISORDER AND PATHOLOGICAL DEMAND AVOIDANCE

Occasionally terms such as Semantic Pragmatic Disorder or Pathological Demand Avoidance are used. These do not currently exist within either of the two main classification systems. They are terms suggested by some research groups. All children on the autism spectrum have pragmatic language difficulties. Children on the autism spectrum who have strong-willed temperaments give powerful resistance to any demands made of them. The research groups in question have suggested some useful strategies for dealing with such difficulties but it remains to be seen whether they are truly separate diagnostic groups. Most clinicians tend to stick to established and recognised categories around which most of the productive intervention research to date has been based.

Conclusion

The diagnostic process will have been emotionally a very difficult one for most parents. We will discuss this in more detail in Chapter 3, 'The Emotional Impact on the Family'. It is important to remember, however, that all children with ASD will continue to make progress.

Most specialists will be pleased to explain the process of assessment and diagnosis with you. If you are uncertain about anything don't be afraid to ask or tell them if you disagree. The aim is always to complete an assessment that will provide information to help you to help your child.

This chapter is by its nature the driest. We hope that most readers will find the following chapters, which are geared to understanding ASD and to what can constructively be done to help children, more interesting.

Summary

- This chapter outlines some of the things that might happen when your child is being assessed for ASD.

- It explains how a diagnosis is made and what the different terms mean.

- The process of assessing children for ASD is likely to occur over a period of time. It may take several weeks or months.

Chapter 3

The Emotional Impact
on the Family

Before diagnosis

At first parents do not know that their child has autism. Sometimes they have a family member or friend with autism. However, at some point suspicions are raised that something is wrong. This may have been by you, as a parent or carer, or by someone else, such as a friend or professional.

Most parents will say that they noticed something was not quite right with their child but they could not say what: this may be especially true if the child is their first or if they have no other children with whom to compare milestones and development. Parents may also have grandparents telling them not to worry. Often, parents will have spoken with their health visitor or doctor or have had their child checked for hearing problems or developmental delay. It is common for parents to be angry with relatives, friends or professionals either for drawing attention to problems when they think there are none or for not taking notice of their concerns.

Before diagnosis many parents will doubt their own abilities. They may struggle to understand why things that worked for their previous children are not working now, or why something that worked for other parents doesn't work for them; or they may think they are no good at being parents. Sometimes professionals may have misinterpreted the child's behaviour, further contributing to parents' feelings of confusion and failure. These are common thoughts but we know for certain that ASDs are not caused by bad parenting.

Researchers have found that people deal with difficult situations and stresses in different ways. Some people may invest enormous amounts of energy in a diagnosis of ASD while others may not see their child's difficulties as fitting into the spectrum.

Coping when the diagnosis is made

Families may go through a range of emotions when they are told that their child has autism. This will vary very much between families, and each family member has his or her own emotional journey to make. Some families have been through a lengthy diagnostic process and some have had to wait a long time for appointments. Some have found the process has gone so quickly that they have little time to think through the implications and adjust emotionally. With some children diagnosis is easier to make at a younger age and with some, diagnosis is not easy because the difficulties are subtle rather than obvious. All of these things will affect how parents feel towards the diagnosis and towards the services supporting them. In general, services are geared to supporting children and families, and professionals will be helpful although they may be under a lot of stress with time restraints and waiting lists.

All parents are different and emotional responses vary widely. You may or may not experience some of the following emotions at different times.

Relief

If parents have felt frustrated at not being taken seriously about their worries concerning their child, or diagnosis has taken a long time, they sometimes temporarily experience relief. They say that finally they can begin to make sense of their child's behaviour and start to get the right sort of help.

Guilt

It is very common for parents to worry that they have done something wrong during pregnancy or in parenting and that this is why their child is behaving as he is. If you are feeling like this you are not alone. But remember, research shows that children do not develop ASD because of something the parents have done wrong in their parenting.

Loss

Most parents have dreams and aspirations for their children both before they are born and when they are small ('she's going to be a ballerina', 'he'll support my football team', 'she'll go to university and marry someone really nice and we'll have grandchildren'). Particularly before their first child they have an idea of how they would like that child to be. As we watch our babies grow into children and young people, most of us have to adjust these ideas as we get to know the individual that is our child and we gradually realise that they have their own personality and individuality. We can help to shape personalities and nurture our children, but we cannot make them something they are not.

This process is heightened with children with ASD as we come to realise that they may never be able easily to do some of the things that we had hoped and wished, or things that we take for granted. Parents may ask questions such as 'Why me?' or wish things had been different. This is a normal response to any loss, including loss of hopes for the future.

Fear for the future

Parents may have fears for the future of their children. When a child is diagnosed with ASD parents experience not only feelings of sadness and loss, but a range of fears for the future which replace the hopes and expectations that they may have had. These are difficult processes to adjust to. Families may have to realign their aspirations for their child, and keep the future in mind as their child develops.

Seeking information

Some families may wish to gather as much information as possible and seek out others who have a shared experience. Others may avoid information and try to put any reminder out of their minds. Many young people and their families now have access to the Internet and will seek out their own information sources. Many such sources are mentioned in this book in the resources section.

Beliefs about where the ASD came from

Different families may have different beliefs about where the ASD came from and this can have quite an impact upon emotions and coping. For example, some families may look at other family members with similar traits or difficulties. This may lead to feelings of guilt in the affected relative, or may lead to blame by other family members ('if only she or he hadn't married him or her'). Some attributions may be environmental, for example, putting ASD down to birth trauma. Each of these may alter the way individuals within the family relate to each other, and towards the child.

Some family members may believe that their child is doomed. This can cause people to think very negatively for a while. Usually, these thoughts change with time and parents begin to think about what they can do to help their children to develop in the best ways possible. In our experience being positive helps a great deal.

Altered relationships in the family

When a child is diagnosed as being on the autism spectrum the family will find that they have to make adjustments. The child will inevitably be treated differently. This will be difficult for parents, brothers, sisters and grandparents. We have found that this process can become easier as people gradually unlock their fears and develop more understanding about why the child behaves in unusual ways at times.

Parents

Stress between parents is very common, particularly if there is any misunderstanding or disagreement about the diagnosis. Many professionals encourage both parents to attend the assessment sessions wherever possible and will try to be flexible. However, they recognise that it can be very difficult to juggle work commitments around appointments. Many professionals will organise an appointment to discuss issues related to diagnosis with both parents. It is also important to remember that emotional reactions to diagnoses are likely to differ from person to person. It may take one parent much longer to cope with the implications than the other.

PLANNING FOR OTHER CHILDREN

This will be an important decision for all parents. In general, if one child in a family has autism then there is about a 2 to 3 per cent chance that another will have autism. Different research studies have found chances of between 60 per cent and 95 per cent among identical twins, with the lower percentage being for a full diagnosis and the higher percentages being found when any symptoms of ASD are included. There is increased research on the genetic aspects of autism, and it is likely that there are different genetic pathways to autism, so these figures above are rough generalisations only. If in doubt, ask your doctor. In some situations specialists in genetics will be able to offer you information.

Brothers and sisters

Brothers and sisters may worry about whether they too will become ill, and may become sad that they cannot have an ordinary playful relationship with their sibling as some of their friends do. They may be frightened of their brother or sister or jealous of the time that their parents are devoting to him or her. They may also be enriched by having a sibling with ASD and may be helpful without being burdened with too much responsibility. There are some good books which have been written to help brothers and sisters understand more about autism, and these are listed in the References and Resources section of this book.

Grandparents

It is hard for grandparents too when they hear that their grandchild has a diagnosis of on the autism spectrum. They will experience a variety of emotions that will be different for everyone and may include shock, denial, grief and worry or a combination of these.

Sometimes the diagnosis will come as a complete shock. In this case, grandparents may not believe what they have been told. They may think that the child's behaviour is due to poor discipline or that the diagnosis is just another word for bad behaviour. They may never have heard of Asperger syndrome. They may perhaps have heard of ASD or know of a child with a diagnosis of it who is very different from their grandchild. They might perceive their grandchild as 'too clever' to have ASD, particularly if he or she has some isolated precocious skills such as learning numbers and colours well before his or her peers. They may try to offer reassurance by saying that the child will 'grow out of it'. Many of the parents we have spoken to tell us how difficult it is for them when their own parents cannot accept the diagnosis. They may have been through a long process themselves, gradually coming to terms with the diagnosis. In their distress they may forget that information and time have helped them towards acceptance and that their parents will need help to understand too.

Grandparents experience grief too. They might become aware that their grandchild may not be able to do some of the things they had hoped. They may worry about the child's future but also about how having a child with ASD will affect their son or daughter.

HOW CAN GRANDPARENTS HELP?

When we ask parents this question, they give us many different responses;

- Try to accept the diagnosis.

- Remember that poor parenting does not cause ASD.

- Try not to be critical (or at least be constructive when you are critical).

- Offer practical help if you can.

- Try not to blame. Comments like 'he doesn't get it from our side of the family' are very unhelpful.

- Just listen. Sometimes parents want to tell you how hard it is for them.

- Get to know your grandchild by finding out about his interests with him.

- Appreciate what your grandchild can do and keep noticing when he develops new skills.

Stigma

Some families (thankfully fewer today than in years gone by) receive negative comments from other people in the community. A typical example is criticism when shopping. Criticism when a child is having a temper tantrum can be hurtful. We may be trying to stick to a particular way of managing things that is hard to practise when other people are watching. Some parents ignore this, some explain that their child has ASD, and we know some who have handed out a card explaining autism. All of these strategies can work. What doesn't work for either parent or child is staying at home for fear of criticism. Occasionally people will be deliberately unpleasant and we should not allow such people to make us feel bad. Discussing healthy coping strategies for these kinds of occurrences will be very helpful.

Helen was the mum of a boy with autism called Jed. She explained that she first became very self-conscious in public and would not take him out. She said that as he became older she became stronger and there came a point where she decided that she would live her life and do all the things she wanted to do with Jed without worrying about what others thought or said. She coped with this by seeing people as belonging to two camps: those who had a broad-minded perspective and those who were not tolerant. She learned quickly who to value and who not to worry about. Friendships were strong and lasting, but she felt that she had fewer 'acquaintances' than she might otherwise have had.

How to get through it all

In general the following may be helpful:

- Accept the diagnosis of ASD and help other family members to do so.

- Find a supportive family and/or friendship-based network.

- Obtain accurate information about ASD.

- Develop a positive attitude, positive beliefs and positive coping strategies.

- Develop constructive relationships with school, voluntary and health services.

- See family life in broader terms and try to keep healthy family routines and attitudes going in your family where possible. It is easy for ASD to become the focus of the family. Consider your needs as parents and your relationship (you have to be OK to look after everyone else, so it is OK to have time out and fun). Consider the needs of other children in the family. They are developing too and still need love and attention.

- Develop resilience to unfair or unpleasant criticisms of your parenting or your child.

- Remember that your son or daughter has his or her own unique personality, skills and attributes. Parents frequently tell us about the excitement and fun they have with their children, their delight in watching their special talents develop and their joy in seeing them make progress.

Summary

- Families may go through a range of emotions when they are told that their child has autism, including loss, relief, guilt and fear for the future.

- It is helpful to accept the diagnosis of ASD and help other family members to do so.

- All parents are different and their emotional responses may vary widely.

- Having a child with ASD has an impact on all members of the family including siblings and grandparents.

- It is helpful to try to develop positive attitudes, positive beliefs and positive coping strategies.

PART 2

How Do Children with Autism Spectrum Disorders View the World?

Chapter 4

Mindblindness

'Mindblindness' refers to being blind to the minds of other people. It means that people with Autism Spectrum Disorders (ASDs) have great difficulty understanding the point of view or the thoughts or feelings of someone else. Some researchers have called this poor 'Theory of Mind', as shorthand for saying that children with ASD have poor understanding of what other people are thinking or feeling: a poor understanding of the minds of others. 'Theory of Mind' (TOM) refers to our ability to make accurate guesses about what people might be thinking or feeling or help us to predict what they are going to do. This is a crucial skill for being able to get on socially. Mindblindness is where we have problems with this. A child with severe autism may have a totally impaired TOM but more often TOM is developmentally delayed. In other words, children on the autism spectrum develop these skills later and to a lesser degree than others.

The Sally Ann test

Simon Baron-Cohen was the first person to use the term 'mindblindness' as a way of explaining some of the problems experienced by people with ASD. There is also a very simple test that is sometimes used in part of the assessment of younger children – the Sally Ann test (Wimmer and Perner 1983). This is a straightforward way of explaining Theory of Mind.

1. Sally has a basket. Anne has a box. Sally puts her marble in the basket.

2. Sally leaves the room.

3. While Sally is not there, Anne takes the marble and puts it in the box.

4. Sally comes back. Where does Sally look to get her marble?

Figure 4.1: The Sally Anne test (after Wimmer and Perner 1983)

Children with poor TOM, or mindblindness, do not understand that Sally does not know that the marble has been moved from the basket to the box. They tend to say that Sally will look in the box. They seem to rely on their own experience or knowledge of where the marble is without considering the knowledge or experience of the other person. They don't seem to see things from Sally's point of view, only their own. Around 80 per cent of typically developing four-year-olds realise that Sally will think the marble is where she left it – in the basket. Only about 20 per cent of four-year-old children who have ASD will say that Sally will look in the basket.

Considering the world from another person's point of view seems to be very difficult for the majority of people with ASD. If we try to imagine being unable to understand how someone else is thinking or feeling or consider their point of view, we realise how confusing and frightening the world must seem and how difficult social interactions must be. It is not surprising, therefore, that young people with ASD appear to be very self-centred and behave differently from other children. This is not the same as selfishness. It is a problem in understanding other people. Some children with ASD are said to treat people like objects.

How does mindblindness show in the behaviour of our ASD children?

If a younger child on the autism spectrum does not have an understanding of the thoughts or motivations of others then she is less likely to use behaviours that communicate to the minds of others or to take into account the thoughts and feelings of others. She might have difficulty with the following:

- pointing things out to others

- making much eye contact

- following another person's eyes when that person is talking about what they are looking at

- using gestures to communicate

- understanding the emotions on the faces of others

- using a normal range of emotional expressions on her own face

- showing interest in other children

- knowing how to engage with other children

- keeping calm when she is frustrated

- understanding that someone else can help her

- understanding how others feel in some situations (e.g. hurt, upset or fearful).

As she gets older mindblindness shows itself in more ways, including:

- a tendency to think about the world from her own point of view, which makes her appear very self-centred

- a tendency to engage in activities that do not depend on other people

- a focus on her own needs only

- a struggle to understand the emotions of others, and so a lack of empathy

- the need to be in control

- a lack of flexibility in interactions

- the use of rigid social rules rather than adaptable ones

- more take than give in the 'give and take' of relationships

- problems with turn-taking

- a tendency to treat people as the same, with no variation for age or authority

- being easily led by others due to her failure to understand the motives of others

- a tendency to relate better to adults. They are more predictable and may be more tolerant

- difficulty with pretend play and an inability to understand about telling lies

- difficulty understanding that her behaviour affects how others think or feel

- not understanding about sharing excitement, pleasure or belongings

- talking excessively about a topic of her own interest without regard to the listener's opinion (e.g. lack of interest or boredom).

Exercise in understanding mindblindness

Along the sea front in San Francisco, just outside a row of shops, a young man famously makes his living by hiding behind a few branches broken from

nearby trees. Dressed in a monkey suit he watches and waits, unseen by most visitors who are busy chatting, shopping or just enjoying the sea atmosphere. Then he jumps out from behind his branches directly in front of someone passing by and shouts: 'Boo!' Most people are startled and might jump or scream before laughing and joining in with the joke. Small crowds often watch from the other side of the road and then give him small change in appreciation of the street entertainment.

In order to make some money out of this, he requires good TOM. He needs to be able to predict the reactions of other people. He needs to think carefully about his chosen 'victim'.

Try to put yourself in his place for a moment. You are now the person waiting, hidden behind a few branches trying to make some money in the same way. You have to make decisions about which people you will choose to jump out on and which you will not. Write the numbers corresponding to the four decisions given on the next page next to the descriptions of the people whom you see approaching to indicate your decision.

When you have finished, ask a friend or relative to do the same exercise and then compare notes.

1 – definitely will jump out on this person or these people. I don't have any worries about it.

2 – It will be fun to jump out on them. There is a small chance of some trouble but I will take the risk.

3 – I am very uncertain. There might be trouble if I jump out on them.

4 – I definitely will *not* jump out on them.

- [ ] two teenage girls
- [ ] a teenage boy
- [ ] a middle-aged couple
- [ ] an eight-year-old girl with a bleeding nose
- [ ] a boy with a small dog
- [ ] an elderly woman in a wheelchair
- [ ] a security guard who is protecting someone famous
- [ ] the local traffic warden
- [ ] a woman with a baby in a pram
- [ ] a mum with two children aged around eight and ten
- [ ] a blind man
- [ ] your best friend
- [ ] two men and a Rottweiler dog
- [ ] an elderly nun
- [ ] your older brother
- [ ] a ten-year-old boy whom you saw taking his sister's ice-cream
- [ ] a policeman
- [ ] a four-year-old child who is crying for her mum
- [ ] your mum
- [ ] your dad.

Answer

There are no right or wrong answers. You will probably find that your answers differ when you begin to talk about why you made your decisions. You will probably have thought about the possible consequences of jumping out on the various people. For example, you may have thought that there was no risk in jumping out on the teenage girls because they might scream and then laugh about the incident, causing people in the small watching crowd to find the event amusing. This might then put them in a good mood and make them more likely to leave some money for you. However, you might have decided not to jump out at the blind man. You perhaps thought that he wouldn't get the joke because he wouldn't know that you had been hiding or know that you were wearing a monkey outfit, or you might have worried that the crowd might turn against you if they thought this was unkind. You are seeing things from his point of view but, more than this, you are guessing what the crowd will think of you and what they think of the reactions and feelings of the person you jump out on. These are important social skills that we take for granted but with which people on the autism spectrum struggle. It is no wonder that the social world may be a challenge for them.

In order to make these decisions, you will have found yourself thinking about the thoughts and feelings of other people and trying to work out the likely consequences of your actions on their behaviour. You may have been thinking not only about your 'victims' but also about the effect on the crowd. Intuitively you will have made a number of complex connections and decisions in a few seconds without even realising it at the time. People with ASD find this very difficult. They have mindblindness. They have great difficulty understanding how other people might think or feel or how they might react.

Are there different aspects to Theory of Mind or mindblindness?

Yes, we know that an understanding of someone else's mind or point of view has different aspects. For example, when we try to understand what it will be like for a nun when a person in a monkey suit jumps out on her, we can consider:

- what she sees and what her *sensory experiences* are (e.g. she sees something different from us)

- what she is *anticipating or expecting* in any given situation or environment, and how that is different from what we anticipate or expect

- what her *feelings* are (e.g. fear)

- what her *thoughts* are (e.g. 'I am in danger' or 'This is funny')

- how she brings all of this together in an *interpretation* of events (e.g. 'A monkey has escaped from the zoo' or 'Another student rag week!')

- what her *plans* are: what she might be wanting to do next or in the future (e.g. laugh and give money, run away or go to the police).

Are there different degrees of mindblindness?

Mindblindness or TOM is not an 'all or nothing' concept. There are different degrees.

The *range* of this skill varies in people with ASD as well as those without ASD. However, in children with autism, the level of understanding of TOM is likely to be within a lower range or band, as shown in Figure 4.2.

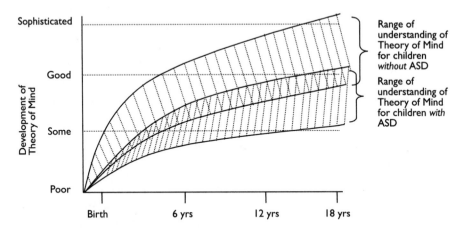

Figure 4.2: The differences in the range of understanding of Theory of Mind in children with autism and children without autism

This figure shows the differences in the range of understanding of TOM in children with autism and in children without autism. It also demonstrates that the level of TOM skills of some children *without* ASD can overlap with that of more able children *with* ASD. Some children with autism will struggle at a very basic level whilst others will develop more understanding. Children and young people with a diagnosis of Asperger syndrome or high functioning autism will usually be more likely to develop a greater understanding of TOM.

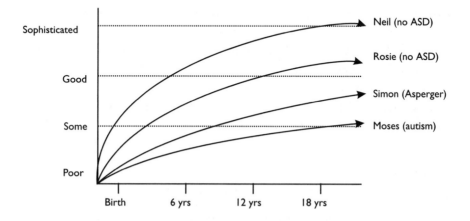

Figure 4.3: The different rates of the development of Theory of Mind for four different young people.

Figure 4.3 shows the development of TOM in four young people. Neil and Rosie do not have ASD but develop TOM at different rates and to different levels of ability. Simon has Asperger syndrome and develops TOM more slowly, but he achieves a good understanding as he approaches adulthood. Moses, who is more severely affected by his autism, makes progress as he gets older but does not achieve the same level of understanding.

Mindblindness or TOM is a core difficulty for children and young people with ASD and very few will reach a sophisticated understanding.

TOM develops with *age*. However, the understanding of young people with ASD develops at a much slower pace and in a different way from that of more typical children. For example, George, a 13-year-old boy with Asperger syndrome, had a similar level of understanding of TOM to that of his eight-year-old brother.

Most typical nine-year-olds understand that different people would react differently in the exercise above, and they would change their behaviour accordingly. Many nine-year-old children with ASD may not. They might:

- treat people as the same without making any variation for their age or authority (e.g. jump out on all people indiscriminately or jump out on no-one)

- focus on their own needs only (e.g. their own enjoyment)

- have difficulty understanding that their behaviour affects how others think or feel and seem unaware of other people's reactions (e.g. being upset).

However, as they grow older, they may develop more understanding. The difficulty seems to be that, for children on the autism spectrum, understanding of other people's thoughts and feelings does not occur intuitively. It has, more often than not, to be taught.

There is a great deal that parents and carers can do to help their children to improve their understanding of TOM (see Chapter 10, 'Developing Social Skills').

Summary

Mindblindness makes it difficult for people with ASD to:

- understand other people's thoughts and feelings

- understand that they are expected to change the way they behave depending on where they are or whom they are with

- predict what people might do next

- interpret different facial expressions or gestures

- understand how their behaviour might upset other people

- understand social rules

- express their own emotions appropriately.

It can make them seem self-centred and uninterested in other children and people.

Chapter 5

Getting the Gist

When we see something, whether it is a picture or a sentence in a book or the real world, we see that it is full of detail. In a picture there are lots of colours, shapes, sizes and objects. Many of us have an ability to draw together lots of information from a situation in order to make sense of it. We can see the whole picture. This is called the 'drive for central coherence' (we call it 'getting the gist'). For example, if we heard church bells and saw a large group of people dressed up in fine clothes and hats, throwing confetti at a couple outside a church, we might guess that this was a wedding.

Children with ASD appear to experience great difficulty in drawing together information in this way to understand the gist of what is going on or what is expected from them. In the example of the wedding given above, the child with ASD might focus on the church bells, or the pieces of paper floating around, but fail to recognise the event as a wedding. If we were sitting in a classroom and the teacher said, 'Take your pencils out', we might understand that a lesson was about to begin and we would be expected to write something down. We relate the details of the words in the sentence to the context. A child with ASD, however, might quite literally take his pencil out of the room. In other words, children with ASD have difficulty getting the gist. They may not understand the overall meaning when presented with the details. They may become preoccupied with detail.

This difficulty in getting the gist applies to the child's use of language as well as his understanding of pictures, stories, events and objects.

Use of spoken language

Language is made up from many different words. When we hear a sentence we use the context of the sentence to comprehend the detail of the words within it. If somebody says 'The lady led the dog down to the beach', we have a picture in our minds instantly of what is happening. This ability to get the gist allows us instantly to know that the word 'led' refers to the action of leading and not the metal 'lead'. We don't need to think about it.

Children with autism may jump to the wrong conclusion because they have problems referring context and detail backwards and forwards to each other. Most people do it intuitively without thinking about it.

We are able to get the gist of the meaning of phrases and sentences intuitively, but sometimes we make mistakes. You may be able to recall situations yourself when you have focused on a particular word in a sentence incorrectly. The whole meaning of the sentence and the social intent that surrounded it may have been lost. A friend of mine recently found herself in a difficult situation on holiday in France. She noticed that there was a large crack in one of the walls and asked a French builder to take a look at it. Unfortunately, in her limited French she asked him to go upstairs with her so that she could show him *l'amour* (love) when in fact she meant *le mur* (the wall)! The words sound very similar but mean very different things. This situation was quickly remedied and both parties saw the funny side of the mistake.

For children with difficulties on the autism spectrum, their own language may seem as confusing as foreign languages seem to the majority of people. Often this is because they struggle to get the gist of the situation because they fail to understand the meaning of words within the correct context. For example,

- A mother commented: 'Oh dear, my foot is wet. There must be a leak in my boot.' Her daughter insisted that she should take off her boot and take the leek out. In this instance the child failed to use the context to appreciate that the leak her mother was talking about was the type of leak that lets water in, rather than the vegetable.

- A grandmother related how she told her granddaughter that she liked to soak her 'bare feet' in a bath of warm water. Her granddaughter became frightened and distressed, insisting on checking that her grandmother had not suddenly grown feet like the bears in her story book.

Interest in parts of objects

Rather than seeing an object as a whole, many children focus on individual parts. This is also associated with not getting the gist. The child may see a doll's house as a series of doors, windows and walls and fail to appreciate it as a whole miniature house. Other examples of this focusing include:

- focusing on some particular aspect of an object such as the wheel or door of a toy car rather than using it as a miniature car to play a pretend game

- focusing on bits or parts of items in a room, for instance a table leg or a small piece of paper on the floor.

If children struggle to get the gist or pull together and understand the overall meaning of events, then it is perhaps easy to see how detail, patterns and sensory experiences become the focus of their attention.

Pictures

The child with ASD may fail to see the whole picture, looking at individual parts instead. He may focus on some tiny detail in a picture or photograph and hence see a feather rather than a picture of his grandmother wearing a hat with a feather in it.

He may count the stripes on the wallpaper or be fascinated by the spinning top on the floor and pay no attention to other things in the picture.

When you show a child with ASD pictures, where we may see a party, a park or a beach he may naturally be drawn to details or patterns he recognises or is interested in, rather than getting the gist or seeing the overall meaning of the event.

Sensory interests

Children may be drawn to particular sensory aspects, focusing on texture, taste, smell, sight or sounds rather than the function of the whole object.

- They might focus on the texture or sensation they get from touching or holding an object.

- They may show more interest in patterns, sensations or music.

- They may prefer to concentrate on one taste at a time – maybe eating the different items of food on their plate in turn or becoming upset if they 'touch' each other or mix.

- They may focus on particular sounds and exclude others.

- They may not be able to process people in terms of a whole but rather as separate 'bits'.

Facial expressions

When children are growing they see various emotions expressed on people's faces and they see them in a context with associated emotions. If they can't understand the context or the emotions, then it will be difficult for them to log the expression in their memory as being associated with similar emotions or contexts. This is what happens for children with ASD, and it makes labelling and understanding emotional facial expressions difficult. It may also be that because they look at individual facial characteristics separately, the overall facial expression is not remembered or recognised.

Learning

Children with ASD may learn by rote rather than intuition.

Seth had to learn by extensive questioning which objects fall into the category of fruit. He went through a period of several months when he repeatedly asked his dad whether different items were fruit ('Is a banana fruit?' 'Is a table fruit?' 'Is a sausage fruit?'), until he had satisfied himself that he knew which items belonged to the fruit category. He seemed to struggle to infer that if one wooden object wasn't a fruit that others would be unlikely to be too and had to go through many similar wooden objects to rule them out.

Being rigid in their learning style, children with ASD may be unable to transfer learning to a different situation.

When Julian was six his dad was angry with him for painting the kitchen table green and told him not to paint the table again. A few minutes later he found him painting the carpet. It took him a moment to realise that his son was not deliberately ignoring him or being mischievous but that he did not know intuitively that painting household objects was not acceptable. He had to be told that he could *only paint on paper*.

Settings

Children with ASD have difficulty in transferring skills or expectations they have learnt in one setting to another. Some children will only eat certain types of food at home, but at Grandma's house they refuse some of these same foods and will only eat something quite different.

'Going into town' for many children means a range of possibilities with visits to different places each time. To a child on the autism spectrum it may mean visiting the same three shops every time in the same order and buying the same things. The child fails to get the gist of the shopping experience and focuses in on learnt, and now expected, routines.

In this way, routines and expected patterns can develop quickly around settings and events.

Getting the gist: Ten-pin bowling

To help to explain getting the gist and illustrate some of the difficulties with poor central coherence experienced by children with ASD, we asked some parents to make a list of the types of things they would enjoy when going bowling. We then asked them to list the types of things their children with ASDs might enjoy if they were to go bowling.

Table 5.1 Ten-pin bowling	
Things parents might enjoy	*Things children with ASD might enjoy*
Company	Lights
Competition	Signs
Skill	Computers
Strike	Balls (colour, size, movement)
Winning	Skittles
Having a laugh	Sounds
Meal afterwards	Tapping the floor
Trip away from the children	Scoring system
Chatting with friends	Sliding along the floor
Socialising	Winning
Sense of occasion	Ramp
Improving	Mechanisms

The differences between the two are clear, in that the *children's* enjoyment was:

- related to objects
- very specific and easy to define
- related largely to details and patterns
- often to do with sensory experiences.

Whereas their *parents'* enjoyment was:

- related to the whole event
- socially oriented
- hard to define
- often to do with more abstract concepts like fun, camaraderie and anticipation.

The social event was the main focus of attention for the parents who had no difficulty pulling together ideas about the whole situation to do with bowling. For their children, the focus of attention was around the detail rather than an appreciation of the whole event. The children failed to 'get the gist'.

Twins story

Two children, who are twins, are going through the same situation. One child has difficulties on the autism spectrum and the other child does not. They are four years old and they experience a trip with their mother in different ways.

As you read through the two different accounts, try to decide

- which twin has ASD

- which descriptions are to do with *mindblindness* or *TOM* (M) and which relate to *(not) getting the gist* (G). Circle the M or the G next to each item depending on which you think applies.

1. **Ben**: The car stops. There is a screeching noise. That must be   M   G
the brakes. They are noisy.

   Tony: The car stops. There is a screeching noise. It is noisy. It is   M   G
not nice.

2. **Ben**: My mum gets out of the car. There is a smell of smoke.   M   G
That comes from the back of the car. I think my dad calls
it the exhaust.

   Tony: My mum gets out of the car. There is a smell of smoke.   M   G
There are stones on the floor. I pick one up. It feels hard
and gritty. There is a stripy fence. One, two, three, four…
I like the patterns I see when I walk by. I hear screeching
noises. I put my hands on my ears. I don't like it. I see a
puddle. Splash, splash, splash. Nice noise. Mum says 'No,
Tony'.

3. **Ben**: I see balloons hanging on the side of the house. A mix of   M   G
different colours of balloons. Hey, I wonder if there is
something fun going on here?

Tony: I see a window and a door. I see balloons hanging on the   M G
side of the wall. A mix of different colours of balloons. Blue
and red and green and pink balloons. There are 11, two
blue, two red, two green and five pink. I'll count that again.
Two blue, two red, two green…

4. **Ben**: Mum takes my hand. That makes me feel safe because I   M G
might be meeting some new people and that might be
scary.

Tony: Mum takes my hand. It feels rough. We walk towards the   M G
wall. I want to count the balloons again.

5. **Ben**: We walk towards the house. I hear some shouting. It is   M G
children's voices. There is also some music playing. It
sounds like nursery rhymes. Hey, this must be a place for
kids. That's good. This is exciting. I wonder what will
happen next. I'll hold on to my mum's hand for a while.
She will make sure I'm OK.

Tony: We walk towards the wall. I hear lots of different noises. I   M G
don't like this at all. What is this? I don't know this. This is
scary. I don't like my hand in that hand. I need to go now.

6. **Ben**: We get to the door. My mum presses a button. That must be M G
the bell. I didn't hear anything ring, but a lady is opening
the door. She is smiling and she says 'hello' to my mum,
and then 'hello' to me. She looks happy and kind. I like her.
She offers me her hand. She has a nice perfume. I look at
my mum. Is it OK to go with her? My mum smiles and
nods. She looks relaxed and happy for me to go. I let go of
my mum's hand and take the lady's hand.

Tony: We get to the door. Mum presses a button. A big gold   M G
button. It shines a lot. The door is opening. A grown-up is
there. I hear 'hello' twice. The lady's hand comes towards
me. What is it for? I don't want it. The hand takes my hand.
It is warm. There is a very strong sweet smell. This is scary. I
know that hand but not this new one.

7. **Ben**: 'Shall I take him to meet the others, Barbara?' she says to   M G
my mum. My mum smiles again. 'Thank you Joanne.' My
mum knows this lady and they seem to like each other. I
wonder who she is. Maybe she is the mum of one of my
friends.

Tony: I hear some sounds and the word 'meat'. I don't like meat. M G
This is all strange. I don't like it at all.

8. **Ben:** She leads me towards a door. I hear more noise. I hear a M G
voice I have heard before. It sounds like my friend. The
door opens. There are lots of colours in this room. There are
toys on the table. I see a cake on the table and it has candles
on it, and there are lots of presents wrapped up in coloured
paper. Hey, this must be a party.

Tony: I hear more noise. I hear a voice I have heard before. The M G
door opens. There are lots of colours in the room. The
wallpaper is yellow with blue stripes. One, two, three, four,
five, six, seven… The hand pulls me into the room. There is
a TV. I see videos on the shelf. I see a 'Thomas the Tank
Engine' video. I see a yellow car. The wheels spin round
and round. I like that. There is paper on the floor and
books and coloured things on the table. I see a cake on the
table and it has candles on it. Five. Four are blue and one is
red.

9. **Ben:** 'Hi, Ben', says my friend, Alistair. That reminds me who M G
that lady is. It is Alistair's mum. He is nice, so she might be
too. This must be his house and it must be his party.

Tony: 'Hi, Tony', I hear. I know this. I see him during the day M G
sometimes. He takes my trains from me.

10. **Ben:** There is lots of smoke coming from those candles. I hope M G
the wax doesn't get on that nice cake. It looks yummy. I
wonder when I get to eat some. I suppose I'll have to wait
until Alistair blows out the candles.

Tony: There is lots of smoke coming from those candles. It swirls M G
in the air in spinning, spinning patterns. That is nice. I like
that. I will watch that. The cake looks yummy. I shall eat
some now. It feels soft and sticky. 'No, Tony.' I put my
hands on my ears.

11. **Ben:** Alistair likes to play, *and* he likes me. 'Hey Alistair, let's go M G
and play!!'

Tony: 'Aa Aa Aaaa Aa!!' M G

Answers

Tony is the twin who has ASD.

1.   *G* Tony focuses in on the sensory experiences (The noise of the car). Ben works out from the context that the screeching sound is to do with the brakes.

2.   *G* Tony focuses in on the sensory experiences (the smell of the smoke, the feel of the stones, the pattern of the stripy fence). Ben works out from the context that the smell is to do with the exhaust.

     M Ben remembers what his dad has said in the past: 'I think my dad calls it an exhaust.' He is possibly thinking: 'That's what my dad would think or say.' He is able to think about what his dad thinks. Ben is showing he can use TOM.

3.   *G* Tony sees windows, walls, doors and balloons. He sees things in parts. Ben recognises that this is a house. He is able to put all the parts together to see them as a whole. Ben also recognises that the balloons mean that there is a 'fun' situation here. He is making a good guess about what might be happening, whereas Tony is mostly interested in focusing on counting the balloons he sees.

4.   *G* Tony focuses on the sensory experience of his mother's rough hand. Ben takes comfort in holding his mum's hand. He knows that this situation is out of the ordinary and might be scary.

5.   *G* Tony is focusing on the noise. He has not been able to bring together all the clues about the situation to make a guess that it might be fun. Ben hears music and adds this information to all the other clues he has that this could be exciting.

     M Ben hears children's voices. He is able to make some guesses about how they might be feeling by their excited voices. To Tony this is more unpredictable noise.

6.   *G* Ben can work out from the context that the button Mum presses is the door bell. Even though he doesn't hear anything, he knows what this situation means. Tony concentrates on the shiny button and then suddenly sees a grown-up and a hand. He also focuses on the smell.

 M Ben seems reassured by the lady's smile and kind voice. He is able to guess from her facial expression that she is happy. He also knows from his mother's facial expression what she thinks about the lady. His mum's smiles and nods mean that this is a safe person and that it's OK to go with her. He is displaying TOM; he is not mindblind. Tony is unaware of his mum's facial expression and concentrates only on the scary new hand.

7. *G* Tony focuses on the word 'meat'. He does not use the word in the context of the sentence.

 M Ben knows from his mother's expression that she knows and likes the lady. He can also guess who she might be.

8. *G* Tony sees individual objects: TV, video, stripes, the wheels of a car, paper, cake and candles. Ben sees the whole picture. He quickly puts everything together about this situation and realises that it's a party.

9. *M* Ben recognises Alistair as his friend. He talks about his personality and knows that he is a nice person. He is also able to think about what sort of a person Alistair's mum might be. Tony knows what Alistair does ('he takes my trains'); he does not think about his personality.

10. *G* Ben knows intuitively that this is a birthday cake and that the social rules in this context say that everyone has to wait for Alistair to blow out the candles before they can eat the cake. Tony isn't aware of these social rules. Instead he focuses on the sensory experiences of the smoke and the feel of the cake.

 M Tony is not able to consider what Alistair's mum might think if he plays with the icing on the birthday cake. So he cannot predict the outcome and is upset by Alistair's mum shouting.

11. *M* Ben is able to understand what Alistair might be thinking or feeling. He knows he likes to play and he knows Alistair likes him. This is all very confusing for Tony, who prefers to be left alone.

Summary

This chapter, 'Getting the Gist', and the previous chapter, 'Mindblindness', have focused on the two main theories which we believe help to explain the way children with ASD see the world and, most important, why they may behave differently from other children. Getting the gist means we can:

- draw lots of information from a situation to make sense of it

- use the context (and relate context to details to find meaning)

- see a picture or a situation as a whole.

People with ASD find this difficult and tend to:

- focus on detail

- concentrate on one small part of a picture or situation

- concentrate on a particular sensory experience, such as:
  - smell
  - taste
  - sight
  - sound
  - feel

- find it hard to 'see' a whole picture and make sense of it.

Mindblindness makes it difficult for people with ASD to:

- understand other people's thoughts and feelings

- understand that they are expected to change the way they behave depending on where they are or whom they are with

- predict what people might do next

- interpret different facial expressions

- understand how their behaviour might upset other people

- understand gestures and non-verbal signals.

It can make them seem:

- self-centred

- uninterested in other children and people.

Chapter 6

Sensory Interests and Sensitivities

For reasons not completely understood children with ASD may develop a range of sensory interests and sensitivities. Possible explanations include the fact that children who have less ability to 'get the gist' (see Chapter 5) may be less interested in overall meaning or in understanding the whole picture and so may be drawn more to the detail or to their sensory experiences. Also, children with ASD find that concentrating on sensory experiences reduces their anxiety. They feel comfortable doing it. It allows them to avoid more anxiety-provoking experiences such as interacting with other people.

Difficulties with imagination may also lead to a tendency to focus on concrete (definite and clear) perceptual experiences. Nature drives children's development partly through play. Imagination injects variety into this play so that the child can achieve more learning experiences. The play 'develops' as a result of imagination. If imagination is absent then play stays where it is and involves patterns and routine. Finally, because of mindblindness, children with ASD do not see the point of play 'with' someone else; as it is often other people who introduce variety into play, solitary play makes the introduction of variety less likely.

Whatever the reason, children with ASD often focus on noise, touch, feel, taste, smells and visual experiences – although not usually all of these. This may lead to preoccupations or compulsions, or oversensitivity to certain sensory experiences (this is discussed further in Chapter 17). For example, some children become very distressed on hearing loud noises that are easily tolerated by most people. This may be because they find it hard to give social meaning to their perceptual experiences or it may be something to do with the way their brains experience perceptions like sound. We don't really know.

Visual interests and sensitivities

It is very common to see children with ASD who like to watch patterns or certain types of shapes or other visual stimuli. They may seek these out on a regular basis and they often notice them in the environment. Some examples include:

- moving their hands back and forth in front of their eyes and watching the shapes and patterns made

- moving forks or other similar objects in front of their eyes

- watching out for electricity pylons and interesting shapes
- dangling coloured beads in front of their eyes
- looking at things through water.

Some children may have an interest in unusual aspects of movement, for example:

- watching certain parts of the body as they move (Jill, aged two, regularly watched her own hands; Sonia, aged six, used to watch her own heels as she walked along)
- looking at things from an unusual angle, perhaps from the corner of their eye by tilting their head or by placing their line of vision at a particular angle to something (Andrew lined his eyes up to the wheels on his train set)
- watching the movement of the credits at the beginning or end of a film
- intently watching balls rolling down slopes
- twiddling pieces of string and watching the movement.

Some children like to watch repetitive movements, such as:

- lining their eyes up in a certain way alongside a racing car track so that the cars repetitively rush past their eyes
- playing with toys that have repetitive movements (e.g. marble runs)
- watching parts of a video with patterns that they like (e.g. the pattern made by the puffing of smoke from a steam train cartoon). They may rewind these sections and play them over and over again
- watching the spinning of fans or brushes on a car wash.

Children with ASD may also find some visual experiences very uncomfortable, examples being:

- bright or flashing lights
- fluorescent colours.

Others may be distressed by subtle changes. When the packaging on food items such as fish fingers or burgers is changed by the manufacturers, some children refuse to eat the food inside, possibly believing that the food is no longer the same.

Temperature

Some children with ASD are either oblivious or particularly sensitive to temperature. One child was happily playing out in the snow in a tee-shirt while his brothers and sisters were wearing coats and sweaters. Another insisted on wearing a coat no matter what the temperature. This may be related to a specific compulsive routine or to a liking for sameness combined with a lack of understanding of social norms. These children may have a particular sensory liking for being warm or cool. It may be that they have not made the link between clothes and their temperature.

Some children with ASD may like to touch or lick cold things (e.g. pipes). Others may like to touch some things that are excessively hot.

> The father of Asha had to be extremely careful when the ceramic hob in the cooker was switched on as his daughter liked to experiment with the sensations she felt by putting her hand on the hot surface.

The temperature of food can be very important to some children, who will only eat certain types of foods when they are at exactly the correct temperature, even when they are favourite items.

> Jason, aged 16, would spend very long periods of time with the shower head mixing hot and cold water, saying he had to get exactly the right temperature.

Vibration

Children with ASD often have an interest in vibration. Children may place their hands or other parts of their bodies (such as their faces or feet) on the washing machine door, the tumble dryer or pipes which have water rushing through them.

Julian, aged six, loved to place his foot on the video recorder when it was rewinding.

Simon, aged five, would rush to the washing machine whenever it was on its final spin cycle in order to stand on the wooden floor that vibrated vigorously.

Anya, aged 11, derived a great deal of pleasure from sitting with her feet in a foot spa.

Touch and texture

Texture can be very interesting to people with ASD.

Luke, aged five and with autism, would rub a cloth against the wall in circles and would go on doing this, seemingly happy, until his parents distracted him.

The feel of skin or hair may interest some children with ASD. They may want to touch or rub their hands on skin or they may want to touch it with their lips or kiss it. Some parents or carers may wish to know when a child stroking their face is showing affection and when it is a sensory interest and of course both motives may be present.

Stuart, aged six, wanted to stroke or kiss the face or hair of people not familiar to him. This was more likely to be due to sensory interest.

Some children may be very interested in different types of texture and will absent-mindedly or deliberately stroke clothes. Some children may constantly wish to finger labels and go to lengths to locate them (e.g. down their trousers). Others may be very sensitive to labels in their clothes and insist that they are removed before putting them on. Some cannot tolerate certain fabrics and refuse to wear anything made from synthetic materials.

Julian could not bear to wear anything with buttons or zip fasteners, which made buying clothes very difficult for his parents!

Smell

Many children with ASD notice changes of smell in their environment. They may sniff their food, objects or other people as they explore the smells. If they have difficulty understanding what other people think or feel and struggle to understand social interactions, it may be that they fall back on sensory experiences such as smell.

Smell is an important stimulus (present in us all from early evolutionary times), and so perhaps it is not surprising that many of us find pleasant smells comforting.

> When Luke was ten he became very distressed one week in class. He would go up to his teacher and smell her and then become very distressed, shouting and stamping about. After four days she realised that she had been wearing a new perfume and so returned to her original fragrance. Luke's behaviour subsequently settled.
>
> Another boy seemed to find the smell of his father's feet very comforting and enjoyed sitting close to his bare feet.

Some parents say that their children regularly smell their food before eating it, apparently checking that it is familiar. In a recent survey we conducted of the parents of 50 children with ASD, 25 per cent said that their children were influenced by the smell of their food.

> Alan, aged 13, found the mixture of smells of different foods in restaurants very overpowering, to the extent that he would sometimes feel sick as soon as he entered the restaurant doors.

Some children find it difficult to cope with the smells of various cleaning fluids. Others may find it different if an environment changes in smell: for example, if a different cleaning fluid is used, or if a familiar adult changes his or her perfume.

Taste

Some children with ASD lick food and surfaces. We have come across several children who lick people's faces or objects such as water pipes. This may be because of an interest in the texture, the temperature or the taste; it is not always easy to know. Some children explore through taste. Some can be very sensitive to tastes and astonish their parents when they notice the difference between different brands of cereals, beans or chips when other people seem to be totally unaware of this.

Sound

Some children with ASD may be fascinated by the sounds in their environment. In contrast to other children, they may be less interested in the meaning behind the sound than in the sound itself. For example, they may hate the noise of their baby sibling crying and hit him or her without realising that this may provoke more crying. They may like to hear their mother raise her voice and therefore carry out an action that has elicited this response before, without understanding that Mum raises her voice in this manner because she is cross. Some children will seek out a noise on a video and play it back repeatedly, or wish to have it at a particular volume; some are fascinated by household noises such as those made by the boiler, extractor fans and so on.

Some children may be very frightened by certain sounds. The laughter on comedy television shows or clapping after performances may be very disturbing. This may be because of the quality of the noise itself or a lack of understanding about the social meaning of the noise.

It is very common for children with ASD to be extremely fearful of loud noises made by lawn mowers, helicopter engines, vacuum cleaners, heavy traffic or school bells. The instant reaction to seeing or hearing these items is often for the child to put her hands over her ears.

Pain

Some experts argue that some children with ASD have higher pain thresholds. Whether this is true is difficult to ascertain, but it is certainly the case that some children will bang their heads or bite themselves without becoming distressed. Some children may have cuts and bruises but not seem aware of them.

Amy's mother was very distressed to find that her daughter had several blisters on her feet as a consequence of her wearing new shoes all day, but was surprised that Amy had not complained of having sore feet.

These responses may be due to habit but may also be related to the fact that the social behaviours that children usually acquire as they develop have not been learnt. For example, children see adults responding to the sight of blood or to household accidents and from them learn emotional responses. Children on the autism spectrum pick up on these much less frequently.

Some believe that children with ASD like adrenaline coursing through their veins and will provoke it by eliciting pain in themselves; others, that the brain releases narcotic-like substances when one experiences pain and that the children like these. There are those who argue for and against these theories. After all, children on the autism spectrum do not seek out all experiences that elicit adrenaline (for example, they do not seek to put themselves in social situations) and most children with ASD do not in fact regularly harm themselves in a way that children with some genetic disorders do. It may be that the sensation is pleasant to them (much like a girl who pulls her hair because she likes the tingling sensation) and their ability to elicit it in a predictable way is somehow comforting. It may be a simple expression of anger or frustration. It seems most likely that the fact that they do not understand the social meaning and emotional side of injury and pain means that they behave in a much more matter-of-fact way.

Intensity

Several authors have written that some people with ASD may experience sensations differently or more or less acutely. (Donna Williams, for example, writes about this.) It is very difficult to know whether one person experiences heightened sensations more than another. Usually we compare our experiences with our own previous experiences. We cannot know exactly how other people experience sensations in order to make a comparison. What we do know is that some people with autism describe things very differently and may centre their attention on sensory experiences that others may ignore. The perceptual experience seems to be different. There is no clear evidence about why this is.

The intensity of sensory experiences appears to be relevant in that many children with ASD seem to be hypersensitive to some things – for example, noise (see Chapter 14, where a child dislikes the sound of the loo flushing). In other instances children may appear to be oblivious to experiences no matter what the intensity (for example, pain; see above). Fears may also develop around sensitivity to taste, smell, texture or other sensory experiences (see Chapter 13).

Mixed sensory interests

Many children have sensory interests that are interwoven.

Luke, aged nine, would go into class and stroke teachers' and pupils' hair. He seemed interested in the texture and would stroke faces and ears as well, but he was also interested in people's hair roots. He would spend more time on hair if the person had had it dyed and he would examine their roots. His teachers thought that he was looking for changes in colour. He would also run his fingers through the hair and smell his fingers. His teachers were convinced that he would do this more if they had recently washed their hair. Finally he would do this more to those other children who reacted by shouting. He would then laugh. He seemed to like this.

Summary

- Many children with ASD develop sensory interests (in smells, tastes, textures, sounds, patterns) and spend long periods of time exploring these.

- Others are very sensitive to various sensory experiences and become distressed when they come across them (e.g. loud noises, bright lights).

- Others seem to have very high or very low pain thresholds.

Chapter 7

Imagination, Time Perception, Planning and Memory

Imagination, time perception, planning and memory are all related. Children with ASD have difficulty in all four areas. It is likely that problems with imagination may set up ongoing difficulties with the ability to plan things for the future and understand the passing of time.

Imagination

Children with ASD have problems with imagination. When we imagine something, we are calling into our minds something that is not present. This is more than memory, because it involves playing with alternatives in our minds or making up new things. It makes use of memories but allows us flexibly to interweave different memories and construct ideas and plans. Imagination allows us to:

- *role play* at things

- *pretend* one thing is something else – symbolic play (e.g. pretend that a stick is an aeroplane)

- *fantasise* – think things that aren't real

- *imagine* different things in the mind

- be *creative* (perhaps with drawing, writing, painting or music)

- *invent* things.

Most people with autism spectrum disorders do develop imagination abilities as they grow older although this may be at a slower rate for many. They can also be extremely creative but are more likely to use alternative creative channels. For example, picture drawing may fall back less on intuition, impression or imagination, and more on logic, memory and juxtaposition. When drawing a house, rather than starting with the outline of the house, the child may start by drawing the bottom of the drainpipe on one side of the house and gradually and systematically work from there. Memory is also regularly used for creativity. Children with autism will play back scenes or events in play, and adults may juxtapose memories or knowledge to build new creations (e.g. pictures, inventions, etc.). In this way some people such as Temple Grandin and Stephen Wiltshire are renowned for their abilities.

Imagination is therefore important in helping to predict the future and in juggling with possibilities. For example, we can imagine lots of different outcomes to a meeting with another person. We can imagine scoring a goal in soccer, having a witty encounter with other people or being an actor or actress. Imagination is used in play and social interaction, but it is also important for problem-solving our way through life. Whenever we are faced with difficulties we create imaginary possible solutions in our heads and then we choose one and give it a go. If it doesn't work we go back to the drawing board and choose another.

What does impaired imagination affect?

As a result of their problems with imagination children with ASD have great difficulty doing the following things:

PLAYING

Play becomes difficult in all but learnt or methodical and logical ways. Make-believe play, role play and symbolic play are all affected. The flexible and imaginative use of toys will be affected. Many children with ASD find playing at tea parties very difficult when they are first introduced to the idea. It is not unusual for them to protest, for example: 'There isn't any tea in the teapot!' The whole concept of imaginary tea seems bizarre to them. Many will, however, copy other children's or their parents' make-believe play but they will not extend this with ideas of their own. As children get older, their imaginative play often improves.

PROBLEM-SOLVING

Thinking about different ways to tackle everyday problems (problem-solving) becomes difficult for children with ASD except where the solutions have been learnt by rote. Even the question 'What would you like to do now?' is sometimes impossible for them to answer.

GETTING ON WITH OTHERS

Social interactions for children with ASD become difficult because they have an inability to imagine the responses, attitudes, thoughts and feelings of others (as you can see, imagination is related to mindblindness). Many parents have told us that they have invited friends around to play with their child only to find that their child ignores them, refuses to share his or her toys or tells them to go home!

SENSE OF HUMOUR

Humour may be affected since much humour (except slapstick) involves imagination. For example, a simple joke like 'Why did the chicken cross the road' has us thinking of all sorts of possibilities before the joke teller says 'To get to the other side' which is the obvious answer. We think it is funny because our imaginations seek all sorts of alternatives before being returned by the joke teller to the obvious answer. We have been humorously tricked. The person with ASD does not find it funny because imagination does not lead them through this process. To get to the other side? Of course! What is so funny about that?

Sense of humour is of course very definitely present in people with ASD. Many families will attest to regular fun and laughter. Slapstick humour, a love of puns and wordplay and often what others regard as a dry, observational sense of humour may all be present.

PROBLEMS WITH UNDERSTANDING ABSTRACT CONCEPTS

Children with ASD have difficulty comprehending some concepts such as sarcasm, irony and abstract ideas including heaven, trust, honour, love and hierarchy. This is not just in the sense of knowing what the concept means but in intuitively knowing how it affects us. For example, social rules are often built around abstract concepts. As a ten-year-old child we do not say to the head teacher: 'Your car needs a wash' but we might do if we were another teacher. A ten-year-old would not say it partly because he would be able to predict that the head teacher might think it rude. However, the remark is not rude in itself. It depends on the circumstances and who is saying it. Social rules deem it rude for a ten-year-old, but not for a teacher. How do we know this? We pick it up. It belongs to a sense of hierarchy and a whole set of unwritten social rules. These are abstract concepts. If we struggle to understand the abstract then social rules become a problem for us.

LITERAL THINKING

An absence of imagination in thinking leaves a child with predominantly logical, fixed, concrete, literal ways of talking and thinking. Idioms may be taken very literally. One of the authors said to one young person with Asperger syndrome: 'I want you to take your vitamin tablet in the morning.' She replied: 'Where shall I take it to?'

Time perception

The present is present now; the future requires imagination

Many people believe that children with ASD possess an altered perception of time. It is certainly the case that children with ASD tend to live very much in the here-and-now. This is because thinking about the future involves imagination. It involves thinking about what might be. The past is logged as memory but it is very factual. Children with ASD are much more likely to be rooted in the present. It is likely that when they consider the future, they do not do so imaginatively in the sense of exploring new possibilities, but in a more literal way. For example, if a child with ASD is told that she is going to Grandma's house she might think she is going right now. Projecting the event into the future by imagination may be difficult. The child may also think about the last time she went there: they went a certain way and had sausage and chips for dinner. The child with ASD, unable to imagine alternatives, may expect that going to Grandma's therefore involves going the same way and having the same food. These problems reduce with age and development but can be very difficult to deal with on a day-to-day basis in a family.

Delay

Children with ASD often have great difficulty understanding any delay when they know something is going to happen. If Mum says, 'We are going to the hamburger restaurant at lunchtime,' the child not only has to project the event into the future but also has to have a mental idea of how much time there is between now and then. He may also have to consider all the things that have to happen in the meantime. This takes quite a feat of imagination. For example, it includes:

- *a period of time:* 'lunchtime'. What is lunchtime and when is it? One father told his son at breakfast that they were going to go to the park after lunch. His son made himself a sandwich, ate it and then stood at the door waiting to go to the park because to him it was now 'after lunch'.

- *a certain length of time passing.* What does it mean? How do we imagine time passing?

- *a series of events.* How do we know which events repeat themselves each day and which are new ones?

- *being in different places.* How do we imagine being somewhere else?

Once we consider this range of tasks we can begin to see why children with ASD find it so difficult to deal with delay. Yet we can be very intolerant of this predicament. It may help to avoid some frustration if we think about this as a period of developmental delay, which will improve as children get older and if they have some assistance from adults.

Planning

To plan something we have to know what the desired outcome is and to arrange in our minds a sequence of steps required to make it happen. We then carry out those steps. Research shows that children with ASD can be very good at planning some things. They are particularly good at planning things they have done before. They can repeat sequences of events. For example, they may be able to find their way back through town even when they have gone a complicated route and their parents are lost. They are not so good at planning where imagination is necessary. For example, they may not be able to work out an alternative route if a familiar road in town is blocked due to road works. It may be that novel tasks require the imagination to generate alternatives in their minds and they struggle with this. Similarly, these children's drawings tend to be of the same things and drawn in a very particular way rather than newly imaginative drawings.

Memory

Some aspects of memory also seem to be a problem. In our experience this is related to:

- *not being able to understand language or the social world very well.* It is difficult to remember something well when you cannot understand it

- *impaired time perception.* Children with ASD live in the here-and-now. If a child with ASD asks you a question and you give them an answer, they may keep on asking the same question over and over again. This may be because words come and go. Once they are spoken they are gone and hard to remember. The child may be repeatedly asking the same question as a way of understanding and remembering

- *a preference for visual memory.* Children with ASD seem to have a better visual memory. This is probably because of language difficulties and the fact that visual images when presented do not immediately disappear in the way that sounds do. Visual images persist and the child can refer back to them. This may be why strategies like visual social stories, visual timetables and the picture exchange communication system (PECS) work much better than equivalent spoken-word-based systems. These interventions are dealt with later in the book (Chapters 10 and 11).

Children with ASD are extemely strong in some aspects of memory. These tend to be the things in which the child has a particular interest. The factual aspects of memory seem to cover for the lack of imagination. When children without ASD go into town they think of all the possible things they can do and places they can go. They use their imagination. The child on the autism spectrum will fall back on memory, remember what he did before and want to repeat it again. Memory can sometimes almost seem like a substitute for imagination.

Summary

With limited *imagination*, it is difficult to:

- play
- problem-solve
- understand jokes and humour
- think creatively in certain ways
- understand social rules.

With poor *time perception*, it is difficult to:

- understand time frames (days and months are hard to differentiate)
- understand any time other than the here-and-now
- imagine the future.

Planning is difficult for children on the autism spectrum if they have:

- a limited imagination
- poor time perception
- no concrete memories to use in the planning.

Memories are difficult to form when we don't understand. So for children with ASD, it's hard to:

- remember complex verbal instructions
- remember social rules.

Chapter 8

Language

Most infants are born with an inbuilt ability to develop communication skills. In children on the autism spectrum these abilities are not as well developed. Some of the communication problems children experience come from difficulties described above such as mindblindness and not getting the gist, but children on the autism spectrum appear to have additional language difficulties. This varies very much from person to person and may be shown in a number of ways. Children with ASD may develop language later than other children and have limited receptive (understanding what is said) and expressive (knowing how to say things) language skills. On the other hand, children with Asperger syndrome will have apparently normal language development in infancy; problems only occur later when abstract language and the social use of language are being developed.

As a baby

Cooing and babbling

At different times in their development babies will coo and babble in response to the noises an adult makes. This goes hand-in-hand with the mimicry of facial movements and smiling at faces. We now know that this is a result of genetic programming that gears babies up to respond to their carers. It is nature's way of hooking parents in emotionally for the benefit of the child.

Children with ASD are much less likely to respond to their carers. They appear to be missing some of the programming that helps them to do this. They do not coo or babble in conversation and parents can frequently feel disappointed by this. If a parent does not know that their child has ASD they may blame themselves for their child's lack of response even though it is not their fault.

As a toddler

Gesture

Some children with ASD don't learn to speak or gesticulate. However, the majority do. Many young children with ASD don't point when communicating, and nodding or shaking the head may be rare. These skills may develop later. Often there is a very different quality in the way talking develops compared with the development of other children. Some use words or gestures but not in a communicative way. Some learn communication skills at a much slower rate.

Apparent regression

Some children with ASD learn words early but then stop talking altogether for several months. When they start talking again their language development occurs at a slower rate.

Repetitive noises or language

Some children with ASD who have little language may use sounds in very vocal ways. This may involve screeching, grunting or shouting. The purpose of these noises is usually not communicative, although the noise may change in tone when the child is excited or angry. Toddlers with ASD who have some language skills may repeat phrases over and over again. These phrases may be unrelated to what is going on around them. A child may repeat made-up words (neologisms) or words they have heard (or misheard) from an adult or the television (echolalia). For example, one child walked around saying 'Daranchella' over and over for weeks.

As an infant

Social language and language we use to have our needs met

Some children with ASD have language ability but don't use language much. It can be almost as if they don't see the point. Some children use words or gestures as a way of having their needs met and not to chat or problem-solve: 'Sam wants…' 'I need…'. The child may have a problem, know what it is, be unable to sort it out for herself but be unable to communicate this. She becomes frustrated, loses her temper and may do something that grabs attention, leading us to sort out the problem. Being unable to understand what is said makes the world a very unpredictable place.

When language and the ability to communicate develop in children with ASD there are often subtle differences in their uses. Some people with ASD are aware of their needs and how to get what they want for themselves. However, they may not understand that other people can also help and so may not approach others, or they may find ways of sorting out the problem in a way that is not acceptable to others, such as climbing onto a kitchen surface to reach the cereal.

Intonation and the production of sound

Intonation and the way language is used may be different in children with ASD. Parents often say that their children's language has a rote, precise, learnt quality to it rather than an easy, intuitive flow. For example, they may learn the root of a sentence and then add words to it: 'Out of the window can you see…a car [lorry, sheep]?' rather than: 'Look Mummy, it's a car!' The child may have an unusually flat, slightly expressionless tone of voice or may not regulate the volume of his voice. Many parents tell us that their children's volume control seems stuck on loud!

Mixing up pronouns

Children with ASD may get the pronouns 'I' and 'you' mixed up: 'You want a drink' meaning 'I want a drink'. They might also continue to refer to themselves by their own names, for example, 'Jonathan wants a biscuit'. Although these things happen to most children, those with ASD may struggle with this concept for a great deal longer.

When conversation develops

Starting a conversation

The child's introduction to a conversation may be unusual. For example, the child might find less-than-subtle ways of attracting the adult's attention, maybe moving the adult's head so that he can talk to her or using the adult's hand as if it were a tool.

Facts, not thoughts and feelings

The conversations of a child with ASD may be about factual information rather than being related to thoughts, feelings and opinions. Indeed, they may have some difficulty understanding what other people mean when they try to talk about their feelings.

One mother was crying soon after the death of her own father. Sara, her 13-year-old daughter who has a diagnosis of Asperger syndrome, could not understand her mother's sadness and seemed unaffected herself by the loss of her grandfather. She was much more interested in asking questions about how he died and what would happen at the funeral. This lack of understanding and emotion was extremely upsetting for Sara's mother who found Sara's attitude at that time almost unbearable.

Repetitive language and borrowed phrases

The language used by children with ASD may be repetitive rather than con-versational. They may borrow phrases they have heard elsewhere, from a video, TV programme, school or adults. These phrases are often used appro-priately but have a slightly odd quality to them, an example being 'I'm hungry mother' (from *101 Dalmatians*). Some professionals call this 'delayed echolalia'.

One-sided conversation

The child may want to talk about his own interests, unaware and uninterested in the response. Even if someone is bored or giving cues that they want to get away, the child on the autism spectrum may not have noticed. Building on a conversation that doesn't centre on the child's topic of interest may be diffi-cult.

Turn-taking in conversation is also difficult for these children. In fact, in many ways a conversation with one of them is not a conversation at all because a conversation implies a movement to and fro, the giving and receiv-ing of information that can lead in many directions. To those conversing with children on the autism spectrum this give and take often feels absent, and the listener may feel that the conversation is only going in one direction, con-trolled by the child with ASD.

Conversational speed

In a conversation the slow processing speed of a child with ASD may make the listener feel uncomfortable and want to stop the interaction. The level of detail from the young person on the autism spectrum may be far too great or some-times too little, with few cues to the listener about what the conversation is about or where it is going. Sometimes a child with ASD may start a conversation halfway through the story, leaving his listener feeling very perplexed.

Miscommunication and literal understanding

Miscommunication is common among children with ASD. For example, the young person may misinterpret what is said. She may hear 'We're not going to the park' as 'going park'. She may have difficulty weaving all parts of the sentence into an understood whole or may not understand the crucial importance of the word 'not' that reverses the whole meaning (see Chapter 5, 'Getting the Gist'). Another example of miscommunication is literal understanding. The child may understand the teacher's words 'Take your seats' in class as an instruction. He may pick up his chair and want to know where to take it.

Other examples we have heard include the following.

Mum: 'Would you take the dog for a walk down the road please, Peter? Just go up and down.' (Meaning: walk the dog up and down the road)

When his mum watched him with the dog, Peter was literally jumping up and down all the way down the road and back.

Dad: 'Hop into bed Jo.'

Jo literally hopped across the room into bed.

Joseph: 'Mum, Sally is crying her eyes out!'
Mandy: (Checking Sally's eyes carefully), 'No, they're still in!'

The social use of language

It is important to remember that children with ASD communicate differently from normally developing children. Their difficulties with Theory of Mind (TOM) and getting the gist make social communication very difficult. They are often unaware of the needs of their listeners and do not pick up the non-verbal clues in people's faces. Their behaviour can sometimes appear to be cheeky because they have not grasped the gist of a comment within a particular social setting. One girl was reprimanded by her teacher when she walked out of the classroom with her pencil after her teacher asked all of the children to, 'Take out your pencils'. A teenage boy with Asperger syndrome was considered to be insolent because he simply wrote 'Yes' in answer to his homework question, 'Was the Victorian age a golden era?'.

Understanding language appears to require a great deal more concentration from children with ASD than for other children. It is not surprising that they sometimes 'switch off', ignore us or seek comfort in some repetitive familiar tasks.

For those children who are very slow in learning about communication or have very little or no speech, there is still a great deal that can be done to help. This is discussed in much more detail in Chapter 11, 'Developing Communication Skills', along with ideas about helping the children who do not have speech to communicate more successfully.

The semantics and pragmatics of language

Since we are talking about social use of language it is a good time to explain some terms that professionals sometimes use, especially speech and language therapists. Sometimes they refer to the *semantics* of language. This refers to the meaning of words and putting words, phrases and sentences together as we speak. As mentioned before there are aspects of this relating to understanding and expression. *Pragmatics* is slightly different in that it relates to how we use language socially. It is to do with knowing when and how to say things; for example, knowing to turn-take in conversation, noticing non-verbal communication such as body language, knowing how to use eye contact and facial expression alongside language, knowing where to start a conversation, knowing what level of language to use depending on whom you are talking to, knowing how to maintain a topic or change one appropriately in conversation.

Further discussion takes place about many of these things throughout the book. Children with autism often have problems with semantics and pragmatics. Children with Asperger syndrome may have normally developing semantic skills but poor pragmatic language skills; for this reason their language is not picked up as a problem until the social use of language becomes more important in communication.

Summary

- Children with ASD often develop language later than other children.

- Some learn words early on but then regress.

- Children with Asperger syndrome will have apparently normal language development in infancy and problems only become clear later.

- When language develops it tends to be repetitive and lacking in social quality.

- Conversations may be more about facts than feelings and be rather one-sided.

- Understanding is often very literal.

PART 3

How Can We Help?

Chapter 9

Managing Behaviour

Parenting is much more than behaviour management. Children are nurtured, loved and cared for by their parents. They are given a sense of security and a place in the world from which to develop. A small part of this is managing behaviour to encourage a healthy developmental trajectory. This chapter explores this aspect of parenting.

Established principles of behaviour management

Being a detective

It may be helpful for parents to go into detective mode at times. For example, if a child is banging his hand on his head he may have a headache, he may be bored, he may like the stimulation or sensation that it provides or he may be frustrated. Which is it? We have to try our best to work it out.

Psychologists and behaviourists the world over have stressed the fact that behaviour occurs in a context. In particular, it occurs in time. Things happen before the behaviour and things happen after the behaviour. What happens before, during and after may affect their behaviour itself and whether it is more or less likely to happen again.

- *Before:* An example of 'before' is that if a child has a good or bad night's sleep this will affect her behaviour the next day.

- *During:* If, during a temper tantrum, a child receives a bar of chocolate it may affect behaviour immediately (ending the tantrum) but also in the longer term (increasing the likelihood of tantrums as the child hopes for more chocolate).

- *After:* If the child is taken to buy a new toy directly after a temper tantrum, this may affect how he is likely to behave in the same situation again (viewing the toy as a reward for the tantrum).

It is not within the remit of this book to go through every scenario, but parents who have certain principles in their heads may be much better equipped to deal with difficult behaviours. Being a detective means looking at what happens before, during and after to see how it affects the behaviour.

The analysis of behaviour in this way can involve many systems that you will see in various books. They include:

1. antecedents, behaviour and consequences (ABC) (Kaufer and Saslow 1969).

2. STAR (settings, triggers, actions, results) as described by Zarkowska and Clements in a book in 1994.

3. the iceberg metaphor as described by Schopler in a book in 1995; See the TEACCH approach (described in Chapter 20, 'Other Interventions').

Does the behaviour of children with ASD require different management?

Understandably, parents of children with ASD frequently ask professionals about the management of behaviour. Their children's behaviour can be understood, but to be managed successfully it requires a slightly different approach from that taken for other children.

Is behaviour communication?

An old adage of people working with children in general is that behaviour usually communicates something. There is a difference with children on the autism spectrum. It is true to say that behaviour communicates things to us, but with younger children on the autism spectrum it will usually not be intended but inadvertent. The child screaming in the middle of the kitchen may be communicating thirst but he will not be consciously communicating this to the mum who is present. She will have to guess and, with trial and error and intuition, will work it out. In this sense the child will not usually be attempting to influence the adult through his behaviour in the same way that other children might.

Mindblindness and the developmental tasks of childhood

In fact, some of the problematic behaviour of children with ASD comes from frustration that the world does not do what the child on the autism spectrum wants. Most children begin life with a notion that they are the centre of the universe. Parents provide food, drink, warmth, etc., when needed. As they get older, children begin to develop a sense that other people are in the world with different views and needs. They see that these different needs may compete with theirs. In healthy households parents challenge their children in small ways showing them that they do not always get the biggest piece of chocolate cake, they are not always first and so on. This provokes anger and rages (the 'terrible twos' and 'frightful threes') but, in time, the children learn to give and take, to share and cope with the competing needs of others. Children on the autism spectrum, on the other hand, have great difficulty with these processes. They go on for much longer thinking that they are the centre of the universe and that their needs are paramount (to the point that they may not be aware of the needs of others). A visit to a school specifically for children with ASD will show you how much they struggle with not being first to get the biscuit. They simply don't understand the need to wait or the need to share. These skills all relate to 'mindblindness' (see Chapter 4, 'Mindblindness').

The here-and-now

Children with ASD tend to live very much in the here-and-now. Future prediction requires both Theory of Mind (TOM) skills and imagination (what *might* happen next), and children on the autism spectrum struggle with both. Strategies that involve delaying rewards can be difficult for young children on the autism spectrum to understand.

What things will be less effective for children with ASD?

The mindblindness associated with ASD means that certain behaviour management strategies work less well for children with autism. This does not mean that none will work (many will), but a little more thought needs to be given to them.

PRAISE AND APPROVAL

Children with ASD will be less motivated than others by praise and approval from parents, e.g. 'If you tidy your toys away, I'll be very pleased'. As they have difficulty understanding other people's points of view or their emotional responses they will often have little or no interest in whether adults might be pleased with them.

INDUCING GUILT

Trying to make a child with ASD feel guilty is also unlikely to succeed e.g. 'You have made me late for work because you have been too slow getting ready for school'. As a result of mindblindness they find it hard to appreciate the effect of their behaviour on other people. They are unlikely even to consider it. In order to feel guilt we need to be aware that others might think badly of us. Similarly, strategies that rely on shaming children, such as saying 'Everybody will laugh at you if you wear your gloves to school when the weather is hot', will work less well (especially when they are younger).

STRATEGIES THAT RELY ON AN UNDERSTANDING OF INTERACTION

Walking away from temper tantrums as a strategy to make the child forget the thing she is raging about and follow you (e.g. in the supermarket or the park), in our experience is not very effective with children with autism. They are angry that they have not got what they want but may not pick up on the interactional aspects of this approach. This does not mean you have to give in to them. The tantrums will diminish when they realise whatever it is they want does not arrive. Calm but firm appears to work. Walking away is also a risky strategy as the child may not be safe if left alone.

As children with ASD get older there may be an interactional aspect to their tantrums. They may learn that tantrums have a desired consequence or effect, or, they may begin to develop a greater understanding of TOM, (see Chapter 4, 'Mindblindness'). Children with ASD develop some understanding of interactions but at a much slower rate than that of other children.

It is very common for parents to say 'we tried that and it didn't work'. Working out why it did not work is an important key to further planned strategies. Plans sometimes don't work but it is also important to think them through carefully, plan them carefully and carry them on for a while. For example, if a child is used to getting a biscuit in the supermarket when she screams out over and over again, and you decide that you will no longer give her a biscuit, then we can predict that certain things will happen:

- The child has been used to getting a biscuit and so will scream.

- When the biscuit doesn't arrive she will scream some more.

- When it still doesn't come then rage, mixed with a knowledge that this has previously worked, will lead to the child persisting with the screaming.

In other words, the behaviour may get worse. It may only be after several occasions of trying that the child begins to learn that the screaming and the biscuit are no longer associated with one another. With children who do not have ASD this may work more quickly because you can explain to them what you are doing and why. They understand the cause and effect between their behaviour and yours. This may be more difficult for children on the autism spectrum who may not associate the arrival of the biscuit with you, and may not realise your 'mind's' role in the process. This means that it will take a lot longer for them learn the process and this has an effect on parents, who will become exhausted more quickly.

Control and what gives behaviour power

We have come across several children on the autism spectrum who have very great power in the house because they are used to commanding what happens and when. This usually happens because of several factors:

1. Parents believing that, because children on the autism spectrum do not understand what is expected of them, they should be allowed to do what they want.

2. Parents believing that no strategy can work and therefore they may as well let the children do what they want.

3. Parents and family members feeling sorry for children on the autism spectrum and so giving them what they want all the time (for example, grandparents may sometimes do this).

4. Parents becoming exhausted or depressed or both because the relentless difficult behaviour becomes overwhelming and they cannot cope.

5. Parents letting children with ASD dictate when they are young leading them to expect to be able to dictate when they are older. Power leads to more power.

6. Aggression from the child making parents afraid that he will harm himself (e.g. banging his head against a wall) or family members.

While all of these things are understandable they lead to 'stuck' behaviour that can hamper the child's development. Families naturally want their child to grow into an adult who can have a place in society. This drive is often a good starting point for thinking about what you are trying to achieve as your child is growing. Whether the child will end up living at home, in a hostel or in a residential placement, she will be in company with other people 'in society'. Behaviour that makes this impossible may seriously affect her life. It is therefore crucial to help children and adolescents with ASD learn acceptable social behaviours and avoid behaviours that work against their future prospects.

Let us look at each of the points listed above in turn:

1. Even if a child does not understand why certain behaviours are not acceptable he can still learn to behave appropriately. If a child regularly plays with his own poo, we teach him not to for reasons of safety and hygiene even though he may not be able to understand why.

2. It is not true that no strategy can work for children with ASD. Some will have much less chance of working, as described above; but many strategies work well. Most take longer to work and they are tiring for parents, but they are worth it in the long run.

3. Giving any child what she wants all the time is not good for her. It sets up unreasonable expectations. If children are used to getting everything they want all the time, they will get a big shock when they go to school and will have a lot of difficulty integrating. As they get older they will find it harder to mix and share.

4. It is important that you recognise and acknowledge exhaustion and/or depression. Respite care and/or treatment and support for adults may be crucial to allow your batteries to recharge.

5. Letting children dictate is unhealthy. The outside world will not let them dictate and they will find it very hard unless they can be helped to understand some of the outside world's ways of working. This does not have to be traumatic if done gradually and systematically.

6. If fear is preventing you from doing what you think is right, this may be where you need support from others to help you to do what you know is right for your child. This may be support from family or the community (friends, church, etc.) or from a professional.

A model for changing behaviours in children with ASD

As you read through this book you will probably find that lots of different thoughts and ideas are being sparked in your own mind about ways you might try to change some of your child's behaviours. Sometimes, very small, simple changes can make huge differences. At other times the situation is much more complex. You may have to think very carefully and in some detail about the behaviour you want to work on and how you can change it. It is for this reason that we include the following model or template to help you to consider the behaviour, the various reasons about why it might happening and what you might do to change it. It is important to try to make sense of the child's behaviour if you are to have much hope of changing it. As children and young people with ASD have a different view of the world, it is helpful to keep reminding ourselves that their behaviour will be related in particular to their difficulties with TOM and getting the gist. Also, as you may have noticed, as parents and carers, we often inadvertently reinforce some of our child's behaviours.

There is a copy of this template in Appendix 1 for you to copy and complete whenever you are faced with a problematic behaviour. We use it in various places throughout the book to give you a flavour of how it can be applied in different circumstances and how these ideas can be put into practice. The rest of this chapter contains some basic principles that you may find useful when you are planning your strategies.

---

1. What is the problem?

This is not as easy as it seems! Take some time with friends or relatives to explore this in some detail. Ask yourself what your child does (or does not do) that you would like to be different. Try to be very specific and not too general (e.g. 'refuses to put shoes on in the morning' is more specific than 'problems getting dressed').

2. Why does your child behave in this way?

Situations and settings: Where does the behaviour happen? Where does it not happen? Is it to do with something in the environment (smells, noises, what other people do, etc.)? Who is around when it happens?	
Triggers and timings: When does it happen? Is it to do with anything pleasant or unpleasant? What are the timings in relation to other things? When does it not happen?	
Mindblindness: Is it to do with mindblindness? Does your child realise he/she needs to communicate his/her needs to someone? Can the child see others' points of view or understand feelings and needs of others in this situation?	

Getting the gist: Is the problem associated with not understanding what is going on and why? Does your child understand the meaning of events and that things have a certain order?	
Imagination: Does your child think imaginatively and does this affect the behaviour?	
Preoccupations and sensory experiences: Is the problem associated with sensory experiences and/or preoccupations? Is the environment too complicated or interesting?	
Social interaction: Does your child do this alone or with others? How does this affect the behaviour?	
Communication: Is the problem associated with language or communication difficulties?	
Emotions: Is the problematic behaviour related to anxiety or mood? Is it to do with your child's temperament? Is there anything else that might be affecting or upsetting your child (e.g. memories, dreams, illness, tiredness, boredom)?	
Sameness: Is it to do with a need for routine or habits? Is there a problem associated with being in control? Has there been a change of routine at home or at school?	
Responses: How have others responded to the behaviour? Does something happen after the behaviour that is important? How does it affect the behaviour in the future?	
Benefits: What positive outcomes happen for anyone (e.g. you, your child or your child's sibling) as a result of the behaviour? (Rack your brains: there usually *are* some!)	

3. What is the goal?

What is your specific aim (e.g. 'Encourage Moses to interact with us for a few minutes each day')? Is the goal of benefit to you or the child or both? Give a thought to the future. You are trying to prepare your child for the future as well as dealing with the present. Check that it meets the SMART criteria below.

- *Specific.* Be clear and specific (e.g. 'Help Ali to say "hello" to Grandma', rather than 'Help Ali to be more sociable').

- *Measurable.* Have an outcome or something that you can see and count (e.g. 'Say "hello" to Grandma when she comes to visit').

- *Achievable.* Start with something that is possible to achieve, otherwise everyone will feel disheartened.

- *Realistic.* There is little point in trying to achieve something that is unrealistic. If the child has not learnt to speak yet, learning to say 'hello' is unrealistic.

- *Time limited.* Be clear that this is something you would like to achieve in a certain time period. It will help you to focus.

4. Plan strategies

With friends or relatives write down as many ideas as possible that come to mind about how you might deal with the problem, matter how silly they may seem – it's often these ideas that lead to creative solutions!

Choose the strategy (or combination of strategies) that you think is most likely to work and that you are most likely to be able to carry through.

5. Checking

When you have a plan, write it down and check:

- the benefits for everybody concerned

- the costs – in terms of emotions, time and resources

- what might get in the way to stop it working? (Find ways of dealing with these if possible before you begin.)

6. Put the plan into action!

7. Monitor progress

If/when problems occur, don't be disheartened, go through this process again thinking about when, where and why it's not working and plan additional strategies.

Figure 9.1: A template for making sense of a child's behaviour and planning ways to help

Preventive strategies

Sometimes children with ASD develop less desirable behaviours out of habit or frustration because they have not learnt new skills to enable them to perform tasks (such as getting dressed) for themselves or because they simply do not understand what is expected of them. Encouraging them to learn new skills and helping them to learn about rules and boundries can help to prevent difficult behaviours from developing.

Encouraging learning and development
CHAINING

Chaining is a good technique for teaching new skills such as dressing. Break down the skill you want to teach your child into small steps. For example, if you are trying to teach him how to put on his tee-shirt think very carefully about the steps he will have to go through.

The first stage would be doing the whole thing for him. Line the tee-shirt up, hold it in the right way, lift it up, make sure the hole is in the right place and then put the child's head through.

You gradually let the child do the early parts of the process (e.g. laying the tee-shirt out on the bed in the right way before picking it up) and you do the rest.

He does more and more of the steps as he succeeds at each one.

BACKWARD CHAINING

Backward chaining is much the same technique as chaining, but in this case you start with the final stages and work backwards. For example:

- You would put the child's tee-shirt on for him but encourage the child to pull down the tee-shirt over his stomach.

- The next stage would be to complete less of the task for him and perhaps get him to put his second arm in to the tee-shirt.

- Building on his success he will, in time, be able to put the shirt on with minimal help.

Many parents with children with ASD find that backward chaining is more useful than chaining. With backward chaining the child achieves a sense of satisfaction and gets to the end result more quickly.

PROMPTING AND FADING

Most children need help to learn new skills. Prompting and fading is another way to help children to learn how to perform new actions.

Prompting can be done verbally or with physical assistance. If you were teaching a child to clean her teeth, for example, you might hold the toothbrush in her hand with her, showing her the movement she needs to perform to complete the task. You could do this verbally, giving brief instructions, if this suited the child's developmental level better. At the next stage (fading), you give slightly less support and continue to reduce support at the child's pace until she is able to complete the task alone.

It is very important to praise your child at every stage of the process. Even though we know children with autism may not understand praise, we still give it. As they get older their understanding increases and experiences of praise will be important to help this understanding grow.

Provide clear rules and cues about day-to-day activities and expectations

Children on the autism spectrum in general prefer a structured day and a clear explanation of what is going on around them. At school they are happier and do better if the classroom is not cluttered and there are clear rules and expectations. The same applies to home.

Early warning signs

Parents are experts in their own children. They often know what the settings and triggers are for negative behaviours. Work out the early warning signs your child gives out before misbehaving and, where possible, avoid situations that may provoke problematic behaviours. This helps when planning everyday activities. Some parents find that it helps to tell their children well in advance about changes to their routine.

Use relaxation and calming techniques where appropriate

Many schools and families use music and aromatherapy at times when they know their children are more likely to be at risk of being highly stressed.

Set boundaries when the child is young

Temper tantrums are hard for parents to cope with at any age. Because the tantrums of children with ASD are often louder and last longer than those of normally developing children, it is very tempting for parents to ignore many behaviours as a way of reducing embarrassing situations. Unfortunately, this does not help in the long term. If it is not dealt with in childhood, the behaviour continues into adolescence when it is considerably harder to control! This doesn't mean that you should be constantly telling your child off, however. Choose the behaviours you may want to change very carefully.

- Don't try to change more than one or two behaviours at a time.

- Ask yourself if it is in the child's best interests that the behaviour should change.

- Concentrate at first on things that:
  - are dangerous e.g. running onto the road
  - will be socially inappropriate in the future e.g. stroking people's legs.

Clear boundaries, rules and expectations stop problems developing.

Visual timetable

Children are given a visual timetable that shows the sequence of events each day. This can be placed on the wall in the morning. It consists of pictures of activities placed in the order in which they will occur. This visual routine could, for example, have a picture of the child having his lunch, and then going to the toilet; and then a picture of him doing his next expected activities, such as washing his hands, going into the playground, etc. The picture of the trusted adult around at the time could be varied each day so that there is flexibility about who takes him. The order and nature of activities can be changed as appropriate. Doing this every day and talking your child through it in the morning creates reassuring routines but also provides the flexibility to change things, giving the child plenty of warning that something has been changed.

Consistency

Once you have decided on an approach, stick with it. Giving in just once will make it worse! Children on the autism spectrum like rules. They like to know where they stand and what is going to happen to them. The structure and routine of rules is helpful to them. They will resist rules that don't comply with what they want to do (like any children) but they do like clear and understandable patterns in their lives.

Other behavioural strategies

Shaping and rewarding alternative behaviours

Shaping and rewarding alternative behaviours means encouraging a child to change a behaviour and learn a new one. It is done by praising or rewarding her as she achieves small steps towards the final goal. Since praise works less well for children on the autism spectrum, offering them rewards is often a better incentive. Rewarding an alternative behaviour is often a good strategy. Children do not need to understand that the reward is a reward as such, they just need to have a pleasant experience. Shaping usually involves moving in gradual steps from one behaviour to another, but it can be done in one big step.

Simon used to hit his little sister almost by habit whenever he walked past her. It was difficult to know the reason for this. He just seemed to like doing it and seemed oblivious to her responses. His father and mother arrived at a plan. Whenever he approached his sister they positioned themselves and took his hand as it came in for the swipe. They would turn the swipe into one stroke of her hair and then lift him away and read him a three-page book that he loved. The most difficult part of this was being in the right place at the right time but they struggled on and after two weeks he was spontaneously stroking his sister's hair and not hitting her.

Helping the child internalise external messages

A similar approach we use that we have not seen described elsewhere is a phased system to try to get internal voices working inside the child. When a small child walks towards the kerb of a busy road, the parent behind shouts 'No'. The child freezes and the parent comes and says, 'It is dangerous, look at the cars'. A small child who hears this message internalises the message. As he grows he hears a warning in his own head when by the roadside. He has internalised the message.

When a 15-year-old child with autism called Annette went outside she would walk into the road without realising the consequences. Her parents were very fearful of letting her out and she would have large aggressive outbursts because of frustration and because she wanted the same freedom as her 12-year-old sister. They had tried to teach her a roadside code but it seemed to make no difference because she never seemed to put it into practice. A staged plan was put into action.

- *Stage one.* Her parents would go out with her and as she approached the road they would come up alongside her and look at her and say clearly, 'Stop! Don't go in the road. It is dangerous'. They did this repeatedly and always said the same thing.

- *Stage two.* After a while her parents said, 'Stop!' but then went up to her and said, 'What am I going to say to you?'. She would then invariably say, 'I don't know'. They would then go back a stage and say 'I'm going to say, "Don't go in the road. It's dangerous"'. After a few weeks though she began to say (much to their surprise) 'Don't go in the road. It is dangerous'. They then said: 'Well done!'

- *Stage three.* At the next stage instead of saying 'Stop' they went up alongside her in the usual way and looked her in the eye. Or the first few occasions she said, 'What?' and they would go back a stage and say, 'What am I going to say to you?'. She would then tell them and they would praise her.

This approach seemed to help Annette internalise what she was being told by the adults around her. More specifically it probably helped her lay down the information in a place in her memory where she could access it in real-life situations. This was probably because the approach was *in* real-life situations and was repetitive. Six months later her parents told us that a university student from the Parents and Carers Together scheme had taught Annette the Green Cross Code and she had seemed very receptive to it in a way that she had not been a year earlier. This may have been growing maturity or the fact that an individual other than her parents was doing it with her (this is often helpful) but, either way, her parents were much happier that she could be safe in roadside situations.

Positive reinforcement

Positive reinforcement is intended to increase good behaviour by rewarding it. Star charts, trips out, comics or anything else that the child finds rewarding can be used. The desired behaviour is made clear to the child so that she knows exactly what is required of her in order to achieve the reward.

When rewarding approved behaviour, it is useful to have a clear idea of things that reinforce or are motivating for the individual child. Usual reinforcers are:

- certain foods

- certain toys

- points/tokens/stars

- certain activities

- time with an adult

- praise.

> Dominic was 12. He had Asperger syndrome and couldn't see the point of homework. He often refused to do it. He especially hated repeating work that he had done in class. His parents helped him design a chart that had steps going towards a reward chest. For each step he could put a star on the chart. The star was for completing each piece of homework. For each star he also received the reward of a certain amount of time on the computer. The reward chest was a computer game that he wanted. He did well with this and his parents faded (gradually reduced and stopped) the rewards. Once in the habit of doing his homework he seemed to settle well to doing it (with the exception of those pieces he was asked to repeat!)

Material reinforcers, e.g. food, may be more powerful for children with ASD. Other reinforcers for this group include:

- things they are preoccupied with (see Chapter 17, 'Preoccupations')

- computer time

- video time

- cards, models, keys, etc., to add to the child's collections

- trip to the railway museum, airport, etc.

Whilst novelty and surprise (which encourages reinforcers to be changed) are very motivating for many children, this may not be the case for children on the autism spectrum. They are more likely to prefer predictable, consistent rewards. It is important to make sure that children understand clearly what is happening (e.g. 'if…then you can…').This means that praise when used has to be very specific: for example, 'If you put your shoes on now, you can have your comic to read'.

Rewards can be used for a variety of scenarios, (for example, when the child is successful in doing something or when the child does not do something for a specified period of time).

Ignoring

> James, aged seven, had little language. He would stand and slam the door repetitively in the kitchen whenever he was hungry. It did not seem to his parents to be a deliberate act to provoke them, but he had learnt that doing this resulted in a plate of biscuits and a drink arriving on the table. His parents realised that this was a problem when he started doing it in the middle of the night and at school. After discussion it was decided that he would have to learn better ways of asking for food and drink. They began to use the picture exchange communication system (PECS; see Chapter 11). At the same time they began to ignore the banging. This was very hard at first because he could be very noisy. However, the two strategies together complemented each other and were very effective.
>
> It is very important if you use this approach to stick to your guns because, unless used consistently, it can make the behaviour worse. This is because if a child is used to getting something after any particular behaviour and then it doesn't arrive, then he does it a lot more. James banged the door a lot in the first two weeks of starting this approach and the neighbours had to be warned. Luckily, they were very supportive – although the strategy was timed for their summer holiday!

Distraction

Distraction is a useful technique for diverting unwanted behaviours in all children. A great deal depends on knowing the best distracters.

> Charlotte could be distracted from her obsession with playing with water when her mother played her favourite music.

Graded extinction

Extinction involves the removal of any responses that might be rewarding for the child's undesirable behaviour. For example, when parents repeatedly respond to a child's cries for more food, drinks, stories, etc., at bedtime, they are inadvertently rewarding the child's cries. If they don't respond in this way, the child will learn not to call out repeatedly. The technique of 'controlled crying' where parents try ignoring the child's crying, is an example of this. It involves parents staying outside the child's bedroom, but after previously decided time periods, e.g. five minutes (see Chapter 16, 'Sleeping', for further details), the parents go into the child's room for a few seconds and calmly say, 'It's bedtime. Go to sleep,' and leave without any fuss. The difficulty with this technique is that the behaviour usually gets worse before it gets better, but with persistence it can be very successful.

Desensitisation

Sometimes behaviour is provoked by fear. Desensitisation is a technique for helping people to cope with fearful situations. It is done very gradually so that the person learns to cope with his fear. The effect is that the fear gets smaller and smaller as he learns to cope.

Sandy hated spiders and refused to go into any room when he had seen one. This would sometimes provoke very aggressive outbursts as his parents attempted to get him to settle. Desensitisation helped Sandy. The aim is to break the connection with fear. He started by learning to cope with looking at a line drawing of a spider, moving on eventually to looking at photographs of spiders, then videos and then plastic spiders and then dead spiders. In the end he could put a glass jar over a live spider and put a postcard underneath it and throw it out the front door. This helped him feel in control of his fear. The idea is to practise coping with slightly scary things until they no longer feel frightening.

1.   Sandy made a list of the scary situations and rated them from 0 (not scary at all) to 100 (the scariest imaginable).

2.   He constructed a hierarchy by putting them in order.

3.   Sandy worked his way down the list.

4.   Each time he moved down the list and succeeded in overcoming his fear, he was rewarded with marks on a chart he had made and for every three he was given a much liked die cast model.

Time out

'Time out', when used by psychologists, really means removing the child from situations where negative behaviour is being rewarded (sometimes it is unclear what the reinforcers are).

Zaffar, who was six, liked rough and tumble but he also like to chew and bite. Mindblindness meant that he had a problem knowing when he was hurting someone else. He would frequently engage in rough and tumble with a parent but, halfway through, would start to bite. He could not understand when the parent was cross. His parents used the simple strategy that they would rough and tumble with him but as soon as he bit they would put him down straight away and say 'No'. They would place him away from them but also move away from him. This was also done at school and proved very effective.

Even though time out is often used to mean secluding a child this is not the goal. The goal is never punishment. The goal is to take away the pleasurable reinforcer. Zaffar enjoyed biting as part of the rough and tumble. He needed a clear message to him to understand that the rough and tumble was fine but that biting was not.

Consequences

Consequences have a big part to play in influencing whether a behaviour happens again. If we go to a friend's house and we eat good food and enjoy the company we are more likely to say yes to going again than if we were cold, we didn't enjoy the food and were bored. Consequences can be positive or negative. Some of the positive ways of encouraging helpful behaviours are discussed in this and other chapters.

Smacking

We do not suggest active punishments like smacking. Smacking may encourage aggression or prompt withdrawal in children with ASD.

Traffic lights

We have devised a traffic light system for a small group of children at the milder end of the autism spectrum. Children on the autism spectrum seem to like it because they are often fascinated by traffic lights. The idea is:

- A child is given a goal that she understands and to which she agrees.

- She is also given a hierarchy of response costs. This means that if she breaks a particular set of agreed rules, there will be consequences. These might be things like missing a television programme.

- She is also given a hierarchy of rewards. These are written down.

- The child is told that she is on green when she is achieving her goal (e.g. sitting at the table throughout a meal). This can be reinforced regularly by the parent saying to the child: 'Well done, you are sitting at the table very well, you are still on green. If you carry that on until the end you will get twenty minutes on the computer.'

- If the child gets down from the table, she is told she is on amber and is warned that she may go to red if she doesn't come and sit down.

- When a child goes from amber back to green by sitting down, she can be praised with healthy dollops of praise and told that her reward is still possible if she remains on green.

Reinforcement is usually built into the traffic light system. In our experience when it is set up well children don't need to have the response costs applied very often once they understand the system. They may test it a couple of times and so it is important to stick to the rules if they do. One parent made a traffic light from board and had it standing in the house (see Gerald's story in Chapter 12, 'Tantrums, Frustration and Aggression').

Conclusion

These are some of the strategies that can be used to help manage behaviours. A range of others are described in this book throughout the chapters in Part 3. The child's level of ability and understanding will influence which strategy is helpful for which child. The most important thing is not so much using any particular strategy as taking a flexible and thoughtful approach to addressing any problems as they arise.

Summary

- Young children with ASD communicate their needs differently from other children. When they scream they may not be *consciously* communicating something to their parents.

- Children with ASD continue to see themselves as the centre of the universe for longer than other children. This means that they may continue to become angry and frustrated about not having their needs met until they are much older.

- Strategies that generally work *less* well with young children with ASD:
  - those that involve others' emotions, e.g. 'Mummy will be very pleased if you eat your meat', or 'People will laugh if you wear your gloves in summer'
  - lengthy explanations.

- Despite the pressures, remember that it is not good for healthy development if children dictate the household rules. They need help to learn that the outside world will not allow them to dictate.

- Plan any new strategies carefully. The model described in this chapter should make it easier to plan.

- The most successful plans are those where the family members work together as this fosters mutual understanding and support.

Chapter 10

Developing Social Skills

Providing help to improve the way children and young people develop social skills is central to helping them to feel more at ease in what is largely a social world. We know from research that early help with interaction skills is likely to reduce isolation and the occurrence of repetitive behaviours. That aside, there will of course be times when people with ASD need respite from a social world and this must be borne in mind.

It is useful to hold in our minds the theories covered in the first chapters, and particularly the chapter on mindblindness (Chapter 4). This background gives us an understanding of why people with ASD struggle so much in social situations. The chapter also makes it clear that there are different levels or degrees of mindblindness. Some young people are very severely affected; others less so. The best interventions will be those tailored to the individual's needs and level of ability at that particular time, rather than those based on chronological age.

It is also worth remembering that one single intervention will not be enough. Seeing a psychologist or a speech and language therapist for ten sessions is not the answer. Social skills develop over years, and so the interventions need to be occurring in the everyday life of the child. There are various techniques that can be used over the years to aid the social development of children with ASD.

In this chapter we will consider:

- achieving a realistic understanding of the individual needs of the child on the autism spectrum

- certain common types of social difficulty (with examples) and how they might be tackled using this understanding

- key strategies for parents and carers
- helping children to understand emotions
- helping children develop imaginative skills
- helping children learn how to interact socially including developing an understanding of social rules and cues
- supporting the development of friendships and relationships
- dealing with things that get in the way.

Achieving a realistic understanding of the abilities and needs of the young person

First, it will be useful to consider some of the main difficulties that make it hard for children with ASD to develop social skills. It is crucial to understand as far as is possible how a child on the autism spectrum views the world and how this affects socialisation. There are many facets to this, some of which have been covered in the previous chapters.

Language difficulties

Language delay will undoubtedly affect social development, but it would be simplistic to say that improved language acquisition will improve social skills. We know that there are several other important factors that impact upon social development.

Mindblindness

This is a key factor affecting social development in children on the autism spectrum. As we explained in more detail in Chapter 4, mindblindness takes away the single most important tool that we use to know how to engage with other people. An analogy would be removing the circuit in the computer that interprets what is being typed on the keyboard. The computer no longer has any way of knowing what the person sitting at the computer is thinking. It cannot respond and so it does its own thing, repeating the screen saver over and over without any understanding that the person sitting at it wants a response from it. It is blind to the needs of the person wishing to interact with it.

Getting the gist

Society is governed by social meaning and is woven together with social rules. The overall meaning of social events gives us purpose and provides meaning to our interactions. We seek fun, companionship and competition. We know when to be serious and when to play. We make jokes, we play games and practical jokes. We plan and carry out tasks together with purpose and we engage in all manner of joint activities. All of these things go way beyond the detail of our surroundings and yet, since children on the autism spectrum struggle with overall meaning, they are left largely with the detail. If a child with ASD goes to a social event and cannot see that such an event is a party, a wedding or a school disco, his sensory interests and interest in detail and patterns will predominate. Similarly, if he goes to the playground he may spend most of his time watching the patterns made by the roundabout or running up and down alongside the wooden fencing rather than seeking out other children. This is in part because of a difficulty in understanding overall meaning, and a problem seeing beyond detail and patterns in the environment.

Sensory interests, special interests and repetitive behaviours

Sometimes children are so preoccupied with their special interests or rituals that any potential social opportunities are missed.

Anxiety

All of us are affected at times by anxiety. It affects us socially. If extreme, it can hamper our performance, our ability to think clearly and our ability to respond with confidence. Children with ASD are no different, except that they are more likely to find the social environment a very scary place for the reasons outlined above. Their anxiety will make it even harder to interact socially.

Slower social development

All aspects of development are by their very nature 'developmental'. That is, we build on things previously learnt and add new learning to them. This follows a natural progression. You cannot learn division and multiplication if you have not learnt what numbers mean, and you cannot learn algebra until you have learnt all of these things. Social development is the same. It is acquired in building blocks that follow one upon the other. If a child gets stuck at a particular point, expecting him to jump three steps ahead is unrealistic. Yet children on the autism spectrum in mainstream school or society may be on a different learning curve when it comes to social skills. The difference means that sometimes they are expected to be more capable than the building blocks they have acquired will allow. It is therefore sensible to prevent stagnation if possible and encourage socialisation skills to maintain progress 'developmentally'. This progress may not necessarily be at the same speed as everyone else's but it should be sequential and advancing.

Lack of intuitive learning

Children with ASD appear to find it harder to pick things up intuitively. Many families will compare their child with ASD to a sibling and say, 'his sister seems to pick it up without even trying, but everything has to be explained to him'. Some children pick up social skills by rote rather than intuitively and this means harder work for those around them in terms of teaching them things that others pick up naturally. It is also harder for the children as they have to concentrate more in social settings and quickly become fatigued.

Lack of experience

Often, because the child may not grasp the importance of interacting with others and because it is so difficult, she will not take the opportunities to learn and practise her social skills as often as others. She may actively avoid other children and adults. Her parents may keep her out of social situations. Her lack of experience adds to her problem with understanding the social rules that other children learn fairly readily. That is not to say that she needs to be flooded with social experiences – this would be too anxiety provoking – but social experiences can be woven into the fabric of life in a gentle way.

Generalisation

Children with ASD can learn social rules but often fail to learn that the same rule applies in slightly different circumstances or situations.

Emma, who was fascinated by people who were overweight, learnt that she should not make comments about people's weight when she was on the bus in the mornings. However, she continued to make remarks at college, in the street and when out shopping. She had to learn that the rule applied in all settings.

Common types of social difficulty

We have put together some scenarios of problems faced by some children with ASD. As we go through each scenario we will try to explain what might be happening in the mind of the child and in the situation in general. After this, there is a more general section on helping children acquire social understanding and skills.

TYPES OF PROBLEM

- seems in a world of his own

- doesn't play with other children

- exhibits socially inappropriate behaviour.

We will take each of these in turn, considering WHAT the problem is, WHY it might be happening, and HOW we might deal with it. We will use three different scenarios to illustrate them.

WHAT is the problem?

Seems in a world of his own

Moses is aged two. He had been given a diagnosis of autism when he was 18 months old. His parents, Julia and Simon, were worried that he did not seem to respond much to them at all. He was very severely affected by his autism and seemed to be getting more and more isolated, very much in a world of his own. He was a very quiet passive boy most of the time and demanded very little attention. He seemed happiest when left alone. He was fascinated with paper and in particular liked to flick through the pages of mail order catalogues. This would keep him occupied for hours at a time. He rocked back and forth making rhythmic sounds as he turned the pages, seemingly very contentedly. When Julia and Simon tried to get him to play with some of the brightly coloured toys they had bought for him, he would scream loudly and become very distressed. It seemed that nothing could distract him from his mail order catalogues and his parents wondered if they would ever be able to get close to him.

Julia and Simon felt very excluded by Moses' behaviour and were determined to find ways to help him to move out of his own isolated world. They realised that this would be difficult but decided to try to tackle the problem together. With a little help, they worked though the template described in Chapter 9, 'Managing behaviour'.

1. What is the problem?

Moses seems in a world of his own. He rocks, flicks though his catalogues, doesn't interact with his parents and gets upset if they try to distract him. He prefers to be left alone.

2. Why does your child behave in this way?

Situations and settings: Where does the behaviour happen? Where does it not happen? Is it to do with something in the environment (smells, noises, what other people do, etc.)? Who is around when it happens?	Whenever he sits on the floor, anywhere, he wants his catalogue.
Triggers and timings: When does it happen? Is it to do with anything pleasant or unpleasant? What are the timings in relation to other things? When does it not happen?	Happens most of the time. Whenever he's not sleeping or eating. He expects to do it after meals. Doesn't matter who is around. He seems to have developed a routine. Does not happen when eating, playing rough and tumble games.
Mindblindness: Is it to do with mindblindness? Does your child realise he/she needs to communicate his/her needs to someone? Can your child see others' points of view or understand feelings and needs of others in this situation?	Yes. He doesn't understand anyone's point of view other than his own because of his ASD. He expects his book to arrive and doesn't know about our thoughts and feelings.
Getting the gist: Is the problem associated with not understanding what is going on and why? Does your child understand the meaning of events and that things have a certain order?	He doesn't seem to understand about playing or interacting with us.
Imagination: Does your child think imaginatively and does this affect the behaviour?	He doesn't have any imaginative skills yet. Maybe that's why he plays with his catalogue.
Preoccupations and sensory experiences: Is the problem associated with sensory experiences and/or preoccupations? Is the environment too complicated or interesting?	He loves the sound, feel, and smell of the pages. He likes the rhythm of his chants and rocking and seems to switch off. It seems worse when the TV or radio is on.
Social interaction: Does your child do this alone or with others? How does this affect the behaviour?	He plays with his catalogue on his own. It never develops. It is very repetitive. We feel excluded by his play.

Communication: Is the problem associated with language or communication difficulties?	He can't say or understand anything yet.
Emotions: Is the problematic behaviour related to anxiety or mood? Is it to do with your child's temperament? Is there anything else that might be affecting or upsetting your child (e.g. memories, dreams, illness, tiredness, boredom)?	He likes to do it when he's bored and sometimes if he is upset. It seems to comfort him. He seems less anxious when he has his book.
Sameness: Is it to do with a need for routine or habits? Is there a problem associated with being in control? Has there been a change of routine at home or at school?	He likes the routine. It has become a habit.
Responses: How have others responded to the behaviour? Does something happen after the behaviour that is important? How does it affect the behaviour in the future?	It might be because we used to give him his catalogues when he was upset or if we needed a break. We don't try to interact with him when he's doing it.
Benefits: What positive outcomes happen for anyone (e.g. you, your child or your child's sibling) as a result of the behaviour? (Rack your brains: there usually *are* some!)	He seems to really enjoy it. It relaxes and comforts him. We can get on with other things easily when he has his catalogues.

3. What is the goal?

At first, Julia and Simon thought their goal would be to make Moses more sociable and although this was their overall aim, they realised that it was not SMART (specific, measurable, achievable, realistic or time limited). After much debate, they settled on a simpler starting point as their goal, which was trying to get him to interact more with them for a few minutes each day. The main problems they perceived were his lack of interaction and his intense fascination with his catalogue to their exclusion.

4. Plan strategies

Julia and Simon wrote down several ideas:

- Take his catalogue away!

- Distract him with toys.

- Change his routine. Don't put him down on the floor.

- Play games – he enjoys rough and tumble.

- Join in with him when he's turning his pages!

They decided that taking away his catalogue would be too unkind and distressing and that toys hadn't distracted him in the past and so ruled these out. They decided to try a combination of the last three ideas.

5. Checking

The plan was that they would play rough and tumble games with him sometimes instead of putting him on the floor with his catalogues. When they gave him the catalogues they would sit with him and join in with his noises and rocking.

- *The benefits.* Might get him to make more eye contact.

- *The costs.* Might be time consuming, tiring.

- *'Is this reasonable for my child?'* It doesn't make too many demands on him and we know he likes rough and tumble.

- *'Is this reasonable for us?'* We will feel very silly joining in with him!

- *'What might get in the way to stop it working?'* Embarrassment.

- *Find ways of dealing with these if possible.* We'll get over it!

6. Put the plan into action!

HOW might we deal with it?

Simon and Julia came up with a clear plan to help Moses. Below is a little more detail to explain how they put it into action.

Mindblindness

Moses didn't understand the need to interact with others, so this meant most of the work needed to be done by his parents. When they played rough and tumble games with him it seemed easier for him as he would make eye contact with them and chuckle happily. When they stopped and put him down on the floor his expression became blank again and it was very hard to make eye

contact with him. In order to try to overcome this, his parents sat down on the floor with him, trying to get their faces and eyes close to his in brief games of peek-a-boo.

Getting the gist

As Moses does not get the gist of playing with his parents, they have to show him and teach him about the order of games. They also want him to realise that it can be fun to do things with other people.

Sensory interests

Many children with ASD are easily preoccupied with the sensory aspects of objects and find people and social interactions dull in comparison. Moses derived a great deal of pleasure from his catalogues and his parents were rightly reluctant to take them away from him. Their intention was to join in with his interest and help him to understand that additional pleasure could be gained from sharing his interest with them. Again, however, they had to do most of the work because Moses did not know that people could be fun too. One at a time, Simon and Julia sat with Moses and started copying his movements and rhythmic sounds. They tuned in to his interests to gain entry into his attentional space. He quickly learnt to tolerate this and later began to show interest in this. His parents were careful to make sure there were no other distractions such as noise from the TV or radio.

Communication

Moses was unable to talk at this stage. He could, however, make sounds. Initially, these sounds were for himself. He could not understand the point of making sounds for or to others. When his parents began to join in with his sounds, he became interested and stopped to listen and look at them. When he made a noise, his parents copied it. In time, he learnt to wait and take turns. Moses and his parents took clear enjoyment in this. These were the first steps in helping him to understand sounds as a means of communication and people as a source of enjoyment!

Routine

Like most children with ASD, Moses liked routine. Routine makes the world a more predictable place. He liked to know what would happen next. His parents were careful not to change his routine too much when they first put this plan into action. They also tried to keep to the new routine of joining him in his play with his catalogue for a few minutes three or four times a day.

Parents' responses

Julia and Simon had been in the habit of leaving Moses to play with his catalogue alone. By gradually joining in with him, they were showing him that being with them could be enjoyable. As time went on they learnt that they could use this technique to help him to use language. Moses' story is continued in Chapter 11, Developing Communication Skills.

In summary, Julia and Simon's plan helped Moses develop in many different ways including,

- helping Moses tolerate someone being with him more often

- helping to build other people more into Moses' routine

- helping him use more eye contact

- helping him develop an early understanding of mutual play.

WHAT is the problem?

He doesn't play with other children. He is socially isolated

Gareth is aged six and has never played with other children. As a toddler he sat and played on his own, usually happily and oblivious to others. He avoided others when they became too noisy. He went to an autistic unit in a special school where there were only seven other children. He learnt to tolerate other children and happily played alongside them.

Gareth made huge progress at the unit. His language skills developed well and his parents and teachers agreed that he would most probably cope in mainstream school with support. He went along to the new school for a trial period for one day a week before transferring full time. He found this very difficult because he missed the routine of his old school. He also appeared to be becoming increasingly isolated and never played or conversed with other children despite their approaches. He had always been interested in collecting things like stones, leaves, conkers and acorns and spent his play times searching for items for his huge collection at home. His parents and teachers were worried that he was becoming even more avoidant of the other children.

WHY might it be happening?
Mindblindness

Gareth has always struggled to understand the points of view of others, and is poor at making guesses about how others think or feel. This means that most of his thoughts are centred around his own interests with little understanding of the needs of others. This was a key reason for his poor socialisation. He didn't understand why the other children approached him and started talking to him.

Liking for routine

When he moved to his new school Gareth missed his routine. This unsettled him. He reverted to his safe routines of collecting stones in the playground whenever he had the opportunity.

Sensory interests

Gareth's fascination for stones meant that he was often preoccupied with them, examining them carefully and rubbing them gently across his lips. This often interfered with any social approaches made by the other children as he was so interested in his stones that he was oblivious to them.

Language difficulties

Gareth's language was delayed but he was able to understand most simple language and could talk eagerly about his own interests. He struggled with more complex language and quickly stopped listening when he did not understand. His use of language was very literal. He was being honest but appeared abrupt to others. For example, when asked 'Would you like to play?' he would say 'No'.

Getting the gist

Gareth rarely understood what was going on in social situations. His preoccupations with sensory interests, special interests and repetitive behaviours dominated, and he had little understanding of camaraderie, the reasons for social play, companionship or the meaning of games, competitions or common interests.

Anxiety

Fear in a new social situation made Gareth become even more blinkered as he attempted to get through the day.

Slower social development

Gareth's experience of social interplay up to the age of six was limited. He had missed many of the building blocks of social development. The children he had spent most time with at the unit had very similar difficulties to his own.

Lack of intuitive learning and difficulty understanding social rules

Gareth had never picked up social rules intuitively. He needed things to be explained to him in detail.

HOW might we deal with it?

Mindblindness

As we discussed in Chapter 4, the development of mind-reading skills is delayed in children with ASD. We are beginning to realise that some aspects of these skills can be taught. Since children with ASD find it harder to pick up as they go along, this means that we (parents, teachers, friends) need to teach it more specifically. The section at the end of this chapter, 'Learning to understand emotions', has lots of ideas about how we can help.

Liking for routine

The routine at Gareth's new school was very different from his old one. His teacher, parents and teaching assistant helped him to adapt to the new system by making a visual timetable for him. He had a chart on the wall for each day with small pictures showing which activities would occur in which order. When an activity was finished he went to the chart and turned the picture over before looking at the next. If there was to be a change in routine for any reason, his teacher would explain this well in advance using his chart. We know that children with ASD find it difficult to hold complex routines in their minds and that the additional visual cues make this much easier and reduce the need for constant verbal checking.

Anxiety

These timetables considerably helped to reduce Gareth's anxiety, although at first he needed to keep on checking!

Sensory interests

As Gareth had always been fascinated with stones and leaves, his teachers knew that this was not going to change suddenly. They decided, however, that they could use his interests to help him to share his knowledge with his class mates. For 'show and tell' time after lunch one day they asked him to bring some of his collection into school. The other children were keen to find out more and he was happy to talk to them about his favourite topic! His teachers extended this idea to include collecting things for the nature table. Slowly, Gareth began to recognise some of the benefits of shared interests.

Slower social development

Gareth's social development was very much delayed. His parents and teachers realised that he was not interested in the same types of imaginative play as his peers. They did notice his interest in chasing games, however. He loved to run about with the others who were very accepting of him even though he didn't understand the rules!

After some time the teachers noticed the other children becoming irritated with him and introduced the idea of the 'Circle of Friends'. This is an idea that was introduced initially in the USA. With the permission of parents and child, a teacher or another adult meets with the child and about six volunteers from the class on a regular basis. They try to identify things that the child finds difficult, especially in the playground. Then they try to think of ways to help and try them out in practice. The adults facilitate this and support and encourage all of the children.

At first, the group focused on the rules of chase games, which helped considerably. The children were very supportive in helping Gareth, particularly as new rules had to be invented to help with some of the rougher elements of the game which Gareth initially interpreted as them pushing him!

Gareth's parents and teachers helped him to develop his imaginative play skills by engaging him in play with miniature figures and dinosaurs for short periods of time. At first he didn't want to play but then he gradually developed an interest in dinosaurs, which was shared by another boy in his class. His imaginative play, although very limited, began to develop. A friendship also began to grow with the boy as the two started collections of dinosaurs.

Lack of intuitive learning and difficulty understanding social rules

When his teachers recognised this shared interest in dinosaurs, they informed both boys' parents. Gareth's parents invited the boy over for short periods of time, helping Gareth to share and teaching him some basic social rules. This was very demanding for Gareth as he did not intuitively know how to behave. His parents took great care not to overwhelm him and only gradually increased the times that they invited the boy over to play. Sometimes they joined in and encouraged the children to consider each other's needs. Gareth's parents also sometimes gave him gentle feedback about friendship and what friends can do for each other. The Circle of Friends helped Gareth greatly. His teachers continued to help to teach him social rules in the classroom when the need arose. His parents continued to do the same.

WHAT is the problem?

Socially inappropriate behaviour

Bernard is aged 12. He is a very able young man who was given a diagnosis of Asperger syndrome when he was 11 years old. His parents had suspected that there was something wrong for many years and had tried to get help from his school and from their doctor. He always did well at school and was described as one of the more able children in his class throughout his early schooling. He was particularly good at maths and science and enjoyed reading about history. He learnt to read when he was four years old and had, ever since, 'had his head in a book'. For a long time he was fascinated by anything to do with the *Titanic*. His parents thought that his Asperger symptoms had not been recognised for so long because of his intellectual ability. They thought people saw his behaviour as a little idiosyncratic at first. Later, however, his behaviour was interpreted as cheeky, bad mannered and manipulative. His responses to his teachers' questions and demands ceased to be funny when he was 9 or 10.

Teacher: 'Take your pencils out.'

Bernard walked out of the classroom.

Teacher: 'Bernard, would you like to take the register to Mrs Jones?'

Bernard: 'No, thank you.'

Teacher: (crossly) 'How many times have I told you not to use your rubber today?'

Bernard: 'Four.'

Teacher: (in a religious education lesson) 'I want you all to draw a picture about what this word means to you.'

She wrote the word 'God' on the board.

Bernard drew a dog 'because it spells dog backwards'.

Some of the other children recognised his vulnerability as he got older and persuaded him into all sorts of pranks, including ringing the school fire alarm.

When he went to high school, he struggled greatly. His new teachers saw his 'idiosyncratic' behaviour very differently. They could not tolerate his talking to them as if he was a peer. They did not know that he hated to be touched and were astonished by his angry response to the briefest of touches. They became angry about his literal responses to their questions and homework assignments. The same boys from primary school, under the guise of being his friends, encouraged him to behave badly and he was regularly in trouble. His school work suffered and he became more and more withdrawn and agitated. One day his teacher told him that if he could not behave properly he should go home. Bernard went home. After several further incidents, he was instructed to go to the head of year where he was reprimanded yet again. Halfway through, much to the alarm of the teacher, he collapsed on the floor. The teacher went to seek help and on her return found him laughing.

WHY might this be happening?
Getting the gist

Bernard could not make sense of the various social situations he was in.

It is easy to underestimate how difficult life in general for young people with Asperger syndrome can be. The problem is that, like Bernard, children and young people with Asperger syndrome may not stand out as being any different from their peers except in very subtle ways which are often misinterpreted as being bad behaviour.

The world is a very confusing place for people with Asperger syndrome. Each social interaction seems to have to be learnt separately and made sense of as if in a vacuum. Previous information cannot readily be used in the interpretation process. Everything seems to be rule-bound. The social world has to be constantly interpreted and often mistakes are made. For example, Bernard's parents were alarmed one day when he did not come home for tea. Later it transpired that he had been to have a drink with a stranger he had met in the library. His parents said: 'We told you *never* to go off with strangers!' His reply was: 'But he wasn't a stranger, I met him in the library yesterday.'

Literal use of language

Bernard interprets language very literally. He is unable to read between the lines in social communication. He knew that his behaviour had caused trouble but did not know why. His view was that he 'could not behave' and so went home as instructed. He was very confused when he was then in trouble for going home.

Exhaustion

Trying to make sense of the social world and use of language can be very tiring. Parents of younger children and some teachers tell us that the children fall asleep in class and often switch off or daydream. Maybe this demonstrates their exhaustion and their need to have some time on their own.

Bernard found the school day very tiring and this appeared to affect his mood and his ability to concentrate on his work.

> In clinic a seven-year-old girl with Asperger symptoms recently told us, 'That's enough talking now', and walked away to play on her own.

Mindblindness

Bernard was keen to have friends and thought that the boys in his class who were setting him up were his friends. He could not read their thoughts or interpret their motivation. He did not understand that what they asked him to do was sometimes for their amusement. He could not work out who were good friends and who were not.

Anxiety

The change of school had caused Bernard to be anxious. He had moved from a small, relatively safe environment to one which was much larger and much less sympathetic. There were different teachers, new subjects and changes of class-rooms several times a day. He was touched and jostled, which he hated. He was shouted at and in trouble almost daily. When his parents asked him about the incident when he had 'collapsed', he said he just needed to switch off and lie down. This seemed to be his way of coping with extreme anxiety. He could not say why he laughed when the teacher returned but we know that laughter is a common response to anxiety.

HOW might we deal with it?
Being proactive

Bernard's parents had been worried about how he might settle into his new school but did not know how best to prepare him. There is a number of specialist teachers now whose remit it is to liaise with parents of young people with difficulties on the autism spectrum and their teachers. Often they will prepare the young person for the transition to a new school by arranging several school visits and talking with them, their parents and prospective teachers. If you are concerned about how your child may cope, it is worth contacting the new school well in advance to ask for advice and support. A meeting at the school may help.

Mindblindness

Bernard is very able. He has some understanding of other people's minds but still struggles with the more subtle, complex social interpretations. He cannot understand deceit, subterfuge or manipulation, for example. He will continue to rely on his parents and other adults to help to explain the behaviours of others. Meanwhile, his parents gave him some rules, which initially included that he should keep away from the boys he called 'friends' and not do anything they asked. Aware of their son's vulnerability, they role-played and videoed some of the situations and scenarios he had found himself in and re-enacted different outcomes. There are several other ideas about helping young people with mindblindness at the end of this chapter under the sections headed 'Learning to understand emotions' and 'Learning how to interact socially'. His parents began to talk with him about the differences between strong friends and weak friends and how to work out which were which.

Training teachers

Most schools and colleges organise training sessions for teachers to help them to understand and work with young people with ASD. Bernard's head teacher organised further training for his staff to help them to support Bernard when he returned to school. Their understanding made a huge difference to him and significantly reduced the number of occasions he was in trouble.

Communication

Bernard's teachers agreed that any incidents at school should be communicated directly to his parents and that they would meet on a regular basis to discuss his progress.

Anxiety

The head teacher asked for the advice of a specialist ASD teacher. She was able to provide a number of strategies to help teachers to support Bernard. One of these was a way of allowing him the opportunity to leave the classroom if he felt overwhelmed or if he felt the need to shout out. Bernard was placed at the front of all of his classes. He had a red card on his desk, which he turned over if he needed to leave the room. His teachers all knew about the symbol and gave him permission to leave. Bernard rarely used this, but said he found it reassuring to know that he could.

Other ideas for helping children with ASD in the social world

There are many other strategies that parents have used, some more successfully than others, and we describe some of these below.

Key strategies for parents and carers

Engaging with children and interacting with them is crucial to everything that comes after. This can at times be hard, but don't give up. Here are some tips to think about.

Some tips to help engage with young children

1. Use the child's own environment – try to get involved with his or her activities.
2. Use the child's skills – if he or she is good at numbers, play number games.
3. Use the child's interests – if he or she likes cars, look at car magazines together.
4. Try chasing and tickling games.
5. Promote shared activities, e.g. visits to the railway museum.
6. Promote shared play, e.g. card or board games.
7. Prompt your child when you want something from him and teach him to prompt you.
8. Some things can be learnt by rote, e.g. greetings.

Learning to understand emotions

Children with ASD have problems understanding the emotions, thoughts or attitudes of other people. There are several different ways in which these difficulties may be addressed.

Explain emotions in everyday situations

This means telling children what you are thinking, feeling or seeing, when they are thinking, feeling or seeing something different. This can be in the course of everyday activities or in more specific circumstances. Such circumstances should be tailored to the needs of the child and include explaining why you or someone else reacted as you did (e.g. happily, angrily, etc.). Other examples could be Circle of Friends time in school (see later) or debriefing (explaining and discussing what went on from your point of view) after an incident or, indeed, any set of circumstances that you felt to be appropriate. It is important to keep what you say as positive as possible and to tailor the amount and level of feedback to the child's understanding.

Emotion projects and scrapbooks

Projects at school can be put together around emotions. Homework may, for example, involve concentrating on one emotion, such as excitement. The young person could be asked to collect and cut out faces from magazines to put in a scrapbook. Class discussion can be based around these scrapbooks.

Emotion diaries

A similar idea to emotion projects for home would be an emotion diary – helping the young person to keep a record of situations where they felt or observed particular emotions.

Attwood emotion thermometer

In order to be able to reflect on the feelings of another person, it is necessary to have some understanding of emotions in oneself. Tony Attwood (1998) suggests that some children benefit from using an emotion 'thermometer' or 'volume control' to measure the degree of intensity of emotions. This helps the child to reflect on her emotions and the contexts of those emotions, and also to develop a keener understanding of the intensity of emotions, rather than seeing emotions just as something people feel or don't feel.

Using an emotion thermometer can be done in an exploratory, educative way with a young person by placing photographs and words at appropriate points on the thermometer, or it can be done in the context of specific situations (e.g. after a classroom disagreement). The emotion thermometer can be used for specific emotions (e.g. worry). The child can identify where she is on the scale in certain situations. It can be incorporated into work on how to manage emotions.

Ahmed would get very angry in school on a regular basis and not necessarily about things that would make other children in his class angry. For example, if his teacher had asked the class to complete a task and he hadn't finished it when asked to put his things away at the end of the lesson, he would become very angry saying that he had to finish the piece of work. When his teacher insisted that he stopped, he would shout, throw things, knock his desk over and sometimes kick his teacher. Ahmed then began to use a laminated emotion thermometer that he had put together with a doctor, his teacher and a learning support assistant. A diagram of this thermometer is shown in Figure 10.1. He talked about how angry (where on the thermometer) he was, and he began to make plans with them about what to do when the thermometer reached certain places (strategies such as counting to ten, speaking to his support assistant, asking for quiet time in the classroom annexe). This worked very effectively. He learnt more about how to monitor his emotions and, more important, he learnt a range of coping strategies.

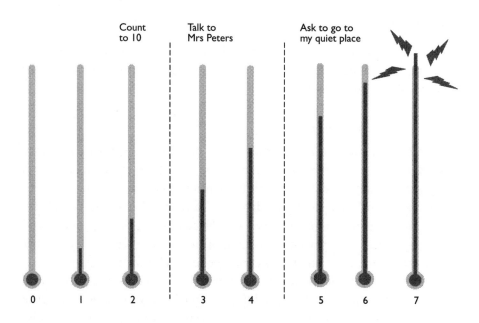

Figure 10.1: Ahmed's emotion thermometer.
Source: Reproduced with the kind permission of Dr Chris Ince, based on Attwood (1998)

Mind-reading literature

A book called *Teaching Children with Autism to Mind Read: A Practical Guide* (Howlin, Baron-Cohen and Hadwin 1999) gives advice on how to help young people with mind-reading. It breaks down the process of learning to understand emotions into different levels. This starts with teaching the child to recognise emotions from photographs and moves on in small steps to helping them to recognise emotions in context, using scenarios. The final stages are about helping young people to understand what the characters in the scenarios might be thinking or what might happen next.

The authors are clear that this is not a recipe book for curing mindblindness or ASD. The book does, however, provide a structure for helping children who are at the threshold of developing an understanding of emotions and beliefs to enhance their skills in this area. It is aimed at children aged between 4 and 14 who have an overall language age of 5 years and over.

MORE COMPLEX MIND-READING SKILLS

A range of more complex skills can be taught. For example how do we know when someone is joking or bluffing? How do we know when someone is saying one thing but meaning something different? These are difficult skills for anyone. They can be helpful skills to acquire because they also help us to know when to make a joke and when not to make a joke. This skill relates in part to mind-reading but also to getting the gist. The context of the situation will be important.

When helping our young people with these skills we can use the Happé Strange Stories (Happé 1994) to assess what kinds of skills our young people have. These tests can also be used to explain things like double bluffs, white lies, persuasion and so on. *Role playing* in groups can also be helpful.

Self-thinking

Older adolescents with Asperger syndrome can find it useful to 'self-think' in social situations before they say anything. Georgina (aged 15) and Mack (aged 16) often said the wrong thing and were laughed at by their friends. In a teenage issues group they agreed they would try to 'self-think' two questions before they spoke with another person in social situations. The two things were: 'What is the other person thinking and feeling' (is he or she happy, sad, angry) and 'What is going on?' (is he or she joking around? Is this serious talk?). They didn't always know the answers but they found that they said fewer things that got them into trouble or were laughed at when they used these techniques.

Understanding facial expressions and emotions

Some software and videos are also available to help children understand facial expressions and body language, including *Gaining Face, Mind-Reading* and *See What I Mean?* (see the References and Resources section at the back of the book: more information, demonstrations of the material and payment details are downloadable from the websites).

Reading stories with emotions and a range of facial expressions

Introducing children to stories where you can discuss emotions may be helpful. This needs to be done in a way, and at a time, when the child or young person is able to understand them. Many stories would be suitable, but some that we have found useful are listed in the Further Reading section at the back of this book.

Groups and emotion-focused games

Emotion and mirror games can be done in group settings. Children can be asked to mirror the emotions of others by literally pretending to be another person's mirror.

Another group game is to send a person outside the room and agree an emotion (e.g. anger). The person comes back into the room and asks each of the others in turn to do an action in the manner of that emotion. For example if they were to, say, tie your shoelace you would have to tie your shoelace 'angrily' and the person has to try to guess the right emotion. This technique should only be used where young people have enough skills to be able to participate without being threatened.

'Sculpting' or 'Freezing' is another game where each child has to make a statue with his or her own body to show an emotion (e.g. fear) and someone has to guess the emotion.

CDs for helping children learn empathy and imagination skills

There are many compact discs (CDs) that can be used for children who are comfortable with a computer to help them explore imagination skills. They also help children explore emotional aspects of story building, and can be a useful fun way of explaining emotions to children. Some of these are mentioned in the References and Resources section at the back of this book. These are programmes that require parents, carers or teachers to be close by or alongside the child to talk him through the emotional or imaginative aspects of the stories he is creating. Left to their own devices children with ASD will tend to write very fact-based stories about what happened (what people or things did and when). They are less likely to use emotions, opinions or thoughts in their stories. The adult alongside them can encourage them and inject small amounts of these things. They will need to tailor this to each child's understanding, and particularly emotional and imaginative levels. This may be quite different from their educational level (for example, in mathematics) and this needs to be taken into consideration.

Developing imagination

Imagination has already been discussed in Chapter 7. When considering how to help children develop imaginative skills, it is important to consider at which developmental stage the child's imaginative ability is. We shall now examine these stages.

Memories and imagination

STAGE ONE

When we see how the development of memory and imagination go alongside each other we notice that the earliest aspects of imagination are the replaying of memories in our minds. We do this as very young children. Some teenagers with ASD who have poor imaginative skills will still be at this developmental stage.

Maggie, aged 16, had atypical autism. Every day she would come home from school and go into her bedroom. She would verbally run through everything that was said to her throughout the day. Her mother would often hear through the door phrases like: 'Maggie, you go and wash your hands now.' 'Yes, Mrs Munster.' 'Sit still, Gerrard, and leave Michael alone…' This would go on for quite some time.

STAGE TWO

After a while, children begin to act out memories. Many children on the autism spectrum act out or play out episodes of favourite television programmes. They do not add new material or flexibly introduce new interactions, they simply play out what they have seen.

STAGE THREE

The next stage is where children take pieces of memories and build them like pieces of a jigsaw into new stories. Children with ASD find this very difficult. They are quite 'concrete' in the way they can use their memories.

STAGE FOUR

This is the stage of development where new ideas almost seem to have no connection with memories. Memories have become so fluid and flexible that new play does not recognisably map onto memories. Abstract play develops where fantasy is unlimited. The child's imagination is free to roam where it pleases without the fixed constraints of single or fixed memories. Again children on the autism spectrum have great difficulty with this.

Planning and imagination
STAGE ONE

At this stage planning and memory are inseparable. If Mum plans to go to Granny's house, the child with autism can only relate this to what Granny's house has meant before. There is little flexibility in what can be done there. The child expects to go the same way in the car, eat the same food and play with the same toys.

STAGE TWO

More is possible as the child has memorised alternative things that can happen at Granny's house. He can choose from these alternatives. He can plan by selecting alternative memories.

STAGE THREE

In this stage children pick memories from other places. They run scenarios in their minds based on a range of experiences they have had. ASD children find this very hard.

STAGE FOUR

Planning is more flexible. It includes limitless possibilities. Spontaneity can take you anywhere. Children with ASD have great difficulty with spontaneous planning.

Symbolism and imagination

As with memory, symbolism and its relation to imagination develop in stages that follow one from the other.

STAGE ONE

Children begin by imitating or copying what they have seen. They copy in concrete ways what Mum is doing. If she is in the kitchen with a bowl and flour and eggs, they want a bowl and flour and eggs. Plastic ones won't do. They are not the same.

STAGE TWO

After a time children begin to be able to use plastic bowls and make-believe eggs.

STAGE THREE

Symbolic play follows on after this where the child can use objects that don't look like the ones they are intending them to be. A building brick becomes an imaginary egg that is broken into an invisible bowl and mixed with a biro that represents the wooden spoon.

STAGE FOUR

Flexible symbolism becomes complex and includes the abstract. The eggs can be magic eggs with incredible powers. The spoon can metamorphose into a wand that can turn the bowl into a high-powered car that drives the child to an imaginary new land where he meets new friends. And all this in the kitchen!

The reason that this is important is that imaginative skills develop like building blocks.

Patricia Howlin and colleagues (1999) also describe ways of teaching pretend play to children with ASD. There are some examples in their book *Teaching Children with Autism to Mind Read*.

A boy, Justin, lines up bricks as part of his play. His older sister is desperate for him to play imaginative games with her and is very frustrated when she tries to teach him to make spacecraft from his bricks. However, it will not be possible for him developmentally to jump from Stage One straight to Stage Four. He needs to have experiences over weeks and months that gradually help him develop. This is key to developing imagination skills.

In Justin's case his father and mother and sister first had to help him tolerate anyone playing with him for five minutes. They copied the way that he played. Once they had achieved the goal of five minutes' play they added more goals. These included letting his dad change the repetitive shapes that he routinely built into different shapes. After a while his dad introduced shapes that could be incorporated into concrete play. His dad built a garage that he and his son could drive their cars into. This all took months of daily playing with his son. His father found it tedious at times but persevered. His son became fascinated with the programme *Thunderbirds* and started collecting videos. Before long they were building Thunderbird landing bays and flying missions around the room. At first these were repetitions from the show, and his son wouldn't let Dad add any material other than what was on the shows. However, with time Dad began to make up new stories and Justin tolerated this and even enjoyed it. Justin's imaginative play still hasn't become very flexible but it has moved on greatly and now one other friend comes around and plays with him.

Joint play and turn-taking

Typically, children with ASD prefer to play on their own. Although they may resist this at first, there are several ways of helping them to engage with other people.

Julia and Simon, the parents of Moses, began this process by joining their son in his play with his catalogues.

This can be extended by watching out for other examples of the child's interest and joining in with his or her games.

Other parents have told us they have played similar games taking turns with the pieces of a jigsaw puzzle. Once these games are established other members of the family can join in too! These are the building blocks of learning how to take turns.

Groups of young children may practise turn-taking when the biscuit tin is handed around. Turn-taking is a key skill in play, including imaginative play.

Moses later developed an interest in stacking bricks. When he was proficient in this Julia started taking alternate bricks and encouraging him to 'ask' for them by looking at her. This later developed into a game where they would take turns stacking the bricks in order.

Play and interaction through music

Music is another great way to learn about taking turns. The numerous musical possibilities allow children to explore their environment with a free rein and some professionals believe that this helps with imaginative skill development. There are many excellent music therapists who specialise in working with children with ASD. Parents can start this process by helping children to take turns with them in banging a drum, for example. Many children really enjoy trying to copy rhythm and pitch from musical instruments.

Role play

As children get older, groups that use role plays may be helpful. However, young people need to be selected for their ability to participate. Some children will find it very difficult and will hate it. Role play has to be organised in a sensitive way and careful attention must be paid to the emotional level of understanding of the child. More concrete activities that the child enjoys will need to be interspersed with any emotional or role play tasks. The role plays should initially be designed around their interests or real-life situations that they have faced.

Giving information

Many children on the autism spectrum have difficulty knowing the difference between real and pretend. This means being careful as to which television programmes you allow them to watch. We have had considerable difficulties occasionally with children who have seen inappropriate videos and then wanted to act them out at school. It also means that when children are allowed to watch developmentally appropriate programmes, parents and carers need to tell them what is real and what is pretend if there is any uncertainty. Just because it is obvious to you, don't always assume this is the case for your child.

Children on the autism spectrum may have problems understanding:

- Father Christmas/the Tooth Fairy
- magic shows
- whether things are real or not (e.g. cartoons)
- abstract phrases or activities.

Adults will need to be aware and give information about these things to children as they grow.

Creative drawing and painting

Many children with ASD will enjoy art. Art activities can be a good way of doing something with your child that can both help social interaction and also encourage exploration of ideas. Children with ASD tend to want to paint the same thing over and over. Encourage a bit of variability. Because the hand can slip, new images can be created and you can interpret for the child what they might be. This seeds imaginative ideas for them.

Playing

Even though play with your child may be repetitive and sometimes boring, regular play with your child will help.

Learning how to interact socially

Learning to listen as well as talk

Learning to listen is an important skill to help improve mindblindness. If our young people are not able to listen to others they will struggle to become aware of others' needs, thoughts or feelings.

- *The conch:* 'Holding the conch' is a technique where only the person holding a certain object (e.g. a certain teddy) can talk and the others have to listen. The object is moved around so that everyone gets a turn at speaking while others listen.

- *Time limits:* A time limit can be put on how long each person can talk. Some children with ASD find this very hard but we have come across several families where these techniques have worked well.

Teaching pointing and gestures

Children with ASD can't see the point of using gestures. This is because gestures are largely there to help communicate something to someone else. If you have mindblindness you don't see the need to communicate to others. Since Theory of Mind develops over time, many people with ASD come to gain an understanding of the need for gestures but they may not be picked up intuitively and so need to be taught. When children are younger, showing them how to point out objects in books may be difficult, but it is worth persevering.

- *Modelling and shaping:* This may involve the adult pointing while reading (modelling) or using the child's finger to point out items in the book (shaping).

- *Joint action games or activities:* You can help young children by playing games that require two people. For example, encouraging games for younger children such as 'Row the Boat' and 'Round and Round the Garden' introduces gesture in the context of joint activity. These games can help children with ASD to get used to gesture and learn to use it even if they don't always understand it.

- *Explanation and information:* Later gestures can be taught more specifically: 'This is something you do when you say goodbye' (wave). 'This is something you do when you want quiet' (place fingers to lips, shhh) and so on.

- *Gesture-based games:* In groups at school or in social skills groups, games can be played to help. A 'gesture name game' is where each person is given a sign made by putting his hand on his face (e.g. touching his finger on his chin). You sit in a circle and make your sign and then the sign of someone else. That person then makes her sign and the sign of someone else, and so goes on. This game encourages watching and gestures and we have found it helpful in social skills groups when playing with young people with Asperger syndrome.

Language-based goals

Developing specific language-based skills is important both to aid communication and, later, to help young people learn the hidden meanings, body language and subtleties of language, which they do not pick up intuitively. Chapter 8 deals with this in more detail.

- *Learning idioms:* Some of our young people have benefited from learning idioms and metaphors. Parents can help by playing idiom guessing games with them; for example, asking: 'What do people mean when they say, 'It's raining cats and dogs'?' We have a long list of idioms which some families take away with them, and some of the many websites available to explore this are listed in the References and Resources section.

- *Humour:* Social skills groups can usefully discuss jokes and what is and is not funny and why. One group we ran for Asperger ten-year-olds put a joke book together and this was used as a fun way of working with humour. Different sections of the book dealt with slapstick (which many children with ASD find very funny), puns, silliness and jokes that 'lead you up the garden path'. Using this joke book allowed children with Asperger syndrome to explore what was and was not funny, and why other people found these things funny (even if the children did not).

Clear boundaries

Most children with ASD do not find it easy to understand and pick up social rules and cues. Clear boundaries in early childhood give children with ASD an understanding of what is acceptable when interacting with others. Hitting other children, for example, would clearly get in the way of children being content in each other's company. Children may not understand all the reasons for rules, but they usually respond to rules, and the rules prevent unhelpful social behaviours later on. On the whole, clear rules without explanations (when the reasons are too complex to understand) work best with younger children. As children become older and situations change, more complex rules will be necessary. For older, more able young people, explanations for these rules will be necessary.

Hugh liked to run around without his clothes on. This was fine at home on warm days when he was little. However, he started taking his clothes off at nursery, in the supermarket and in the street. His parents taught him a new rule: 'Only take your clothes off at home'. For obvious reasons this rule had to become more complex with time. 'Only take your clothes off upstairs at home...and for PE lessons at school...and when you go swimming...and if a doctor asks you to at the surgery, etc.' Explanations were added as he gained more understanding.

Preventing bad habits/thinking of the future

It is easy for bad habits to develop around our natural propensity as adults to be tolerant of unusual behaviour in our young children, especially when we feel sympathetic to their difficulties. One thing that needs to be borne in mind for our children with ASD is that habits can be formed that can be very powerful and difficult to break.

Freddie liked to stroke the legs of people wearing tights when he was three or four years old. The adults around him found it amusing and tolerated it well, but his interest in the feel of the nylon continued as he became older. As a teenager he did not realise that women other than his mother did not like it or that some were scared by it. He would become angry or upset if he was stopped. Stopping it earlier on in his life would have been kinder to him even though he would not have understood why and might have become distressed. Tolerance is good but we also need to protect our children from habits that will hamper socialisation in the future.

Learning what is appropriate and not appropriate

Many families we have met have said that they specifically teach what is and is not appropriate in certain circumstances.

Emily was ten and learnt that when Grandma left the house she kissed her as a way of saying goodbye. She quickly turned this into a rule and wanted to kiss anybody who left the house. The plumber got a surprise when she kissed him goodbye. Her mother had to explain the difference between people, explaining rules about whom it is normal to kiss goodbye and whom it is not.

Conversation building and learning to listen as well as talk

Conversation building and learning to listen as well as talk are important skills dealt with in Chapter 11, 'Developing Communication Skills'. Turn-taking skills are a very important part of learning about conversations.

Learning social conventions

Families need to teach certain social conventions and tailor these to the developmental needs of the child. Such social conventions include:

- saying hello
- saying goodbye
- goodnight routines
- conversational rules
- giving and receiving praise
- saying thank you
- saying please
- saying sorry.

Shared-space skills

Young children often find the first few days at school very difficult because the rules are very different from those at home. They adapt remarkably quickly, however, because the rules are clear and there are consequences for breaking the rules. At home the situation is quite rightly much more relaxed. Where there is regular conflict, however, it may be worth having a few clear rules!

Teaching specific social behaviours and using social stories
SOCIAL STORIES AND SOCIAL RULES

Social stories were devised by Carol Gray (see References and Resources section at the end of this book). These are stories to help those with Asperger syndrome or high functioning autism to understand social concepts and others' feelings, and can be adapted for virtually any situation. The aim is to write simple social stories about your child specifically for him or her. They can be written about things your child has achieved or about situations with which they might struggle. The idea is to write a short story about the child, his or her family, likes and dislikes, and then to write about the situation which is difficult. The story goes on to explain what happens and what the child is expected to do. One parent wrote a social story to help her son to wait quietly in McDonalds.

> We go to McDonalds and sit by the window. George takes out his crayons and draws quietly. He sits on his chair. George will try to wait quietly for his fries to come. Sometimes it takes a long time before he gets his fries. George likes fries! When his mum puts them on the table, he eats them all up. His mum says, 'You are a good boy for waiting quietly. Well done!'.

A teacher we know wrote one recently to help a boy to understand that PE could be fun at school.

There are books about how to write social stories for your child as well as books with stories already complete. Once a story has been written, your child can illustrate it with you. The next step is to read it with your child two or three times a day for as many days as necessary, to help him or her to understand the situation and the expectations more fully. The fact that the story is written down with the child's name in it and is clear about what happens seems to be a very powerful way of helping children understand and learn social behaviour.

INTERNALISING AND REMEMBERING SOCIAL RULES

Children with ASD do not easily learn social skills or social rules. Adults may tell them what to do or not do in certain situations, but parents often say that their child still finds it hard. When children who do not have ASD approach the fire they may hear their parents saying 'Don't touch that, it's hot'. After a few occasions they 'internalise' (they take inside themselves) these words and hear them in their own heads. Children with ASD find this process more difficult.

Katherine was 14 and had a diagnosis of Asperger syndrome. She had four siblings who were mostly patient with her and a family that felt family routines and family life were crucial. They had a family meal each evening. Katherine regularly interrupted everybody else and the family felt it time to help her learn to stop interrupting and take her turn in conversation. They used a strategy suggested by the psychiatrist.

Phase I involved one of her parents saying 'please don't interrupt, Katherine, X [name of person] was speaking'. They were advised to use eye contact and a particular hand shape when saying this.

In Phase 2 they would say: 'What am I going to say to you, Katherine?' If Katherine didn't know they would go back to Phase I.

Phase 3 involved them saying her name 'Katherine?' when she interrupted, keeping the same hand shape and eye contact. If she said 'What?' then they would go back to Phase 2. The idea was to try to help her hear a voice inside her own head with the answer.

At Phase 4 they used the eye contact and hand shape, and if she carried on with the interruption they returned to Phase 3. This worked very effectively.

This kind of strategy can be used for different targets but would only be used for one thing at a time. It is important that it is not punitive. It is always used with an encouraging approach and can be very effective. We also use it for children with ADHD who also have problems hearing internal messages of control.

Social-use-of-language programmes

There are several programmes available which are designed to aid the development of the social use of language. Some that we have come across are listed in the References and Resources section at the back of this book.

Supporting the development of friendships and relationships

Understanding development

It is crucial to understand the sequence of the healthy development of friendships. The ability to make and keep friendships usually follows in a certain pattern. It begins with a child playing alongside other children, getting used to being with others and doing the same things. Later, turn-taking develops and the child may start to give help to another playing nearby. Children may ask for help and copy each other in chasing games, hide and seek and other games. Common interests are discovered and a common memory for shared events. Children learn rules and wish to stick by them seeing things as unfair if the rules are broken. They begin to select whom they are with, making guesses about threats from others and making predictions about common interests. They find other children who like the same things. They become aware of the attitudes, feelings and thoughts of others and this develops in sophistication. Children become aware of how things that they do impact on others either by making them happy or by hurting their feelings. They spend more time together and may prefer being with their own sex. They begin to develop group play and belonging and adopt group attitudes (e.g. 'We don't like boys'). They develop a sense of a friend as being more than 'the child next door' or 'the child who is nice to me' and understand that being kind and honest with each other is part of friendship. In adolescence peers take on an important role in the lives of young people and a keener sense of belonging and close friendship develops.

Mindblindness

Mindblindness has a lot to answer for in the way that these developmental processes are hampered in autism spectrum children. Given that much of this developmental process is markedly delayed in our autism spectrum children, how can we help them?

Starting from your child's developmental level

The approaches we might use will depend on the age and ability of the children. We should bear in mind, however, that because of their social impairments, children with ASD will not develop friendships in the same way as normally developing children. Some children will show no interest in developing peer relationships and be unconcerned about them. Others may want to make friends but not understand why they should consider the needs of the other person in this relationship and hence be unable to maintain friendships.

Recognising vulnerability

A significant problem for many children may be that their vulnerability will be exploited by other young people. They may believe their peers who say that they will be their friends if they do certain things such as steal, throw bricks through windows, trip someone up, etc.

This highlights the importance of teaching clear rules and taking care to teach the best rules for the circumstances. The new rule of 'Don't do anything these boys tell you to do without checking with a teacher first', helped to get Bernard through the next few weeks at school. Adults have a large part to play in the process of helping young people with autism and Asperger syndrome to develop social rules and to protect them from bullying.

> Bernard was persuaded to tie a young girl's wheelchair to a fence because a group of boys at school said that he could join their gang if he did so. He was excluded from school for a week as a result of this and his parents and teachers did their best to explain the seriousness of this behaviour and how hurtful it was to the girl. The day he returned to school the same boys encouraged him to call her derogatory names. He was very puzzled to find himself excluded again. His teachers were very angry with him, thinking he had learnt nothing from the previous week and that he was being deliberately defiant. However, as far as he was concerned he had not broken the rule 'Don't tie up people's wheelchairs'.

Home-based ideas for helping children to develop friendships

Helping children with ASD to make friends is very complex. It is a developmental process. Some children will get 'stuck' at various different points in the process and others may never show any interest at all!

- *Turn-taking and sharing:* You may need to help your son or daughter to share, take turns, accept other people's opinions, cope with praise or criticism, learn to compromise and many other social skills!

- *Learning that other people can be interesting:* Teaching about friendships begins with helping children to understand that other people can be interesting. Without this understanding, children will not appreciate the value of other people and certainly won't grasp the meaning of friendship. Moses' story in this chapter shows how his parents successfully engaged with him even though he was a very solitary boy.

- *Learning that other people can help:* Parents can also teach their children that people can be useful for helping them find socially appropriate ways of having their needs met.

> Moses learnt how to ask appropriately and politely for drinks instead of randomly screaming in the kitchen.

- *Learning social rules by rote:* As they get older, children can be taught various social rules such as how to comfort someone if they are upset. None of this comes intuitively to children with ASD and parents often tell us that they spend many hours repeatedly explaining social rules. Even though some children learn *what* to do regarding different social rules, they do not usually truly understand *why.*

- *Being with other children outside school:* Inviting children home from school for short periods of time can be helpful. However, because children with ASD are mindblind, they will need their parents to show them what to do and how to play when they have a friend over.

- *Explaining confusing experiences:* The social world is very complex and confusing. Children with ASD will need your help to make sense of it. They may ask about confusing incidents sometimes but at other times it will be helpful if you explain incidents when you see that they find something puzzling.

- *Learning social routines:* Parents who are more sociable themselves will intuitively encourage their children to respond to others with greetings and polite social 'chat'. This may seem false and rather rote-learnt at first but, with practice, will begin to seem more natural. Demonstrating and practising good eye contact and smiling can also help.

- *Encouraging shared interests:* It is possible to encourage likely friendships by watching out for shared interests with other children. An interest in Play Station games has marked the beginning of several friendships that we are aware of.

- *Encouraging successful educational pursuits:* Many young people with high functioning autism or Asperger syndrome may be very successful in some academic subjects such as mathematics, information technology, physics or art, and may find common interests with others or even go on university where some will thrive in some areas of college life.

- *Encouraging and supporting pen pal arrangements:* Some parents have encouraged their children to become pen pals because letters can be carefully constructed with help and advice in a way that

face-to-face encounters cannot. They are therefore less
threatening.

- *Learning social skills*
  - Some families use videos of examples of where friendships are
    going well and less well (e.g. from favoured television
    programmes) and talk about them together.
  - Some families like to read more on the subject (see References
    and Resources section at the back of this book).
  - Many families prompt and reward young people for successful
    experiences, guiding and shaping their responses as they do.
  - Social stories can be very helpful (Gray and Leigh White 2002).
  - Some families keep a friendship diary to help young people
    reflect successful and unsuccessful encounters.

School-based ideas for helping children to develop friendships
CIRCLE OF FRIENDS

As discussed above this involves other young people being tasked to befriend
and assist a child in school. Many educationalists believe that all of the
children involved benefit from Circle of Friends, but parents of the other
children need to consent to the process and the group needs support and monitoring (see References and Resources section at the back of this book).

BUDDY SYSTEMS

Sometimes schools are able to organise buddies for children with ASD. This
seems to work best when children volunteer to help. The idea is that they may
help by making sure the child with ASD knows which room to go to next,
which books she might need or asking if she wants to play or go to the library
together.

GROUP WORK

Group work in schools helps children get used to being with each other. Early
on, when children sit round a table together for a biscuit or a drink, they may
scream when they have to wait, but they gradually learn social routines and
turn-taking is introduced.

CIRCLE TIME

This is a well-known technique used in schools for helping children develop their social skills, and to promote tolerance and an understanding of the needs of others. It would only usually be used by an experienced facilitator, but more teachers of classes at all ages use reflective discussion in their classrooms.

NASEN sell an in-service Circle Time manual for teachers (see References and Resources section).

VIDEO FEEDBACK

Some of the young people's therapeutic groups we use have video feedback. This can be very helpful to some children who have a poor perception of how they come across to others.

> Josh, a fourteen-year-old boy with Asperger syndrome, was able to see that he always stood very close to anyone he spoke with and was able to compare this with everyone else in the group. After seeing this contrast on video he was able to adjust where he stood and family and friends noticed a big difference.

We have found role play about specific situations very useful in helping children to practise social rules. They need to be repeated and preferably played back several times on video to be effective, however. Also, some of these skills are difficult for the children to apply in different settings due to the children's inherent difficulties with generalisation.

The role of the child and young person in developing friendships

Many friendships depend on the young person's temperament and interests. Some people with ASD are temperamentally more sociable than others and will seek people out. Others much prefer their own company. Some have special interests and hobbies and will make friendships around these. Ideas to help with friendships include:

- joining special hobby and interest groups
- learning how to play games like chess, Monopoly, Diplomacy and card games
- reading books on friendship

- reading books about autism and Asperger syndrome written by young people with ASD (see References and Resources section for examples).

Sexuality

YOUNGER CHILDREN

Young children enjoy exploring their bodies. It is normal for boys to play with their penis and for girls to fondle their vagina. When they are very young, parents ignore this behaviour, recognising that it is part of development. As children grow older they learn from the adults around them what behaviour is appropriate in different places and what is not. When a child is aged seven, for example, parents may have no problems with him exploring himself in the bath but may not wish him to do it in the supermarket.

Children with ASD have more difficulty picking up these rules about privacy. They may have little idea about what behaviours, at what ages, may offend other people. Some children appear to regard their private parts as a portable toy and become fascinated with the sensory aspects of this toy. They will need some help from their parents or carers about the most appropriate times and places to touch themselves in different places. At around the age of three or four they can be gently distracted from fondling themselves in public. Similarly, older children with ASD may want to go on touching their mother on the breasts in a way that they might have done when small and breastfeeding. They may need clear messages about this as they are growing. This is not cruel. It is to help their social and sexual development along its path.

It is important to remember that children with ASD will not be aware of the usual social constraints due to their mindblindness. They will not pick up disapproving looks from adults or be aware of causing any offence. At the same time as discouraging play with sexual parts in inappropriate places, it is fine to give the message that it's OK to do this in private.

Children and young people with ASD may also need help learning about when and where to wear clothes and when it's OK to be naked.

> Luke used to like to run around with no clothes on at all at home. He wanted to do this at school and it took parents and teachers quite some time to help him understand that it was not appropriate at school.

Although this is fine when children are young, it can be very embarrassing for parents and siblings if this is still happening when they are teenagers. In our opinion, it is better to tackle behaviours such as these (i.e. behaviours that are acceptable in young children but may be problematic in the future) when the child is young and before they develop into habits, which may be difficult to change.

> Earlier in this chapter we described how Emily, who liked to kiss strangers, was taught not to kiss everyone she met (e.g. the plumber). She showed no signs of picking up for herself that this was not appropriate and her parents worried that if this carried on as she grew, it might cause her to suffer ridicule or aggression.

It is crucial to make sure that children are safe and this includes teaching them not to approach strangers with behaviours that may in some circumstances make them vulnerable.

ADOLESCENCE

It is helpful to talk to children about their bodies, including naming sexual parts, so that as they get older, you can prepare them for the changes that will occur. As they approach adolescence they will need to know about menstruation, the growth of body hair, orgasms etc. Young people may have to be reminded about places where it is OK to masturbate and where it is not OK. You may have to be specific about this.

> Sam, aged 17, learnt that he should only masturbate in his bedroom. This was fine until one day when a kindly but embarrassed neighbour came to tell his mum that Sam often stood at his bedroom window masturbating in full view! This was soon remedied when she told him to pull down the blind in the bedroom.

Social relationships are very difficult for people with ASD. This, combined with the development of sexual feelings in adolescence, can be problematic. Young people may struggle to know how to approach others and can sometimes be inappropriate in their advances.

Sean, aged 12, developed an interest in women's breasts and found himself in a lot of trouble at school when he started touching girls' breasts. Due to his mindblindness, he did not understand how the girls might feel about this. He was curious and not tuned in to the social rules in our society that deem this unacceptable. His parents and teachers taught him a clear rule about this, 'Do not touch girls' breasts'. They kept the rule simple at this stage. As he grew older they discussed sexuality and touch in much more detail and gradually helped him to develop more sophisticated rules. They also spent some time teaching him about social interactions in general.

In our experience it is important to give sexual education to young people with ASD. Many parents have said to us that they shy away from this because they don't think their child will understand. However, many of these young people have struggled precisely because of this poor understanding of social and sexual rules and morality. Young people can learn rules that make them safe, and finding straightforward ways of doing this is worthwhile in the longer run.

Dealing with things that get in the way of learning social skills

Sensory interests, special interests and repetitive behaviours

Unusual or odd behaviours or actions can get in the way of social interaction either by making communication impossible or because other people become wary or critical. There is more on this in Chapter 17, 'Preoccupations', Chapter 18, 'Compulsions, Routines and Rituals' and Chapter 19, 'Mannerisms and Repetitive Movements'.

Daniel, aged five, was so preoccupied with twiddling string that opportunities to engage with others were missed.

May, a six-year-old, could not read a book with her teacher because she wanted to look at the light through the flicked edges of the pages and would have a tantrum if not allowed to do so.

Reducing compulsive behaviour

While some behaviours help children become more calm and so enable them to engage more socially, some behaviours work against socialisation. A child who has a 90-minute compulsive routine in the morning and who has to go back to the beginning when it goes wrong may drive other members of the family to distraction. Everyone will be left feeling exhausted and irritable, both of which will affect interactions. There is more on compulsive behaviour in Chapter 18.

Personal hygiene

It is important to teach children about daily hygiene routines as early as possible. Habits formed early on in life are more likely to continue into adolescence and adulthood with relative ease, e.g. daily bathing, cleaning teeth, changing clothes, etc.

Dealing with conflict

This is a very important social skill. Children and young people will need help in dealing with this. Chapter 12, 'Tantrums, Aggression and Frustration' deals with this in more detail.

Bullying

Sometimes children with ASD stand out as being different from other children and they can become the focus for the unkind behaviour of other children. Parents can help to prevent this in various different ways. It helps if teachers and supervisors understand about ASD and the vulnerability of your child. Children can be given advice about blending in by being aware of the fashions and the ways in which the other young people wear their clothes and hair.

When Sophie started high school, she was puzzled by the other girls who were laughing at her feet. Her mother later realised that wearing ankle socks was the source of the ridicule.

When the father of one of Marcus's classmates died, Marcus asked lots of questions about the death and the funeral. While none of these questions was unpleasant, Marcus did not tune in to his friend's difficulty in answering such personal questions. Other classmates later criticised Marcus. He did not understand why they were so angry.

Children with ASD are more likely to say the wrong thing at the wrong time or misinterpret comments made to them. This can sometimes make them the focus for ridicule. Sometimes they say hurtful things to others.

Some children with ASD lose social perspective, believing that either everyone hates them or that everyone likes them. They polarise or generalise their understanding of how they are seen amongst their peers. They need careful advice, guidance and information to understand that different people have different views at different times. Some of the other suggestions made in this chapter such as Circle Time, buddy systems and helping children to learn more social and emotional understanding are all helpful here. Even if children learn this by rote instead of intuitively, it can make children less likely to be bullied.

All schools have bullying policies and parents can ask to see them. If worried go and see your child's teacher or head of year.

Minimising anxiety

Since the social world is so unpredictable, it can produce a lot of anxiety in children with ASD. Reducing anxiety may be very helpful. We have come across numerous different strategies for doing this used in schools and homes.

- Two schools we know use aromatherapy as a way of reducing anxiety.

- Calming music may help if it is not disliked by the child.

- A quiet calm atmosphere is often soothing.

- Time out. Some children will find going to a quiet place for a short time helpful. This is not a punishment.

- Routine reduces anxiety. Knowing what the course of events is going to be can be very reassuring. Visual timetables may help here.

- Some sensory interests and habits or rituals can make children stand out and interfere with socialising but they can also be very comforting. If they are not damaging then children should be allowed to use them to calm themselves.

- All sorts of things can cause anxiety and attempting to minimise this will be important. However, this does not mean being overprotective. For example, fear of noise might hamper social interaction, and the child will need help to overcome it.

Helen was a three-year-old who would be calmed by watching a certain video before meals.

Mark was a teenager in a special school who tore bits of cardboard when he was distressed. He was taught by the teachers that this was the only thing he could tear and they kept a box with his cardboard in it.

Sunita (aged six) liked to fiddle with the corner of her cotton handkerchief.

Understanding consequences and social problem-solving

Johnny was 17. He was poor at working out the consequences of events. He regularly, prompted by 'friends', did things that got him into trouble. Once his friends told him to tell the teacher that her car had a flat tyre. He did this because he believed them, but got into trouble because it wasn't true. The psychologist taught him the 'social problem-solving' technique. He found it easier to deal with these situations after this.

Social problem-solving skills are a systematic way of analysing what to do next. You may find it helpful to fill in Figure 10.2. with your child.

As yourself the following questions:	
1. What did I do?	
2. What happened next?	
3. What were the good things about what happened?	
4. What were the bad things about what happened?	
5. What six other things could I have done instead?	
6. What good things and what bad things would have happened for each of these?	

Figure 10.2: Social problem-solving chart

Some children with Asperger syndrome find this a very clear and structured way of making more sense of social situations.

Summary

- Developing social skills is a very complex process for children with ASD but there is a great deal that can be done to help.

- Remember that social skills do not develop intuitively for people with ASD and so have to be learnt using a combination of many of the techniques described in this chapter.

- Social development happens in stages that progress one from the other. Work out the level your child is at and work from there.

- Children with ASD may need:
  - help understanding and interpreting emotions
  - help with understanding social rules and social cues
  - help with development of all kinds of relationships.

- Your child will benefit from different types of help at different ages.

- Encourage imaginative play developmentally by:
  - understanding at which stage your child is
  - playing with your child regularly.

- Social situations can be extremely stressful for young people with ASD. Ensure that anxiety is kept to a manageable level when possible.

Chapter 11

Developing
Communication Skills

In Chapter 8 we outlined the many different forms of communication problems for children and young people with ASD. These vary from subtle difficulties with the social use of language to more severe instances where the child may never learn to use verbal language effectively. Similarly there is a huge range in children's abilities to use non-verbal communication.

It is important to remember that children with ASD view the world quite differently, and the theories described in Part 2 of this book are essential in helping us to understand why children with ASD struggle so much with communication.

Communication and social skills are very much linked to each other and so there were additional ideas about improving communication skills given in Chapter 10, 'Developing Social Skills'. There are two specific common difficulties discussed in detail and then lots of ideas to help children improve communication. There are additional ideas for helping with the development of communication skills at the end of the chapter.

Understanding the problems

Children with ASD may have problems communicating because:

- they have a language delay caused by developmental delay

- they may not see the need to communicate or may get the subtleties of communication wrong owing to:

- problems with mindblindness (not understanding the need to communicate with someone else, or misreading how they will be understood)
- problems with getting the gist (not understanding the need or the subtleties of communication in any given social setting)

- they may be preoccupied with other things such as:
  - their sensory interests
  - their special interests, etc.

If we want to help children's communication skills, then understanding the nature of the problems is half the battle. Our help will be much better targeted if we know which of the above is relevant in any given situation where communication is a problem.

Motivation

Any intervention plan to assist with communication should concentrate on the child's interests and needs. They will be much more motivated to communicate about the things relevant to them rather than those that are important to you! You might need to try several different ideas.

'He can't talk, so he can't communicate'

It may seem that some children with ASD who have no language cannot communicate. However, when we think about this carefully, it becomes clear that the child's behaviour is a form of communication. The child's way of communicating may not be socially appropriate and we may not always understand what their behaviour means but there is a message for us to interpret.

> Moses used to sit at the kitchen table and quietly wait. This was his way of getting a drink when he was thirsty.

Before discussing general strategies to help children improve communication we will go through specific problems.

TYPES OF PROBLEM

- Not asking for things or initiating communication with other people

- Being rude without realising it

WHAT is the problem?

Not asking for things or initiating communication with other people

Moses, aged three, had learnt to tolerate his parents sharing his play with his catalogues, but they were keen to help him to develop new skills. They knew that he could make sounds but they wanted to help him to learn how to use language to communicate. His parents struggled to work out what he wanted most of the time. He had recently got into the habit of going into the kitchen and screaming. He did not point or use gestures or show his needs in any other way. Julia and Simon had to guess what he might want. Most of the time they were really good at guessing, but sometimes the screaming would go on for what seemed like hours.

Simon and Julia used the same process as in chapter 10 to try to become clearer about what they wanted to be different and how best to help Moses.

---

1. What is the problem?

He doesn't say anything or ask for anything in any way. We have to guess. He just sits and waits. Occasionally, he has tantrums because we can't always work out what he wants.

2. Why does your child behave in this way?

Situations and settings: Where does the behaviour happen? Where does it not happen? Is it to do with something in the environment (smells, noises, what other people do, etc.)? Who is around when it happens?	It happens when he wants something and we don't know what it is. It can happen anywhere.
Triggers and timings: When does it happen? Is it to do anything pleasant or unpleasant? What are the timings in relation to other things? When does it not happen?	When his needs are not being met.

Mindblindness: Is it to do with mindblindness? Does your child realise he/she needs to communicate their needs to someone? Can the child see others points of view or understand feelings and needs of others in this situation?	Yes. He doesn't understand that he has to tell us what he wants. He just expects it to happen. He doesn't know that our minds and thoughts are different from his.
Getting the gist: Is the problem associated with not understanding what is going on and why? Does your child understand the meaning of events and that things have a certain order?	He hasn't grasped the whole idea about communicating.
Imagination: Does your child think imaginatively and does this affect the behaviour?	
Preoccupations and sensory experiences: Is the problem associated with sensory experiences and/or preoccupations? Is the environment too complicated or interesting?	He spends a lot of time with his books, chanting and rocking.
Social interaction: Does your child do this alone or with others? How does this affect the behaviour?	
Communication: Is the problem associated with language or communication difficulties?	He can't say or understand anything yet nor does he use gestures like pointing.
Emotions: Is the problematic behaviour related to anxiety or mood? Is it to do with your child's temperament? Is there anything else that might be affecting or upsetting your child (e.g. memories, dreams, illness, tiredness, boredom)?	He does seem to be quite strong willed and it's definitely worse when he's tired or ill.
Sameness: Is it to do with a need for routine or habits? Is there a problem associated with being in control? Has there been a change of routine at home or at school?	Yes, we are probably encouraging him not to communicate without realising it. He has no need to tell us because we communicate for him.
Responses: How have others responded to the behaviour? Does something happen after the behaviour that is important? How does it affect the behaviour in the future?	When he sits and waits we give him things to eat or drink. If he cries we give him something else.
Benefits: What positive outcomes happen for anyone (e.g. you, your child or your child's sibling) as a result of the behaviour? (Rack your brains: there usually *are* some!)	A lot of the time he gets what he wants.

WHY might it be happening?

Mindblindness

Because Moses has a very limited understanding that others have thoughts and feelings, he has no awareness that he needs to communicate that he wants a drink. He is aware that he is thirsty, but has no understanding of how the environment provides a drink for him. His understanding may be limited to simply expecting it to happen. The drink arrives because he is thirsty, not because he has successfully understood his mother's role, motivations, thoughts or intentions. He simply does not know that he can communicate his need to her mind because he has no awareness of her mind. Since pointing involves communicating with someone else's mind (and directing their gaze to what you want), he does not point. He does not understand the reason for pointing since he does not understand his mother's mind.

Sensory interests

Moses was still preoccupied by his mail-order catalogues. Julia and Simon still had to work very hard to get him to make eye contact with them. Often, his preoccupation seemed to be more interesting to him than they were and over-rode social behaviours like social smiling and eye contact. They had experienced some success in joining in with him when he was turning the pages of his catalogue and were keen to build on this success.

Language difficulties

Moses still hadn't developed any useful speech or gestures. Simon and Julia knew that he could vocalise but they also knew that he was unable to use or understand language.

Getting the gist

Moses didn't seem to understand the connections between anything. Everything was like a series of isolated incidents. He did not have an understanding of the social rules of greeting or of polite ways of asking for things, nor did he perceive social conventions when asking for things.

Parents' response

Julia and Simon were very attentive parents. They were very much attuned to Moses' needs and were in the habit of providing everything he wanted. This is a very normal response and an essential factor in developing loving and caring relationships between children and parents. It serves the purpose of keeping children happy and knowing that their parents are responsive to their needs.

In their first two years of life, normally developing children learn skills to attract their parents' attention to their needs. They learn to point, make verbal requests, understand their parents' responses and to wait. Their parents no longer have to anticipate or guess what the child wants. However, like many parents of children with autism, Julia and Simon were still at the guessing stage with Moses just after his third birthday. He had not shown signs of developing communication skills and they had consequently continued to respond to him as they had in the past. Moses had learnt that simply sitting at the table and waiting usually resulted in his getting something to eat or drink. If not, screaming helped and, if not, a full-blown tantrum usually did the trick. Julia and Simon's anticipation and quick responses had inadvertently reinforced Moses' tantrums (making them more likely to happen).

HOW might we deal with it?
Mindblindness

At the age of three, Moses has no understanding of his parent's thoughts or feelings. He does not know that he has to find a way of telling them what he needs. He knows, through a series of trials and errors, that some things he does will result in his needs being met (e.g. sitting at the table brings a drink).

The understanding of how others think (Theory of Mind) will develop very slowly for Moses. His parents have already started to help him by joining in with his preoccupation with catalogues. One of the things he is learning through this is making eye contact. Eyes have been described as the windows of the mind and eye contact involves shared communication. Moses has little understanding of the need for eye contact and so most of the work needs to be done by the other person. This means getting into a position where eye contact is easy – at his level directly in front of him – and lining up the eye contact for him. Playing his favourite games has helped his eye contact. At this stage the best games for eye contact were tickling games, rough and tumble and catalogues!

Sensory interests

The Son Rise or Options approach (see Chapter 20) encourages parents to involve themselves in the play of their children even when this play is unusual. Simon and Julia had already had some success in joining in with Moses' game with his catalogue where he turned the pages repetitively and chanted to himself. He liked it when his parents joined in with his chanting and when it had turned into more of a shared game whereby Simon or Julia introduced new chanting sounds that he copied. He especially liked slow, repetitive rhythmical sounds so his parents started saying his name and their own names in this fashion. Soon, although he did not recognise their meaning at first, he was saying, 'Moses', 'Mummy' and 'Daddy'.

Getting the gist

Getting the gist is something that will also, in part, come with age and explanation. Simon and Julia helped Moses with this by putting meaning to activities with words: for example, announcing 'Catalogue Time!' when they were starting to play with his book. They also started adding meaning to other social behaviour: coming in from work, saying, 'Hello, I'm home', and giving him a hug, rather than expecting him to pick social rules up intuitively.

Parents' response

Julia and Simon were in the habit of anticipating Moses' needs or responding to his sitting at the table or screaming. Hence, Moses did not see the need to make requests for himself. They wanted to find ways to encourage him to ask to do this. They explored a variety of options before working on an intervention plan. There are several ideas about helping with communication skills in the last section of this chapter. Simon and Julia embarked on the following plan for Moses:

- *Early Bird:* They joined a local Early Bird course. This is a course for parents of young children with a diagnosis of ASD. It is designed to help parents to understand their children's difficulties, share their experiences and learn different ways to encourage social interactions and play (see Chapter 20 for more details).

- *Using his topics of interest:* They had experienced some success by joining him in interest in his book and decided that they would try to encourage Moses to request this in some way rather than their simply presenting it to him. Julia started by taking the book as usual but instead of giving it to him straight away, she sat on the floor with him, held on to the book and waited for him to make eye contact with her.

- *Pointing:* Julia also started to teach him to point by pointing to the book herself and saying 'book'. She then added the word 'book' into their chanting game. She started by actually touching the book with her finger but then left increasingly longer spaces between the end of her finger and the book to help him to begin to understand that there is an imaginary line between a pointing finger and an object.

- *Withholding:* With practice, Moses started to copy the gesture of pointing and tried to say 'book'. Neither word nor gesture was very clear at first but slowly improved. As the weeks went by Julia was able to withhold the book until he gestured towards the book and tried to say 'book'. This was a major achievement and formed the building blocks for the next stages.

- *Changing routines and shaping:* Moses' book was kept on a shelf out of reach. The morning routine was that, after breakfast, he would sit on the floor and wait for his book to appear in front of him. One day, Julia decided to change this routine as a way of encouraging him to request it. She sat in front of him as usual but did not place the book in front of him. He made brief eye contact with her but then looked puzzled and distressed. Julia found the following tantrum very difficult to cope with but comforted him and persevered. When he had calmed down, she took him to the shelf, held out his hand towards the book saying 'book', and then continued with their old routine. Over the following days he learnt to stand by the shelf, looking towards the book and sometimes gestured with a nearly pointing finger. This helped to shape his behaviour in small steps in his development towards requesting the book from his mother.

Simon and Julia used similar techniques to help him to request a drink and biscuits.

- *Computers:* Moses had recently started showing interest in his parents' computer and so they decided to get some children's software. There is a variety of software to buy and some available free of charge on the Internet (see the References and Resources section for further information).

Julia and Simon bought a CD called *My First Incredible Amazing Dictionary* by Dorling Kindersley (available from most computer stores).

At first they played some simple games with Moses but before long he was using the computer with very little help. The computer was soon a favourite activity and became another tool for helping Moses to engage with his parents. He was so motivated by the computer that he spontaneously began to request their help and share his excitement with them. They made sure that they were around. One of his favourites was a naming game and before long Moses was copying and learning to say the words (even mimicking the narrator's accent!).

Over the years, the computer played an important part in helping Moses to learn and build on new skills.

- *Picture Exchange Communication System:* PECS is described in more detail in Chapter 20. There is also information on the Internet including when and where courses are available.

The idea is to begin by helping the child to exchange a picture for a desired object. The child presents the card and is quickly given the object. The child builds on this skill by learning to discriminate between different pictures and, in time, to construct simple sentences. The prompts are not verbal (although words can be used at the same time) and so language difficulties do not hamper its use. Despite the fears of some, it does not seem to adversely affect language development and, if anything, improves it. We know of some children who have been helped to move from using single words only to using full sentences after being introduced to the PECS system.

When Moses started nursery school, his teachers introduced him to the PECS system. They also showed his parents how to use the system so that he could practice at home. His first PECS card was 'milk'. It had velcro on the back and was kept at his height on a velcro strip on a low kitchen cupboard. With help, at home and at school, he quickly learnt to exchange the card for a glass of milk. When he had learnt to use several cards, he was given a special book. Each of his cards was laminated and had velcro on the back. His book also had strips of velcro to hold his cards in place and make them easy to find.

Moses made good progress over the following year. His parents did not know if it was due to his own development, the computer, their efforts to encourage his communication or a combination of several factors but they were delighted that finally he was beginning to communicate with them.

WHAT is the problem?

Being rude without realising it

James, aged 11, was bright but had a tendency to say things at the wrong time to the wrong people. In other words he was rude without realising it. He told his teacher that she smelt of sweat; he asked a football supporter on a train why he had drawn on his neck (he had tattoos) and he frequently pointed out people in the street whom he regarded as 'fat'.

WHY might it be happening?
Mindblindness

James had a poor understanding of the feelings of others. He could not tune in to distress unless it was very obvious. Since most people he met and insulted generally did not say that they were upset by his comments, he tended not to learn from his experiences. He could not pick up on the subtle messages he was getting that people were hurt or shocked.

When his parents did explain it to him, he couldn't understand why people could be upset by the truth.

Sensory interests

James was fascinated by the detail in his environment and noticed anything different. Many of his comments were about the things that he saw and was interested in.

Language difficulties/literal thinking

James had a literal way of looking at the world. He liked facts and concrete reasons for things. He genuinely could not understand things like fashion or why someone would want to have a tattoo or a pierced ear or belly. He was drawn to commenting on these things. If his teacher said 'The red table can sit down', he would comment on how this would not be possible. Some of his friends thought that he was being sarcastic, but he was being honest.

Getting the gist

James didn't really understand social rules and cues. Many of them were too subtle for him. If his parents explained that it was OK to ask his family their age but not the very proper old lady next door, he would not understand why. He often missed the point of the social context.

Other people's responses

Most of the family members were so used to James that they never commented on his social mistakes. They thought that he was just James being James. Sometimes they laughed in a gentle way. None of this gave James the message that there was a problem. Sometimes his classmates laughed at him but he either didn't understand that this was negative or he saw it as a good thing. Some of the responses made James feel that his comments were a good thing and might have made him more likely to make them.

HOW might we deal with it?
Mindblindness

James' parents decided to give him much clearer feedback about what was and was not appropriate to say. They decided they would do this in a gentle and caring way but that they would give him regular information. This seemed to help James understand the feelings of others and he began to be more careful about what he said.

Sensory interests

The family used James' fascination with detail to their advantage. James was quite bright and began to do 'experiments' to see if he could observe things in the way people behaved (facial expressions and body language). He began to discuss this with an older sister who was at university and would come back home regularly. He enjoyed these talks.

Language difficulties/literal thinking

At school James did a very helpful session on idioms and began to collect them in a notebook. He would discuss these at home, and even though he often had difficulty understanding them he learnt what they meant. This helped him in social situations.

Getting the gist

The family set about explaining social rules to James and at his school review this was also discussed so that his support assistant could help. It was made one of his annual review targets and, because he was present at the end of the review meeting, James took it very seriously. The school used personal and social development classes to discuss some of these things. James also entered a social use of language group run jointly by a speech and language therapist, an occupational therapist and a psychologist. He did well and took great pleasure in explaining the rules to new members.

Other people's responses

James' parents asked other family members not to laugh at him and to let him know their feelings if he had offended them. James found this hard at first, but it did make a difference to his comments. He still struggled with very subtle things but overall improved a great deal and continues to do so as he gets older.

Ideas for helping non-verbal children to improve communication

Pictures and photographs

In order to teach children to communicate we have to help them to understand that words, pictures and symbols have meaning. The starting process for this is teaching the association between pictures and objects. This can be done in games naming objects. It can then be expanded into activities, initially using real actions (for example drinking from a cup) and then using the abstract (for example pretending to drink from a cup). In this way a picture of a cup can be used to express a need for a drink. Once this has been learnt, more pictures can be added.

Two ways in which pictures can be used more systematically include the Picture Exchange Communication System (see page 168) to improve communication, and the visual timetable where a series of pictures can be used to explain a sequence of future events. We have found both of these to be very helpful for many children. Some children may not reach this stage but are still helped by single cards to indicate what they will be doing next.

Objects

Some children find it too difficult initially to understand the connection between a picture and an activity. In this case it is best to start by using a real object, perhaps showing shoes to indicate that a child is about to go outside. A child might communicate the need for a drink by putting a cup on the table.

Parents might want to help their child to find a more appropriate way of seeking help. They might, for example, use a technique called 'shaping' (see Chapter 9).

Use simple language

Our language is usually too complicated for children with ASD. Many parents are shocked to discover how much language they use and how complex it is if we watch a video of them in their house with their child. Keeping sentences short and keeping language simple can be very helpful. Using the child's name first and sticking to simple nouns and verbs may work wonders in some instances: 'George, give Mummy the book' is more effective than: 'Would you like to pass the book over to me please?'

Face-to-face contact

Children will respond better to us if we get down to their level and face them and make eye contact with them. This is the case for all children but is particularly important for children with ASD. Because children with ASD may use little eye contact, it is tempting to think it is not important. However, they may never learn it unless they experience it regularly.

Give time for responses

Children with ASD often have language processing problems. It takes them longer to understand what people say. It is therefore important to give them more time than you would other children to listen, understand and work out how to respond. Slow down what you say and wait longer for a reply. Some parents have been astonished by what a difference this can make.

Computers

Sometimes children with ASD respond well to information on a computer screen. There are many games and teaching programmes readily available (see References and Resources section for examples). At one time it was thought that the use of computers would automatically lead to the children developing obsessions about computers and hence would reduce their social contact. In fact, the use of computers often helps to encourage communication as many children are greatly motivated by them and are keen to ask for help and share their enjoyment. It is important, however, to offer several alternative activities and to be cautious about allowing your child too much time exclusively on the computer as obsessions can easily develop.

Using your child's skills and interests

Use your child's skills and interests to help his or her development. If he or she is interested in different makes of cars, for example, try making games of them that involve the child naming or matching them to words or symbols.

Curtis was fascinated by the logos on the packaging of his videos. He enjoyed playing games of 'matching pairs' with his parents which involved them making cards of several different logos (two of each), turning them face down and taking turns to find the two matching ones. His first words were 'Walt Disney Records' and 'Universal'! He quickly learnt to recognise hundreds of logos and to read the text that sometimes accompanied them. He also learnt to recognise the Roman numerals indicating the date on which the video was released.

His parents were keen for him to extend his vocabulary to incorporate the social use of language. They encouraged him to ask for his logo cards by playfully repeating 'Curtis wants...logo cards' before giving them to him. Curtis began to join in by repeating 'logo cards' with them initially. Later his parents left longer pauses until eventually he said 'logo cards' without their help. Soon after this, he learnt to request his cards by using the whole sentence himself.

Professionals may talk about this as helping the child to 'internalise external cues and messages' but it really means the child needs more help than others to take on board communication rules and cues and use them for himself without being prompted by others. Lovaas (see Chapter 20, p.304) uses some of these principles to encourage learnt communication skills. Curtis couldn't do it intuitively. He needed help to learn these rules so that eventually he could think of them for himself. As time went by his parents helped him to request other items in the same way. Although there was a stilted or 'learnt' quality to his language, he was able to make his needs known much more easily.

Start early with visual and non-verbal communication

Teaching non-verbal communication skills has many benefits. For children whose development may be delayed in several areas, non-verbal techniques are more appropriate as they rely much less heavily on thinking, speech and memory skills. Words, which are just sounds, disappear very quickly, but pictures, symbols and objects are in the child's view and touch for much longer, allowing her greater periods of time to make sense of the information and store them in her memory. This is very important. The ability for many children to communicate and understand by non-verbal means is helpful in reducing their behavioural problems and improving social interactions. Most important, learning non-verbal techniques does not interfere with the development of verbal language but establishes the building blocks for verbal communication in many children.

Motivation

Children often need incentives to change their behaviour. The best incentives are those that motivate the child. Parents are in the best position to know what motivates their child. Whether this might be looking at car magazines, playing with keys, tickle games, playing with pieces of Blu-tack, etc. The more motivated children are, the more likely they are to find ways of expressing their desires. They will be more receptive to learning new ways of communicating if it gets them something they really want. So, if you are trying to teach a new skill such as pointing or exchanging a picture for an item, choose something that you know highly motivates your child.

Music and music therapy

Sometimes, young children with ASD show no interest in spoken language but are fascinated by music and singing.

Laura ignored her mother when she called her name, when she tried to talk to her and even when she tried to help her associate her favourite doll with its name. She also refused to make eye contact with anyone. However, whenever she heard singing or nursery rhymes, she would stop, look around, smile and make eye contact with the person singing. Her mother was delighted when she discovered this as she felt that previously she had been unable to make emotional contact with her. Singing soon became a very useful way to attract Laura's attention and to teach her some simple concepts.

Music is also a useful way to teach children other skills such as turn-taking. Turn taking is an important skill in learning to have a conversation. One person speaks; the other stays quiet and listens. A simple game with a drum and two sticks (or a pan and two spoons) where you copy your child's drumming sounds and he copies yours, is a good foundation for developing the skill of taking turns.

In some areas, music therapy is available. This can be of real benefit for many children and young people with ASD.

Dan occasionally used isolated words. He loved music and quickly settled into music therapy. He enjoyed the instruments and also the therapist's voice. Within a few sessions he was echoing her songs, in perfect pitch: 'Dan likes the big bass drum.' Soon after this he began adding his own words: 'Dan likes beans and chips!'

Music therapy can encourage interaction through sound. We have seen some very good responses in children with little or no language. It seems as though asking them to communicate through language is much too hard, but helping them to do it in a reciprocal way through music can be very helpful.

Making it essential to communicate

The majority of parents are really good at anticipating their child's needs and wants. They might see their child look at a toy or an item of food and give it to him without thinking. However, this means that the child does not have to communicate his needs and does not learn how to do so. Similarly, the routine of the day with regular meals and drinks means that he doesn't really get hungry or thirsty. There are a few simple ways of helping a child to learn how to communicate:

- *Withholding:* This means holding back – not giving your child the object immediately but encouraging a response of some sort. This might be eye contact with you, a point, a nod of the head or a verbal request. Much depends on your child's developmental level and what you are trying to achieve. If your child is verbal then *waiting* until she asks for help gives her time to realise that a phrase may be appropriate, for instance, 'Open the lid please', before you do it for them.

- *Changing the routine in small ways:* Deliberately 'forget' to do something you normally do. For example, only put jam on one instead of the usual two pieces of bread for your child as a way of encouraging him to communicate this.

Teaching pointing

Most young children with ASD do not use pointing as a means of communication. In order to use the pointing gesture for this purpose a certain degree of Theory of Mind is essential. If we did not credit another person with a mind capable of having different thoughts from those of our own there would be no reason to point something out to her. The pointing gesture can, however, be taught in a rote fashion initially as an aid to communicating more effectively.

First, help your child to point to something he can touch by demonstrating to him. Take a book, for example, and point out objects with your finger. Practise this each time you read and help your child to copy your gesture. Do the same with objects – pointing out, for example, 'cup', but touching it rather than pointing from a distance. Your aim is to help the child progress slowly to the understanding that there is an imaginary line between the end of your finger and the object in question. You do this by gradually leaving more space between your finger and the object. If you want your child to learn to point to his favourite orange drink on the shelf, start by lifting him to it and pointing with your finger on the bottle and in time gradually move further away.

Children with very limited ability to communicate

Some children with ASD may remain very limited in their ability to communicate but can benefit greatly from being helped with understanding what other people are trying to say to them. Many of the ideas in the section above can be used in the same way. Pictures and photographs are particularly useful; for example, pictorial calendars help to explain which days are school days, weekends and holidays. A photograph of the car or taxi and a photograph of school help children to anticipate the routine of a school day. A small picture board showing the daily activities in sequence helps predict what will happen next. Any changes in routine can be explained in advance with simple pictures.

Ideas for helping verbal children to improve communication

Creating opportunities

Parents can do a great deal to assist their children's language development. There are many ideas throughout this chapter. However, one of the most effective techniques is to provide and create opportunities for speech. Ask questions which require increasingly complex replies, depending on your child's developmental level. Create opportunities for your child to tell you about her special interests. Talk to her yourself about what you are doing or thinking. Correct her mistakes gently but clearly without criticism. Praise her attempts.

Rhymes

Most young children like rhymes. As time goes by they become more familiar with them and may join in with you. They might also be encouraged to say the last word of each line if you pause to allow them space to complete it.

Teaching scripts

Children with ASD do not usually pick up the normal social scripts we might use routinely and may need some help to learn some basic responses, such as when and how to say 'Hello' and 'Goodbye'.

Self-talk

Talking as you work with your child exposes him to language in a meaningful and practical way. If you are cooking, for example, talk through the process out loud. 'First, we put the water in the pan. Then we put in the rice…' Similarly, encourage him to join in.

Give clear instructions

Try to keep it clear, simple and to the point. If you are asking your child to do something out of the ordinary, remember he might be very literal in his understanding. One grandmother sent her grandson into the boys' toilet saying, 'Go and wash your hands and use plenty of soap'. He came out with his hands covered in wet soapsuds. She hadn't told him to rinse the soap off his hands and then dry them!

Video social skills and role play

More complex social scripts can be taught and reinforced by the use of video. Try acting out how to greet people and start a conversation, record it on video and then play it back, commenting on the most successful strategies.

Teaching turn-taking (boundaries and timers)

Many parents grow weary of being talked 'at' by their more able children with ASD. The children fail to realise that their topic of interest might be boring for others and fail to pause and allow the listener to comment or even to make an excuse to get away! This is something that can be helped by videoing role play scenarios and demonstrating different ways of having conversations.

Explaining the rules of turn-taking can help. Some parents we know have used timers to time turns, or have used a 'talking spoon' (like the conch we mentioned in Chapter 10): at the tea table, for instance, whoever holds the spoon gets to talk and the others have to listen. The spoon is passed round when different people want to talk. It helps children to realise that we can all have a turn and it also helps them to wait and to be quiet while someone else is talking.

Repetitive language

It is very common for people with ASD to repeat words, phrases, questions, dialogues, sentences – in fact any forms of speech – many times. This can be very irritating for friends and relatives. Not surprisingly, parents frequently ask for help in trying to change this behaviour. However, before we can do this, we need to think about *why* it is occurring – what function does it have?

- It may be your child's way of learning new language. It could be the only way to make contact with you.
- Possibly, it is a way of seeking care.

- Maybe it is caused by anxiety.

- Perhaps it is related to your child's preoccupations.

- It may be being used to block out demands in situations when your child feels unable to cope.

- Or it could be a combination of all these factors, depending on the situation.

Figure 9.1 in Chapter 9, 'A template for making sense of a child's behaviour and planning ways to help', should help you to work out some of the reasons or purpose of the repetitive language.

There may be many benefits for your child in continuing with his repetitiveness and you may decide that to try to help him to moderate it is the best solution. If it is related to anxiety, i.e. it is a way of seeking reassurance or trying to resolve a difficult situation by rehearsing it, talking it through with your child might help. If it is related to his obsessions, you might decide to help him to put some limits around it.

Jordan, a 16-year-old boy with Asperger syndrome, liked to talk about automatic door-closing devices and would talk at length about them to anyone who would listen. His parents realised that in many ways this allowed him the social contact he enjoyed but within his own safe limits. He could control the conversation and it was predictable. It meant that he could avoid the uncertainty of less familiar topics, while at the same time indulging in his obsession!

His parents, bored with the topic, set him some rules. He was only allowed to talk to them about door-closing devices twice a day and for no more than ten minutes each time. They were also very concerned that he was beginning to be seen as a nuisance in the local store where the devices were sold, as his conversation with strangers was socially inappropriate. The rule was that he was not allowed to talk to anyone in the shop about door-closing devices without the shop manager's permission. He could go in and look at them. Meanwhile, his parents realised that Jordan needed their help in developing other topics of conversation. They practised talking about his favourite television programmes and films, for example. They also tried to teach him some listening skills, how to recognise some of the signs of his listener's boredom and how to stop talking!

Teaching idioms

Some children will respond very well to being taught idioms and some abstract aspects of language. One technique to help with this is 'paralleling' where an idiom is used and then its literal (real) meaning is put alongside it: for example, 'It's raining cats and dogs. That means there is lots of rain'. Some children may also enjoy making a visual dictionary of idioms by downloading images from the Internet or from clip-art.

Discouraging inappropriate language and swearing

Sometimes you might want to stop your child from talking! Children often learn that certain words and phrases produce interesting responses from people and they continue to use them despite our best efforts to discourage them. Swearing is particularly effective in public places and serves a variety of functions. You will need to work out what these are before you begin to try to change the behaviour in earnest. It could be a way of getting something the child wants (e.g. sweets to keep her quiet in embarrassing situations), a way of getting out of doing something (e.g. being taken out of a shop if she doesn't like shopping) or a way of getting a response from people. It can then be dealt with appropriately. Chapter 9, 'Managing Behaviour', should be helpful in devising a plan.

Helping other people to adjust their language

Although parents will be very much aware of the need to keep their language simple when talking with their children, other adults will rarely appreciate the need to do so. This can be particularly problematic when, as is commonly the case, the child's speech is better than their level of understanding. Sometimes teachers use complex instructions and fail to understand why the child hasn't completed tasks.

> In a class with seven-year-old John, the teacher, who was cross with him for not sitting in the circle, said: 'So you don't want any lunch then?' He had absolutely no idea what she meant.

Teachers might also become annoyed and frustrated if the child is very literal in his response. It is possible that teachers who are not particularly familiar with the communication difficulties of children on the autism spectrum will misinterpret some responses as rude or cheeky. If difficulties of this nature arise it may be helpful to explain the child's difficulties to the adults concerned or possibly contact your local specialist autism teacher for advice.

Speech and language therapy

You may have been referred to a speech and language therapist (SALT) who will be able to offer advice about how to help your child's communication skills. He or she may also have some information about specific programmes such as the Hanen programme or Adapted Hanen (see Chapter 20) aimed at early interventions for parents.

Summary

- Set realistic goals.
- Break information down.
- Repeat information.
- Give the child extra time to respond.
- Remember that being punitive, as a central strategy, won't get you far.
- Consider what you are trying to achieve in the long as well as short term.
- Remember that communication is much more than speech.
- Use simple language.
- Explain social communication rules when the child makes mistakes.
- Use visual cues, e.g. photographs, pictures and objects to aid communication.
- Remember it is hard work but productive!

Chapter 12

Tantrums, Aggression and Frustration

Many of us will be familiar with the way toddlers' tantrums turn into sheer rage within seconds! Being denied a favourite toy or treat can quickly turn happy toddlers into kicking, screaming, stamping, distraught little people who are unable to control their frustration. However, as they grow older, most children and young people and adults learn to control and contain their frustration most (although not all!) of the time. Some of this is due to growing maturity and some due to embarrassment and social constraints.

Children with ASD will be less aware of social constraints. Their mindblindness (see Chapter 4), means that they will not consider other people's disapproving looks or comments. Also, the frustration and rages of those who are unable to communicate their needs effectively may escalate. A further factor in the escalation of rage in children with ASD might be adults' responses. Most adult onlookers will tolerate a two-year-old's tantrum in the supermarket. They are often much less tolerant of an older child. They can be very critical towards parents, sometimes accusing them of being bad parents and unable to control their children. Not surprisingly, parents often find the embarrassment too great to bear, become upset themselves and give in to the child's demands. On giving in to the child's demands, they are inadvertently reinforcing the child's tantrum. The next time the family go shopping, the child knows that having a tantrum achieves what he wants. The screaming becomes associated with the reward. If parents don't give in, the child may have louder and longer tantrums until he gets what he wants. Sometimes the tantrums develop into self-harming behaviours, such as head-banging, or into aggressive behaviours, like hitting out at others. These behaviours are more difficult to tackle the longer they go on. This chapter has some ideas about how to tackle some of these behaviours as well as thoughts about preventing them from escalating.

Tantrums, rages and aggressive behaviours occur for a reason. Sometimes the reason is clear. At other times we have to become detectives!

> One parent couldn't work out why his daughter, Josie, had a tantrum every time they went to a particular park. Eventually, he realised that it was because she wanted to go to the water fountain she had seen on her visit there many months previously!

Often reasons for tantrums can be broken down to one or a combination of the following:

- wanting to do or to have something the child is prevented from doing or having

- not wanting to do something

- boredom or frustration

- fear

- to elicit a response from the environment and the people in it.

We will discuss these in more detail in some of the examples below.

TYPES OF PROBLEM

- Hits others because he can't have his own way

- Doesn't want to do something and has a tantrum or goes into a rage

WHAT is the problem?

Hits others because he can't have his own way

Gerald, aged nine, showed very little interest in his little sister Florence when she was born. As she learnt to walk and talk the two children played happily alongside each other. It was only when Florence began to be more assertive that problems arose. Although she was three years younger than Gerald, Florence was socially the more able. Arguments began to break out between them, resulting in Gerald head-butting or slapping Florence. Many of the disagreements started when Florence refused to play Gerald's preferred game or when they both wanted to watch different television programmes. Their parents found that they were spending more and more time refereeing arguments, comforting Florence and getting angry with Gerald for hurting his sister. They had tried shouting, time out, removing privileges and rewards for good behaviour but nothing seemed to be working. They decided to work through the model described in Chapter 9, 'Managing Behaviour'. Their ideas are summarised below.

1. What is the problem?
Slaps and head-butts his sister

2. Why does your child behave in this way?

Situations and settings: Where does it happen? Where does it not happen? Is it to do with something in the environment (smells, noises, what other people do, etc.)? Who is around when it happens?	At home, at Granny's, at his aunt's house, sometimes at school. When his sister won't comply. When he's upset. When they disagree about the TV.
Triggers and timings: When does it happen? Is it to do with anything pleasant or unpleasant? What are the timings in relation to other things? When does it not happen?	Whenever Florence won't do what he wants her to do. Worse when he's upset or worried. Sometimes he provokes a disagreement when he is bored. It's worse on busy school mornings. He hates to be rushed. Does not happen when they are out on family trips.
Mindblindness: Is it to do with mindblindness? Does your child realise he/she needs to communicate his/her needs to someone? Can the child see others' points of view or understand feelings and needs of others in this situation?	He doesn't understand Florence's point of view. He has a poor understanding of her pain. He isn't good at predicting the consequences of his behaviour.
Getting the gist: Is the problem associated with not understanding what is going on and why? Does your child understand the meaning of events and that things have a certain order?	He has a poor understanding of friendship. He doesn't appreciate the give and take in relationships and doesn't share easily. Incentives don't work for him. He thinks about the here-and-now rather than the future.

Imagination: Does your child think imaginatively and does this affect the behaviour?	He has too limited an imagination to be able to come up with alternative strategies for himself.
Preoccupations and sensory experiences: Is the problem associated with sensory experiences and/or preoccupations? Is the environment too complicated or interesting?	Hitting out at Florence helps to release his tension. In the past he used to hit his head on the floor to release his tension.
Social interaction: Does your child do this alone or with others? How does this affect the behaviour?	He enjoys some of the interaction he gets during and after the behaviours. He lacks the social skills to manipulate the situation in more healthy ways.
Communication: Is the problem associated with language or communication difficulties?	He struggles to communicate his needs. He can't tell his sister how he feels.
Emotions: Is the problematic behaviour related to anxiety or mood? Is it to do with your child's temperament? Is there anything else that might be affecting or upsetting your child (e.g. memories, dreams, illness, tiredness, boredom)?	He is worse when he is anxious. He gets anxious when he is being rushed. Gerald finds it difficult to control his own impulses. He gets tired after a busy school day and is very easily provoked just after he gets home.
Sameness: Is it to do with a need for routine or habits? Is there a problem associated with being in control? Has there been a change of routine at home or at school?	Gerald likes routine. He likes to know what will happen next. Florence constantly challenges this.
Responses: How have others responded to the behaviour? Does something happen after the behaviour that is important? How does it affect the behaviour in the future?	When Florence tells us, Gerald gets extra attention. Sometimes he gets sent to his room, sometimes one of us tries to defuse the situation with distraction e.g. playing on the swing. He sometimes likes to see Florence cry. Florence also has a part to play. She likes to get him into trouble. She also blackmails him: 'I won't tell Mum you hit me if we watch my video.'
Benefits: What positive outcomes happen for anyone (e.g. you, your child or your child's sibling) as a result of the behaviour? (Rack your brains: there usually *are* some!)?	He gets our and his sister's full attention. He gets to play on the swing with Mum. It seems to defuse intense emotion and act as a kind of release.

3. What is the goal?

No hitting or head-butting at home

Gerald's parents began to realise that, although they wanted to change Gerald's behaviour, his sister was not always an innocent bystander. Any plan they put into place would also have to involve Florence as she could easily sabotage its success.

4. Plan strategies

Gerald's parents came up with the following ideas:

- Distraction. Keep him busy – out on trips.

- Monitor the children carefully and trying to avoid disputes escalating.

- Explain the new rules carefully: for instance, 'No hitting'.

- Find alternatives for him to hitting; for example, telling Mum he's getting upset.

- Help him monitor and label his emotions.

- Find some immediate incentives for good behaviour e.g. star charts.

- Switch off the TV when the children argue.

- Mum use playing on swing as a reward for good behaviour rather than a distraction after Gerald has hit his sister.

- Lots of praise for playing nicely.

- Try to find calming activities when the children are tired.

- Get up earlier to give them more time.

They decided that they could not keep Gerald busy all of the time. It wasn't realistic to keep going out on trips. It was also impossible to monitor the children all of the time. However, they decided that it would be useful to try out a combination of all of the other ideas. The plan was that they would explain the rules to the children about 'no hitting' and that if Gerald found himself getting cross, he should go to his parents, who would praise him for this and distract him with little jobs. To help

Gerald monitor these situations he and his parents decided to refer to the heightened emotions he experienced as 'getting in a muddle'. He could use this phrase as shorthand to discuss things in a preventive way with his parents. They also set up a 'traffic light' system to help the children to recognise when they were beginning to reach a point where they were getting too cross with each other (see below for details). Finally, they set up a star chart reward system for good behaviour.

5. Checking

- *The benefits.* Might help Gerald to understand that hitting isn't acceptable and also give him different strategies when he is 'in a muddle'. Might help him to realise that good behaviour leads to rewards.

- *The costs.* Might be time consuming, tiring for us, the parents.

- *'Is this reasonable for my child?'* It doesn't make too many demands on him and seems achievable – particularly if we do not extend the plan to school at first.

- *'Is this reasonable for us?'* It will probably be very difficult at first. We expect that Gerald will keep coming to us to tell us he's 'in a muddle'.

- *'What might get in the way to stop it working?'* We might get tired and cross.

- *Find ways of dealing with these if possible.* When we do, we'll take it in turns to deal with the situation.

Gerald's parents came up with a clear plan to help him. The following gives more detail to explain how they put it into action.

HOW might we deal with it?
Getting the gist
Gerald doesn't understand the idea of sharing or turn-taking. His parents wanted to help him to learn to play cooperatively with his sister and understand that this was generally a better strategy than hitting her!

Not being rushed

Gerald hated to be rushed. His parents tried getting up earlier on school mornings, which gave him time to get ready. When he was dressed and had eaten his breakfast he was allowed to watch a video until it was time to leave.

Routine

Gerald liked routine. He needed to know what would happen next. He had developed a sort of routine or habit around hitting his sister. He would get upset because his needs were not being met, hit his sister and either get into trouble from his mum, get what he wanted from his sister or get to play on the swing with his mum. His parents thought that by teaching him an alternative routine they might be able to avoid the hitting part! The new routine was explained slowly and carefully to both children. The new rule was: 'No hitting or head-butting.' When Gerald began to feel cross (he called this 'getting into a muddle'), the rule was that he should go to his mum or dad and tell them, 'I'm in a muddle'. His parents would praise him for coming to them and would give him something to distract him – usually something he found fun to do.

Communication

Gerald found verbal communication difficult. He was able to use phrases and sentences but this was hard work for him. He had found hitting and head-butting an easy and effective way of having his needs met. Not surprisingly, his parents wanted to teach him a more socially acceptable response! He also found it difficult to understand what people were saying to him, particularly when they were using lots of words in a cross voice.

Gerald's parents realised that they had been expecting a great deal from him. Since he could talk they assumed that he could understand everything too. In fact this wasn't the case. They decided to try to use simple language and to use visual cues to help him to understand more clearly. They tried the 'traffic light system'. This is described in more detail in Chapter 9, 'Managing Behaviour').

During the first few days, Gerald was almost constantly going to his mum or dad in the mornings saying that he was in a muddle. They had anticipated this and had allowed themselves extra time by getting up earlier; they also supported each other to stay calm. When Gerald came to them, they gave him something to do to help him to calm down, such as giving him a small job or a game to play with. Sometimes they tried to make him laugh by making a

The 'traffic light' system

The children and their parents made a set of traffic lights out of coloured card. The lights were set to green. If an adult heard a disagreement escalating he or she would set the light to amber and ask them to calm down, saying: 'Official warning!' They were also to be reminded that if they didn't stop, they would go to the red traffic light. When the situation calmed, the traffic light would be returned to green.

Gerald's parents hoped that the traffic lights wouldn't have to go to red but realised that there should be consequences if they did. They decided on a short 'time out' period if the red light was shown. The children would sit in separate rooms until they were calm for three minutes. An egg timer was used to help the children to understand the concept of the three-minute time period.

deliberate mistake so that they could help him to defuse his 'muddle'. After four days, he wasn't going to his parents as often and after two weeks, he went to them less than once every morning.

If Gerald started to become a little aggressive without realising it, his parents reminded him that the traffic light was on green but it would have to go to amber if he didn't calm down. On the few occasions that it did go to amber, his mum or dad reminded him that he would still get a green sticker. He hated the traffic light going to amber and quickly learnt to calm down so that it could be returned to green as soon as possible. He learnt that he could calm himself down. During the two-week period, the lights never went to red, the children achieved all of their rewards and the house was a much calmer place.

Over the next two weeks, the traffic light system also went to Granny's and to Auntie Sue's house. The only time that the lights went to red was at Granny's one day. The children had been fighting about TV programmes, had ignored their warnings at amber and the red light was on! Gerald and Florence were distraught! Their granny quietly took them to calm down in 'time out' for a few minutes. Gerald was particularly upset but he complied with the rule. Although everyone found this very difficult, it was an important learning experience. The children learnt that there were consequences to breaking the rule and that they would be carried through. The adults learnt that the strategy was a useful one and that Gerald was able to cope with the consequences of his behaviour.

Mindblindness

Gerald did not really understand why he couldn't have what he wanted when he wanted it. For him, hitting and head butting his sister had the benefit of being able to release his tension and frustration and often resulted in his getting some extra time doing one of his favourite things (playing on the swing with his mum). He wasn't aware of her pain or her point of view. Nor did he understand his mother's response, which was inconsistent (sometimes angry and sometimes distracting him with play). His mindblindness prevented him from knowing these things intuitively. He would therefore benefit from a series of rules to help him. His parents worked out a plan to help him with social rules including teaching him the new rules and routines described above.

Additionally, they wanted to teach him that good behaviour was perceived positively and would result in rewards. They ensured that they praised good behaviour (i.e. when he was playing nicely with his sister, telling them when he was upset instead of hitting Florence or simply just sitting quietly watching TV with the family). In order to give both children extra encouragement at this stage they also used star charts.

The star charts is a chart with green stickers and red stickers for both children. For every session that each child's traffic light stayed on green or amber, he or she each got a green sticker on the chart and for every session his or her traffic light went to red, he or she got a red sticker. (A session was a short period of time defined by activities, e.g. before getting dressed, before breakfast, after breakfast and before leaving for school.) They could each earn up to ten green stickers a day. After five green stickers they had won a small reward such as playing on the swing with Mum or reading a comic with her. At the end of the week, if they had thirty green stickers or more, they could have a new comic.

Over the coming months, Gerald learnt to control his aggression toward his sister without involving his parents most of the time. His behaviour also improved at school without the need for them to transfer the techniques they had used at home.

WHAT is the problem?

Doesn't want to do something and has a tantrum or goes into a rage

Moses, aged seven, made good progress as a result of his parents' help and his growing maturity. He had started to construct simple sentences and to communicate his needs in a variety of ways. Unfortunately, this was still very difficult for him and at times he had prolonged tantrums out of sheer frustration. He went into a rage whenever he had to do something he didn't want to do. There were many things that he didn't like doing. He hated shopping, but shopping for new shoes in particular had become a battleground! Simon and Julia had tried on three separate occasions to get him to try on new shoes but each time he had major tantrums and refused to cooperate. Simon and Julia had begun to despair that they would ever get him to wear new shoes.

WHY might this be happening?

Getting the gist

Moses doesn't really get the gist about new shoes. He doesn't understand the idea that he has grown out of his old shoes and needs new ones. He doesn't understand the point of shopping generally. As long as his needs are met he is happy.

Communication

Although he can say more now, Moses cannot explain why he doesn't want new shoes.

Environment

Moses dislikes loud noises, bright lights and busy environments. Shops are noisy, bright and busy. He possibly feels over-stimulated and uncomfortable in shopping environments and simply wants to be somewhere safe like home.

Liking for sameness

Change has always been difficult for Moses. He has relied on things staying the same in order to feel safe. Sameness allows him to know how things look, feel and smell, and to predict how they will be. Anything new is scary and unpredictable. New shoes present a threat.

Parents' response

Julia and Simon are anxious about taking Moses shopping for new shoes, knowing that it is going to be a battle. In the past they left shops as soon as he started to have a tantrum, hoping he would stop. The last time they went shopping they were determined that he would have new shoes but ended up leaving out of embarrassment because he had kicked the shop assistant and thrown shoes all over the shop floor! Later, they realised that in, allowing Moses to leave in this way, they were making a tantrum in a shoe shop more likely to happen next time because his behaviour allowed him to leave the shop.

Mindblindness

Moses could not understand how embarrassing this was for his parents in the shop.

HOW might we deal with it?
Getting the gist

Moses will get the gist about the need for shopping in time. Meanwhile, his parents started to help him with this. When he asked for milk one day when there was none left, Julia took him to the fridge, saying 'Milk gone. Let's go shopping'. They went to the shop and just bought milk. She did this often when they ran out of his favourite things until he began to get the gist about shopping.

Communication

Moses needed visual cues as well as verbal explanations to help him to understand. His mother used photographs of different shops to help him understand where they were going and what they would buy. She also found that writing a simple social story with him helped.

Environment

Simon and Julia recognised that going shopping was stressful for Moses. They tried to pick quiet times to go shopping – early on a weekday morning for example. They also tried to go for just one item when he was with them, so that he could get used to shopping. They attended a small local parents' support group where they found out that shoes were a big problem for many parents of children with ASD. They were able to obtain advice from other parents about shoe shops which were more peaceful than others and where the shop assistants were much more tolerant of children with ASD.

Parents' response

Armed with renewed resilience and advice from the parents' support group, Julia and Simon prepared carefully for their shoe-shopping trip. They visited the shop in advance and explained the difficulty to the shop assistant in preparation (many parents find it a very helpful strategy to get the shop assistants on their side). They agreed on a quiet time to take Moses. They selected some shoes in advance that were similar in colour and shape to his old ones and made a note of these. Julia took a photograph of the shop and put it into a social story (see Chapter 10, 'Developing Social Skills') for Moses about the trip. She read him the story several times in the days prior to the visit.

These preparations made the trip a little easier – but Moses still had a tantrum! This time, however, they came away with his new shoes. At first he refused to wear them. His parents left them out next to his old shoes for several days until he became more familiar with them. Then they took away the old ones and after some protests he agreed to wear them.

Moses' parents continued to take him shopping for short trips and with time he learnt to tolerate them and even enjoy the trips for his favourite things.

The anger cycle

Most of us will have experienced anger many times in our lives. We can be sitting or walking quite calmly and gradually or suddenly, we become upset by something. The trigger might be the unexpected sound of a car horn, being jostled roughly in a crowd, feeling that we are being treated unfairly or finding ourselves threatened by someone. The list is endless. When this happens, we move from a comfortable, calm emotional state to feeling more alert, threatened and ready to defend ourselves. Our bodies prepare themselves for action. Our hearts start racing and we feel a surge of energy as our adrenaline goes into action. Our response is 'fight or flight'; either to run away or to fight off the threat. If the threat continues or another trigger upsets us when we are in this state of high arousal, we can move into the next stage where we lose control (see Figure 12.1), become less rational and sometimes become verbally or physically aggressive. This state of extreme high arousal usually occurs in short bursts before we are able to calm down. During this early calming phase, however, we can easily be provoked again into the extreme high arousal state. When we do calm completely, we tend to go into a low emotional state, where we feel drained, sleepy, exhausted and want to be left alone. Fortunately, the extreme state is very unusual for the majority of us. We learn to monitor and control our behaviour and find alternative strategies to those of hurting others or ourselves.

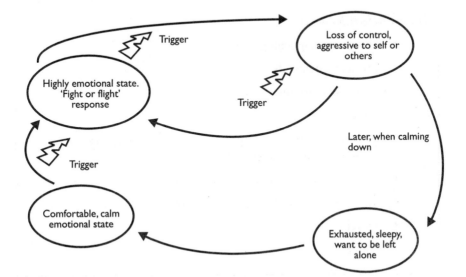

Figure 12.1: The anger cycle

It is important to understand this cycle when we are trying to help young people with ASD who experience extreme rage. It may, at first sight, seem that the rage occurred for no reason, but careful reconsideration of the incident is likely to provide clues. Having worked out possible causes, it is easier to prevent possible triggers in the future.

Dealing with aggressive behaviour

It is possible to reduce the distress and hence the increased arousal caused by these factors once we are aware of them.

We can help young people to find safe ways to remove themselves from noise and over-stimulating environments. We know of some schools that provide a quiet room, for example.

We can try to keep demands to a manageable level.

Where there are known conflict situations, we can make compromises rather than turning the situation into a battle.

One girl liked to be first into her taxi, which wasn't always possible. She also liked to sit in the front seat. The compromise rule that she learnt was that they would take it in turns to sit in the front seat.

We can also learn to be aware of the impact of sudden changes.

Possible triggers for anger

- Things not happening as expected
- Too many demands
- A change in routine
- Noise
- Over-stimulation, e.g. bright lights; colourful displays; noisy, jostling crowds in supermarket
- Being prevented from completing rituals
- Uncertainty/lack of structure/waiting
- Travel
- Conflict.

Robert, a 13-year-old boy with Asperger syndrome, had expected his next lesson at school to be art. During registration he was given a message that he was to go to his year head teacher's office first. After registration, he ran out of the classroom with his art folder. His teacher ran after him thinking he was running away. The boy ran faster and became frightened about being chased. When his teacher caught him he was very distressed, in a high state of arousal, and he started hitting out at her. When he had calmed down later he was able to explain that he was running to his art lesson. He could not cope with the unexpected change in plan to go to his year head's room. He thought the teacher who was chasing him was going to be angry with him and in his fear became aggressive towards her when she caught him.

One of the most difficult tasks for teachers and parents is to understand how the young person with ASD may be thinking or feeling and remember that her social and emotional understanding may be at a different level from that of similar-aged children.

If a young person with ASD has moved into the highly emotional stage where she has started to become threatened or threatening, we can help by trying to calm the situation down and thus prevent her moving into the next stage where she loses control and becomes aggressive.

Much depends on the situation and your knowledge of the young person, but some hints on calming down the situation include:

- Stay as calm as possible (this prevents the emotional tone being raised).

- Avoid grabbing the young person (unless she is in danger (e.g. beside the road).

- Distract the child from the source of the anger (e.g. by playing pattern games).

- Play calming music.

- Take or send the child to a quiet place.

- Simply walk with the young person and listen to her calmly. It isn't usually possible to reason with someone when they are angry.

- Offer another release for the anger, e.g. tearing cardboard.

Our ultimate aim is to show the young person different ways of managing her anger so that she does not reach the stage of extreme arousal where she loses control and becomes aggressive.

Even with all of the above precautions, it sometimes happens that a young person loses control. If this happens it is important to keep her and others as safe as possible. There is little that can be done other than damage limitation and avoiding anything that may make the situation worse. Younger children can be removed as gently as possible to a quiet space. In very extreme circumstances, it may be necessary to resort to special clothing for a child.

> Tony's parents agreed that, for his own safety, he should wear a protective helmet for a short period of time.

If a teenager reaches the stage of extreme arousal resulting in aggressive behaviour, it is often safest to remove other young people from the room so as to allow him to calm down on his own.

Several children have used emotion thermometers to tune in more to their emotions and develop plans for dealing with high states of emotion (see Chapter 10, 'Developing Social Skills' and Appendix). These can be successful.

More ideas for avoiding and dealing with tantrums

- Use social stories (see Chapter 10) to help the child to understand and cope with situations he finds difficult.

- If the child is getting upset or having a tantrum and you can't work out the reason, check whether it could have anything to do with the environment: labels on clothes, bright lights, sounds, colour, crowds and smells.

- Consider whether the behaviour is to do with change or transitions. If it is, try making a visual or written storyboard about what to do next, e.g. getting out of bath – pull plug, step out of bath, get towel.

- Give the child several warnings before expecting her to end favourite activities. To help with time, try using egg timers. Have another activity to follow, e.g. 'Computer time then supper time!'

- Use visual timetables to help the child to understand what is going to happen or where he is going (see Chapter 9, 'Managing Behaviour').

- When children have tantrums because you want to take a different route somewhere, try helping them to understand by making a large map or model of your local area and play games with cars and miniature figures taking different routes.

- Help older children cope with turn-taking and losing by using high frequency games such as 'Snap' and 'Connect 4'. Teach them how to be a good loser and winner, by saying things that show what a good loser does and says (modelling).

Summary

- Children with ASD will often go on having temper tantrums until they are much older than children without ASD.

- Temper tantrums in children with ASD often last for longer periods of time than those of other children.

- It is usually better to try to change children's behaviour when they are young.

- It is important to get a good understanding of why your child might be having tantrums or showing aggressive behaviour before you try to change it.

- Children with ASD don't have to understand the strategy you use for it to work.

- Having clear rules that you stick to with your children is not cruel. It helps them learn that the world has boundaries and this helps them for the future.

Chapter 13

Feeding

Eating and feeding problems are very common for children with ASD. They vary tremendously and cause parents huge amounts of concern. Some children start with extremely good eating habits but then restrict their diets to only three or four foods; others are difficult to wean from liquid to solid diets from the beginning. Mealtimes can be a battleground and a source of anxiety for parents.

TYPES OF PROBLEM

- Will only eat a few specific foods

- Difficulty weaning to solids

- Will only eat or drink in specific places

We will take each of these in turn, considering WHAT the problem is, WHY it might be happening and HOW we might deal with it.

WHAT is the problem?

Will only eat a few specific foods

Joanne, aged six, had always been a very fussy eater. She gradually reduced the types of food she would eat to the extent that for the last year she had been eating exactly the same things each day; Weetabix for breakfast, cheese sandwiches and and apple for lunch and Tesco's own brand fish fingers and beans with chips for dinner. Her father had not been too concerned as he had been assured that Joanne was probably getting all of the required daily nutrition from this diet. One day Joanne suddenly spat out her fish fingers and beans. Later her father discovered that her first front baby tooth had come out. She had a tantrum the next day when her father produced her usual meal. Any alternative, other than chips, was met with a further tantrum. Her dad became worried that Joanne's diet was becoming increasingly restricted and feared that she might reach a point of only accepting one or two foods.

WHY might it be happening?

Sensory sensitivity

Joanne is very sensitive to texture, taste and smell. Any variation, such as a change to a different brand of fish fingers, seemed very difficult for her to cope with.

Need for routine or sameness

Mealtimes had a certain routine quality for Joanne. She liked them at the same time, in the same place, with the same crockery and cutlery and the same food. Over the years her father had changed his own behaviour to make sure everything was just right so that his daughter would eat. If something like the cutlery changed, for example, there was a risk that she might stop eating something else.

Language difficulties

Joanne cannot talk and cannot explain the problems to her father, so she often gets cross and has tantrums.

Poor understanding

Joanne doesn't understand that her father is worried about her. She has poor Theory of Mind.

Her father's response

Joanne's dad was becoming more and more anxious and spent a lot of time trying to persuade her to eat other food. Joanne would then throw these foods on the floor and her dad would become cross with her. In fact this behaviour was developing into a routine and Joanne's dad was becoming more frustrated and tired.

Association with something unpleasant

On the occasion when Joanne stopped eating fish fingers and beans, it was possible to trace her distress to her discomfort at having found a loose tooth in her mouth while eating these foods. Many of us will be able to recall similar situations that have stopped us from eating something, at least for a short time. (Finding a small slug on a lettuce and mushroom salad in a restaurant stopped one of the authors from eating both mushrooms and lettuce for several weeks!)

HOW might we deal with it?
Sensory sensitivity

Joanne had always been very sensitive to sound, texture, smell and taste. Her father realised that whenever she showed a preference for a particular food, he would buy it for her and stop buying other foods. In hindsight he thought that prevention might have been a better approach. Instead of allowing particular preferences to develop he could have presented her with brands she liked less, for example; he might also have mixed two brands together, so that she became used to slightly different tastes. Her father realised that, given her now very restricted diet, this might be more difficult. However, he decided to start by adding a few chips of a different brand to her plate each day, which

Joanne happily tolerated. Gradually introducing new sensory experiences became helpful.

Need for routine or sameness

Joanne had settled into a routine of having the same food at particular times of the day. Children with ASD like routines as they make life more predictable. One of the problems for children with ASD is in not being able to make predictions or guesses about what might happen next, particularly if they have poor language skills. So, keeping things the same makes things feel safe. It is very important when changing a routine, therefore, to keep as many other parts of the situation the same and to introduce change gradually and sensitively.

Joanne's father decided gradually to introduce some of her favourite foods from different times of the day into her evening meal. He knew that Joanne liked apples, so after her chips he put a bowl of apples on the table and invited the family to help themselves. On the first day Joanne did not take an apple, but on the second day she did and quickly established this as part of the routine. He then moved on to giving her a piece of her favourite cheese (on a separate plate) with her chips, which was also accepted. The problems started whenever he tried something new and Joanne had a tantrum. However, he persevered. He recalled that she had liked crisps in the past and put these on a plate next to her chips. At first they ended up on the floor but after several days she tolerated them and even tried one a few weeks later. He continued with this technique, with slightly different but previously favoured foods and had variable success. Joanne did, however, learn to tolerate different foods on a plate near to her as she became familiar with them, and even developed a liking for some!

Her father's response

After talking about the problem Joanne's dad began to realise that his own anxiety might have been making matters worse. Dinnertime became a very stressful event as he tried to tempt Joanne with alternatives. Anything other than chips on her plate ended up on the floor and invariably he became cross with Joanne. It seemed that, in some respects, Joanne was enjoying the time her dad was spending in encouraging her and in tidying up the mess. She also seemed to get quite excited when her dad lost his temper with her. At first he thought she was 'winding him up' – deliberately trying to make him cross – but then he realised that the severity of her autistic symptoms made this impossible for her. She was unable to consider the thoughts and feelings of other people (mindblindness). It was more likely, he decided, that he was reinforcing her behaviour. She had possibly learnt that the consequence of throwing food was a very interesting response from her father. So, he made his responses as calm as possible.

He decided that he would try to reduce his stress over dinner by initially simply giving her chips and ignoring her if she threw any food.

Association with something unpleasant

All children's associations with unpleasant things are very difficult to break. It may be best to avoid reintroducing food that has been associated with distress to a child for a little while. It can be reintroduced at some future point. As these associations seem to occur frequently for some children with ASD, it is particularly important to keep trying to introduce other foods into the diet on a regular basis.

WHAT is the problem?

Difficulty weaning to solids

Sophie, aged three, is a very quiet, content, petite child. She had always been breast-fed and easily pacified by a quick feed. The problem began when her mum tried to wean her onto solids. Sophie refused anything other than breast milk. She spat out spoonfuls of food and turned to her mother, becoming very distressed until she was fed. Her mum was becoming increasingly concerned that she might not have enough milk to help Sophie continue to grow and that Sophie would never be weaned!

WHY might this be happening?
Sensory sensitivity and distress

Sophie was very sensitive to changes of texture and taste. She became distressed when a spoon was placed in her mouth and looked to her mum for comfort in the way she had always done – seeking to be breast-fed. She had established a habit of crying as soon as she saw her father with a bowl and spoon and rejected it before the food reached her mouth.

Her mother's response

Sophie's mum worried greatly about her daughter's health. She was concerned that Sophie was underweight for her age and so happily breast-fed her on demand.

Need for routine and sameness

Sophie was in the habit of generally pottering about the house and turning to her mum approximately every 20 minutes for a feed. This was comforting for her and her mum was readily available.

Communication difficulties

Sophie was unable to use or understand any verbal language. Her mother was unable to explain to her what was happening. As Sophie could not interpret non-verbal cues such as smiling and gestures of reassurance from her mother, she became confused and distressed.

HOW might we deal with it?
Sensory sensitivity and distress

Sophie had recently started to explore some objects such as plastic toys, by putting them in her mouth. She was happy to do this, but only with objects of her choice. Her mum noticed one day that she had picked up a biscuit and happily chewed on this for some time. She then experimented with other types of finger food, which Sophie either chewed on or spat out. This seemed like a major breakthrough and, although she was not eating much and was still largely breast-fed, it was a start.

Her mother's response

Sophie's mother realised that she needed to break Sophie's habit of breast-feeding so regularly. She knew that Sophie needed to move on to solids now that she was older and that maintaining a largely milk-only diet was insufficient for her needs. She knew that practically and emotionally reducing breast-feeding would be much more difficult than it had been when she had weaned her son at the age of six months. One day she commented to Sophie's grandmother, 'I wish my milk would just dry up so it would be easier to say 'No' to her.' As this was not the case, she decided to try leaving Sophie with her grandmother on some afternoons. Sophie coped remarkably well without a feed for over two hours and was content with a biscuit. Sophie and her mum built up the times she was away in the afternoons over a period of weeks, during which time she began to sample crisps, chocolate bars and juice. Following from this, Mum found it possible to say 'No' to some of Sophie's frequent requests for breast-feeds and reduced feeds to three and then later to two times a day.

Need for routine and sameness

Sophie continued to need routine but was able to establish a new one based around her three and then two feeds a day. She did, however, insist on her favourite finger foods being readily available at all times. This created a new problem! This was dealt with later.

After a while, Sophie was feeding only once at night as part of a bedtime routine. The feed was then substituted with Sophie's own red cup and spout. This was put into a sequenced bedtime routine, which the family agreed would initially be gone through with Dad and Grandma. Sophie threw the cup on the floor and screamed the first time, but every night it was offered as part of the routine. One night, in desperation, Grandma began drinking from it. Sophie shouted 'No!' and took if from her grandma and began drinking. There was a further night of tantrums the first time that Mum tried to do the routine, but she stuck to it and stayed calm, and Sophie settled into her new routine after this. The objective of weaning Sophie had been achieved.

WHAT is the problem?

Will only eat or drink in specific places

Becky, aged four, started nursery, but she refused to eat or drink anything throughout the three-hour period she was there. After three months the situation was still the same and her mum was worried that she must be hungry and thirsty as she was very keen to eat and drink when she came home. Her teachers had tried coaxing her with her favourite things and her mum had stayed through snacktime to encourage her to eat, but nothing had worked.

WHY might it be happening?
Need for routine

Becky's daily routine had been seriously disrupted when she started nursery. She didn't know what to expect and was likely to be very distressed about this. Nothing was familiar.

Generalising

Becky had no experience of nursery before she started going there. She did not know what to expect. She had been in the routine of eating at home but not anywhere else. It may be she perceived eating as only occurring at home. Most children with ASD have difficulty generalising: transferring different skills to different situations.

Communication difficulties

Becky spoke only a few words and was unable to tell the adults why she couldn't eat at nursery.

Mindblindness.

Becky did not know intuitively what was expected in this situation.

Anxiety

Many of us lose our appetites when we are anxious. The new social situation made Becky anxious.

HOW might we deal with it?
Need for routine, communication difficulties and anxiety

Becky's mum recognised that Becky needed to understand what was happening and how she should behave. She discussed the problem with the teacher and together they made picture charts showing photographs of the nursery routine. The first was a picture of Becky taking off her coat, the next of her doing puzzles and the next sitting down with her snack.

Becky gradually learnt the order of the day and nursery became more predictable and safe. Becky's anxiety decreased over time as she became used to the new surroundings and routine.

Generalising

Becky's mum wondered whether using familiar plates and mugs with her own favourite food would help her daughter to eat at nursery. On the days when she didn't go to nursery, they 'practised' snacktime at home. They prepared the snack together on her favourite Winnie the Pooh plate with her Winnie the Pooh mug. After a few weeks, they packed her familiar snack on her favourite plate and took it to nursery. For the first few days, she still did not eat. However, her mother persevered and packed her snack each day. Then, suddenly, Becky began to eat from her plate and drink from her mug. As she became more familiar with the idea of eating at nursery, her mother gradually introduced slightly different foods so that she wouldn't become fixed on a particular snack. Later, she also successfully introduced different plates.

Other interventions to try

Children need to learn about foods in a comfortable, relaxed and non-pressurised environment. When they feel safe and comfortable, they are more willing to risk something new. Try to make mealtimes pleasant and enjoyable, as relaxed as possible. Let them see other people enjoying eating different foods. Allow them to eat their favoured foods within this environment for some time before gently trying to introduce new foods in the following ways:

- *Try to work out what types of food your child likes and build on these:* Make a list of the foods and liquids that the child currently accepts and likes. Organise them by taste (e.g. strong or bland), texture (crispy or soft), colour and smell. Then try to think of other foods that are very similar to those they like and experiment gently with these. If your child likes softly boiled cauliflower, for example, you might want to try mashed potato (both are soft, savoury and white) or try mixing a little potato with the cauliflower first.

- *Make small changes:* Some children with ASD are hypersensitive to even small differences. Often they will only eat one brand of fish fingers or beef burgers. If this is the case, try adding just a little of a different brand to the plate.

> Sara went through a phase of eating only green foods. She gradually learnt to accept differently coloured foods by being introduced to apples of varying shades of green and red!

- *Try different types of favoured food:* This might involve trying different flavoured yoghurts or crisps, different types of cheese, fried potatoes in different shapes, etc.

- *Mix together favoured foods:* If your child likes bananas and fromage frais, mix the two together to help him to learn about different combinations and textures.

- *Try using foods in play:* Some children with ASD do not like the feel or smell of many materials, including food. Hence, the thought of putting them into their mouths fills them with horror. By gradually learning to cope with different textures through play, this fear usually subsides. Dried pasta is good for making collages and salt dough can be made into different shapes for decorations. Bread or biscuits are usually good fun to make at home. Faces or stick people can be made from all types of food. Care should always be taken, particularly in the early stages, to ensure that there is no expectation at all that the child should eat the food prepared in play. The major focus is for the child to feel familiar and comfortable about food products.

- *Getting used to lumpy food:* If your child has a very sensitive mouth, she may not have explored toys or other objects in her mouth in the way most young children do. This is an important developmental stage, not least for learning about how to manage objects in the mouth. Lumpy food may very well feel uncomfortable and your child may not know what to do with it. This experience can be made a little easier by only gradually making her food less smooth and also helping her to remove unwanted food from her mouth with your finger or helping her to spit it out.

Sam used to vomit when he saw a bowl of spaghetti on the table having once gagged on a strand of spaghetti. He could cope with seeing dried spaghetti, so his mother used this as the point of success and started from there. They glued it to paper, painted it and made patterns. Then they did the same with partially cooked cold spaghetti. Eventually, Sam could cope with seeing a bowl of fully cooked spaghetti at a distance and then on the table. It was always clear to him, however, that there was no expectation that he should eat it. He still doesn't eat spaghetti but he is no longer sick when he sees it!

- *Work from the point of success:* Becky was eating happily at home. Her mother's task was to think of ways she could transfer this success to nursery. In very extreme cases, the sight or smell of some foods can cause children to be sick. By working from the point at which the sight or smell is tolerable, it is possible to reduce and eliminate many aversive responses.

- *Persevere and build up familiarity with different foods:* Encourage your child to have a small amount of different foods on his plate but make it clear that he doesn't have to eat it. He might decide that, having tasted it once, he doesn't like it. This is OK. However, having the food on their plate occasionally helps children to become more familiar with it and more tolerant and accepting of it.

Summary

- Use food-like textures in play so that the child gets used to different feels and sensations.

- Create a relaxed environment for eating with other members of the family if possible.

- Make eating routine.

- Introduce different foods on a regular basis.

- Don't over-react to rejection of foods.

- If problems arise, build on different types of favoured foods by making small changes, e.g. to brand or flavour.

- Work from points of success.

Chapter 14

Toileting

Many children with ASD will learn to use the toilet without any difficulty. The process may be delayed and take longer than for children without ASD, but otherwise be uneventful. For others it may be more problematic. This chapter covers some of the more common difficulties associated with learning to use the toilet. It concentrates mostly on achieving bladder control. Problems with bowel control and soiling are covered in detail in the next chapter.

Why is toilet training more difficult for children with ASD?

- *Communication.* They may have very little use of language. They may have difficulty communicating their needs or may not understand the association between words and actions.

- *Social awareness.* Due to 'mindblindness' they may not be aware of the need to communicate with adults. Also, they will not be motivated by social pressure in the same way as other children. For example, they are unlikely to be interested in using the potty 'to please Daddy' or to show that they are 'a big girl' or 'a big boy'. Nor will they be motivated by shame, e.g. 'People will laugh if you are still wearing nappies'.

- *Routine.* Children may be quite happy with the nappy changing routine and be resistant to change to a new routine.

- *Sensory awareness.* They may not be able to read the bodily cues about the need to use the toilet.

It is, of course, important for the child's social development for him to learn to use the toilet. It makes aspects of everyday life much more comfortable and acceptable for everyone concerned. Incontinence can also be embarrassing for siblings and other family members, as well as expensive and demanding for parents and carers. There will be a very small minority of children with ASD who may never successfully master toileting, but it is usually in everyone's interests to persevere with the toilet training process.

How will we know if our child is ready?

Some of the following are indicators that children are approaching readiness:

- Having a dry nappy for two or three hours.
- Pausing or standing still when wetting or soiling.
- Noticing when wetting or soiling.
- Showing interest in others going to the toilet.
- Voluntarily weeing when not in a nappy and taking interest in it.

There are many different types of problems to do with learning to use the toilet. Some of the common ones include:

- not knowing what to do
- seeming afraid
- not being dry at nights
- having irritating habits
  - using too much paper
  - aiming badly
  - insisting on a certain colour of loo seat
  - finding flushing too noisy

TYPES OF PROBLEM

- Doesn't seem to know what she is supposed to do
- Seems afraid

We will take each of these in turn considering WHAT the problem is, WHY it might be happening and HOW we deal with it.

WHAT is the problem?

> Doesn't seem to know what she is supposed to do

Maria had just had her fifth birthday. Her parents had tried to toilet train her several times over the past two years without any success. She just didn't seem to make the connection about what she was supposed to do. They were sure that she was ready because she could easily be dry for several hours at a time. She was also very interested in watching puddles form on the carpet as she wet the floor when her nappy was off!

WHY might this be happening?
Getting the gist

Maria had not grasped the idea about toilets. She didn't understand that certain behaviours (going for a wee or a poo) were associated with a particular place (the toilet).

Communication

Maria had very little speech. Also she lacked the awareness that other people could help her to meet her needs if she communicated it to them.

Sensory experiences

Most of the time, Maria wore a nappy and seemed comfortable wearing it. When her parents had tried putting her onto the toilet or a potty she had hated the experience, and jumped off as quickly as she could. Her parents wondered if the seats were too cold, uncomfortable or frightening in some way.

Environment

Maria really liked to be in the bathroom. She loved water and bubbles and would spend hours playing at the sink if her mother would allow her to do so. She also liked to throw paper down the lavatory and flush it repeatedly. The bathroom had become one of her favourite places to play! Perhaps it wasn't surprising that she didn't make the connection between the bathroom and going for a wee!

Parents' responses

Nappy changing time for Maria was a very pleasant experience. Her parents usually chatted and played with her. Even when she wet the carpet, she seemed to enjoy her parent's reaction and then trying to play in the bowl of water they brought with a cloth to clean up the puddle!

HOW might we deal with it?
Parents' responses

Maria's parents decided that the time had come to train Maria and that this time they would plan their strategy very carefully. They decided that they would devote as much time and energy as necessary to this and accept that their lives would be taken up with training Maria for a concentrated period of at least three weeks! They considered all of the things that might have been making it difficult for Maria to learn about using the toilet, including their own responses. With the help of her teacher they devised the plan below. Carrying out Maria's toilet training plan involved a great deal of hard work, encouragement and persistence!

1. Keep a chart of the times she wets and soils her nappy for one week to find out when and how often she wets and soils (Figure 14.1)

2. Make a note of any fears or special interests she has that are to do with the toilet.

3. Set aside several days (in the holidays) to start training.

4. Make sure she is wearing easy-to-pull-on pants.

5. Make a little card with a picture or photo of a toilet on it.

6. Use the information from the chart to plan when and how often to take her to the toilet: if she usually needs the toilet 20 minutes after breakfast – take her to the toilet about 15 minutes after breakfast. If she usually wets soon after her mid-morning snack, take her to the toilet a few minutes after her snack. Be patient and sit with her until she does a wee or a poo. You can sometimes encourage this by giving her drinks while she is on the toilet.

7. Just before taking her to the toilet, show her the picture of the toilet.

8. Make a visual timetable showing the sequence of events. Toilet. Pull pants down. Sit on toilet. Wee. Wipe with toilet paper. Get

off toilet. Flush. Wash hands. Dry hands. Leave bathroom. Play with Lego.

9. Give praise and rewards for sitting on the toilet.

10. Use star charts to reward successes. [Maria was not interested in praise but loved gold stars.]

11. If she seems worried about anything specifically to do with the bathroom try to make it safer, e.g. buy a special child seat to go over the toilet seat and a footstool to make it more comfortable.

Chart for recording times when child wets and soils – to be used BEFORE toilet strategy begins. W = Wet; S = Soiled; D = Dry							
Time	Monday	Tuesday	Wednesday	Thursday	Friday	Saturday	Sunday
6.00							
7.00							
8.00							
9.00							
10.00							
11.00							
12.00							
13.00							
14.00							
15.00							
16.00							
17.00							
18.00							
19.00							
20.00							
21.00							

Figure 14.1: Wetting and soiling chart

Getting the gist

Maria's parents were keen for her to get the gist about using the toilet. As well as taking her to the toilet at frequent intervals for the first few days, they watched out for times when they thought she might be pausing or straining and took her again. If she had an accident, they took her to the toilet immediately and continued the routine in the bathroom, making sure that any attempts to clean up didn't distract her. Her parents decided that they would not punish her for any accidents and try very hard not to get cross with her. In addition, her mother took the opportunity, when it was convenient, to take Maria to the toilet with her to reinforce the idea about what the toilet is used for!

Sensory experiences

Her parents realised that Maria was unhappy sitting on the toilet because she thought she might fall in. They bought her a special child's toilet seat with her favourite Sesame Street characters on it. They also put her cassette recorder in the bathroom and switched on her Sesame Street tape while she was sitting on the toilet, and they read her favourite books to her.

Environment

As Maria loved playing in the sink, hand-washing tended to take a very long time! Her parents wanted to teach her that this sink was for washing her hands after she had used the toilet and discouraged her from playing in the basin in the bathroom. They decided to limit hand-washing time by letting her use a timer to indicate when it was time to finish. They also encouraged her to play outside at other times with a bowl of water instead.

School

When Maria returned to school three weeks later, she had made huge progress. There were still many accidents but these were ignored as far as possible. Her teacher used the same symbols and visual timetable that Maria had used at home. She still needed to be taken to the toilet regularly but after a few weeks settled into a routine which fitted in with her classroom timetable alongside some of the other children.

WHAT is the problem?

Seems afraid

John, aged eight, was very afraid of toilets. His parents believed that the plumbing in his old nursery school was much to blame for this. The pipes made loud unexpected gurgling and rattling noises and, when the toilets were flushed, John found it almost unbearable. He screamed and ran out of the toilets with his hands over his ears. He was so upset by the toilets there that his teachers and parents agreed not to force him to use them. Unfortunately, thereafter he became hyper-vigilant about toilets and did anything he could to avoid them. Even going past lavatories caused him to shout out and put his hands over his ears. However, he was able to use a potty and would also urinate outside in the garden. He seemed not to be afraid here and would wee almost anywhere outside, once catching the cat unawares by accident. The problem was that he was now getting too big to use the potty and his parents also wanted to discourage him from urinating outside, as this was no longer socially acceptable.

WHY might this be happening?

Situations and triggers

John's parents knew that toilets were a trigger for him to become unsettled and cover his ears. He had even started to do this when they were out shopping and no toilets were in sight. Finally, his parents realised that he did this in anticipation, as he could smell toilets from some distance!

Sensory experiences

John had always been very sensitive to loud noises and from an early age had covered his ears on hearing sudden harsh sounds. He used to react badly to traffic noise, lawnmowers, aircraft and tractors in much the same way as he did to toilet flushing sounds, but seemed to be able to cope with these noises now.

Communication

John was quite severely affected by his autism. His verbal communication was very limited. This meant that his parents had to try to work out what he wanted by being attuned to him whenever possible.

Emotions

John's parents were sure that fear played a large part in John's reaction. They noticed that he became agitated even when he passed the bathroom door at home.

Other people's responses

Due to his extreme reaction at nursery, John's parents had decided not to make him use the toilets there. He went to the toilet at home before going to nursery and came home at lunchtime. They had hoped that when he started school, he would cope with the new toilets. Unfortunately, this wasn't the case. When his teacher insisted that he went along with the other children, he became hysterical. Over the following days he started getting upset in the mornings, seemingly not wanting to go to school. He also began to be wary of the toilet at home. Again, his parents decided not to force him to go into the toilets at school. He started coming home at lunchtime to use the toilet.

Over the coming months John's fear grew gradually worse and he refused to go near the toilet at home or any other toilets. As time went on, the people around John learnt about his phobia and it became accepted that he 'didn't go into toilets'. Without realising it, people around him were reinforcing his belief that toilets were scary places.

Benefits

The benefits for John were clear in that he didn't have to be in an environment that he found frightening. Unfortunately, though, in permitting him to avoid something frightening, his parents were not giving him the opportunity to learn that perhaps toilets weren't so scary after all.

HOW might we deal with it?
Fear

John's parents were sure that he had developed a phobia about toilets and sought advice about ways to deal with it. They decided to use a desensitisation technique. This technique is described in Chapter 9, 'Managing Behaviour'. The long-term goal was to get John to wee in the toilet at home. His parents knew he was a long way from this and set a more realistic goal of getting him to cope with being able to stand next to the toilet at home. As he was unable to draw up his own list of fears, they made one for him, using their great knowledge about him, his likes and particularly his fears.

John had a favourite sheepskin rug that he liked to sit on and stroke for comfort. His parents used this to get him to sit nearer to their downstairs toilet. They started to move it *very* gradually towards the door over a period of several weeks. They sat with him reading his favourite books. They also deliberately left the toilet door open. In the beginning he kept closing the door every time he passed. Then, his mother, knowing that he liked star charts and stickers, made him a chart and put it on the inside of the toilet door. Each time he passed, leaving the door open, they put a sticker on the chart. At first, he kept his hands over his ears but in time he became distracted and stopped doing this. One day his mum put his rug inside the door and persuaded him to stand on it whilst he put his stickers in place. Before long, the walls in the downstairs toilet were covered with stickers and John could happily enter the room without difficulty.

His parents used a similar process to help him to use the toilet. At first he used the potty in the room and then progressed to the toilet.

Flushing remained difficult for a long time after this but at least he was using the toilet at home! (There is a brief section on coping with flushing noises below.)

School

When John was confident about using the toilet at home, his parents and teachers worked together to help him to use the toilets at school. They used a similar desensitisation strategy to the one they had used at home. Fortunately, his school was now in a building with modern plumbing so the noise was less of a problem for him. John had also learnt to cope with the flushing noise of the toilet at home. His parents thought that smells were still a potential problem and supplied the school with cans of the same air freshener they used at home.

In order to encourage John to go into the school toilet, his teachers made him a new sticker chart similar to the one at home. They placed this on the inside door of the toilet block and started out by taking him there when no one else was around. Gradually, they moved on to placing the chart on the inside door of one of the cubicles. They took this stage very slowly, not putting him under any pressure to use the toilet. After several weeks, he spontaneously started using the toilet himself. His teachers continued to take care to help him to use the toilets at quieter times and to keep them as fresh smelling as possible!

Other common toileting problems

Not dry at night at all

If your child is under 12, is still not dry at night and never has been, it is most likely that her nervous system has not yet matured enough to control night wetting. Using star charts or some of the other mechanisms mentioned will not work in these circumstances because it is not within the wilful control of the child. Remember, about 5 per cent of ten-year-old boys *without* ASD will wet at night and 10 per cent of five-year-olds. This often runs in families. You may have to wait until the child is older and the urinary and nervous systems have matured further. In these circumstances, don't worry!

Dry some nights and not others

The best advice for dealing with night wetting after the child has gained control is to:

- avoid caffeine drinks in the evening

- give your child plenty to drink in the day (not the evening). Many parents think the opposite and restrict children's fluid intake. This does not work because it leads to a small bladder capacity

- use a waterproof cover for the mattress.

If a child has been dry for a while and then begins wetting again, this may be due to some upset in the child's life. Think carefully about changes in routine or new stresses. Sometimes children get urinary tract infections that make wetting more likely. If it is possible to catch a urine sample your family doctor can check for this.

However, most children go through a phase where they have only partial control. This phase usually passes. If not, in some circumstances the 'pad and bell' can be used if children are dry for some nights but not others. This involves a pad connected to an alarm that goes off when it gets wet. It is a small device clipped or taped into the pyjamas or pants. Some children on the autism spectrum will not tolerate these devices. The bell goes off and the child wakes and then uses a potty by the bed (or walks with assistance to the toilet), and the connection is made between a full bladder, and waking and going to the toilet. Many areas have clinics for this (enuresis clinics) and if you think this may work with your child then you can talk with your family doctor to arrange this.

Occasionally medication can be used. There are two types. These are tricyclics (antidepressants used in much smaller doses that seem to act on the urinary control system) and drugs that reduce the amount of urine being made at night (antidiuretic hormone). In many cases these work until you stop them and then the problem often comes back, and so they are less commonly used than they used to be.

Uses too much toilet paper

Nial had developed a habit of using half a roll of toilet paper to wipe himself every time he went to the loo. He had blocked the lavatory several times and had developed a very sore bottom. The problem was that he didn't know when to stop. His grandma had told him that he must use 'plenty' of toilet paper to make sure he was clean and as he was very literal in his thinking, he used plenty of paper every time. His parents couldn't persuade him to use less. They tried removing the roll of paper and only leaving a few sheets for him but he became very upset and insisted on having more.

When his grandma realised the problem, she put a strip of his favourite dinosaur stickers in a line on the wall underneath the toilet roll holder, allowing for about five sheets of paper. She told Nial to measure the paper to the line of dinosaurs and tear off that amount.

Bad at aiming

Ray's dad seemed to spend vast amounts of time cleaning the bathroom floor when Ray had used the toilet. When he watched him, he noticed that Ray was far too busy looking at the patterns on the wallpaper to aim correctly. To help him along, his dad put a ping-pong ball into the toilet bowl and challenged him to aim at the ball! His dad also painted the wall a plain colour. This worked.

Insists on a certain colour loo seat

Hazel, who was 14, would not use any toilet unless the seat was white. She would check all of the cubicles in public places until she found one with a seat of the correct colour. If she couldn't find one, which was often, she wet herself. Her head teacher at school even started changing black seats to white ones when they were broken so as to reduce accidents. Other places were less accommodating, however.

Eventually the problem was solved by making white cardboard toilet seats covered in sticky-backed plastic which Hazel put on top of any differently coloured seats. She and her occupational therapist spent many hours making differently coloured cardboard seats and even painted different patterned ones, in the hope that she might start using these too. The plan was that if she could use differently coloured home-made seats, she would progress to being able to use differently coloured public seats. Unfortunately, although seat making was fun, it didn't inspire Hazel to use them! The home-made seat covers *had* to be white before she would use them. Several years later, however, we discovered that she was happy to use disposal paper toilet seat covers which her mother bought from high street pharmacies.

Flushing is too noisy

Edward was afraid of the flushing noises in toilets. When he had finished on the loo, he ran away as quickly as possible with his hands over his ears. His parents took photographs and video recordings of themselves walking into the bathroom, flushing the loo and walking out again. His mum sat Edward comfortably on her knee with his favourite blanket and showed him the photographs, which she had made into a small book with a social story. After a few days she turned on the video without the sound and played this to him several times. After a few days she put the sound on very quietly and in time gradually turned the sound up.

Summary

- Toilet training often takes longer for children with ASD due to their difficulties with communication, social awareness and sensory sensitivities.

- Be as sure as you can that your child is ready before you start toilet training.

- Keep a diary of times your child wets and soils before you begin.

- Punishing children or getting angry with them when they have accidents is likely to make the situation worse.

Chapter 15

Soiling

'Soiling' describes going for a poo in inappropriate places. This might be in your nappy, pants, behind the sofa – in fact anywhere except in the toilet.

It should be remembered that there might be differences between children who have never learnt to poo appropriately and those who have but, for a variety of different reasons, are not currently doing so. Sometimes children's muscles and nerves have not developed enough and they will in time. This can be frustrating, but lots of clever strategies will not work if your child's nerves and muscles are not yet ready.

In addition, other factors may be at play in this situation. For example, if a child persistently stops himself pooing then he may become constipated and if this goes on for long enough this may affect how his bowel works (e.g. by causing stretching of the rectum).

The following is a list of common problems in children with ASD.

TYPES OF PROBLEM

- Refuses to sit on the toilet or only poos in a nappy

- Smears faeces on the walls or elsewhere or plays with the poo

- Only goes to the toilet in one place or particular places

- Seems frightened to 'let go' and becomes constipated

We will take each of these in turn considering WHAT the problem is, WHY it might be happening and HOW we deal with it.

WHAT is the problem?

Refuses to sit on the toilet or only poos in a nappy

Anton was a seven-year-old boy with atypical autism. He had never used the toilet other than to urinate. Every night on arriving home from school he would be put into a nappy by his mother. If this did not happen he would have a temper tantrum. He would then poo in the nappy at some point in the evening. He would not approach his mother after this, but his mother would be able to smell when he had done this and would then change his nappy without any resistance from him. This was a routine he was used to. A new nappy would be put on him which he would then wear overnight.

WHY might it be happening?
Liking for routine

Anton likes to do things in a certain order and dislikes his routines being altered.

Things that keep the behaviour going

Anton seemed to like the snug feeling of the nappy. He could not sleep without it, even though he rarely wet it at night.

Sensory interests and fears

On the two occasions his mother had managed to get Anton to sit on a toilet to open his bowels Anton had become very distressed. She thought that he did not like the sound of plopping in the water, because he became distressed by any loud hissing, whooshing or splashing noises (e.g. swimming pools, lorry brakes, etc.).

It is possible that Anton disliked the sensation of sitting on the toilet. This could be to do with the coldness of the seat or even unexpected things such as the colour or texture of the seat.

Difficulty understanding social rules

Anton had little understanding of why it was necessary for him to sit on a toilet when he was perfectly happy emptying his bowels in the nappy whenever he was ready. He did not understand what others expected of him (mindblindness).

HOW might we deal with it?

Liking for routine

Using the nappy had been an established routine for a long time and it was not likely that Anton would change it on his own. For any strategy to work it had to be made into a new routine with which Anton was comfortable. His parents might start by sitting Anton on the toilet without expecting him to poo, with activities he enjoys before and after the toilet to build into a pleasant routine. For one family this involved the child sitting on the toilet before his bath in the evening, which he loved.

Things that keep the behaviour going

If Anton is reluctant to stop using the nappy because he likes the nice feeling of it, then a substitute may be a good idea, but one that does not involve him pooing. For example, a favourite warm pair of socks or teddy bear might help. One child with this problem tolerated not wearing the nappy in the evening once he had learnt to poo on the toilet, but still wished to wear it at bedtime. His parents found some warm pants with soft, brushed cotton material and he liked them better if they were tight ones. He seemed to be happy with these and never soiled in them.

Sensory interests and fears

If Anton has a fear related to his senses (e.g. fear of a cold seat, a particular colour or the sound of flushing toilets) it is possible for his parents to deal with this. A toilet seat cover or a change of colour may help. The difficulty may be in finding out what the problem is if your child is not saying or is unable to say what it is. Most parents are very good detectives. For example, one family noticed that the flushing sound was very like other noises the child was afraid of. When they stopped flushing until the child was elsewhere in the house, far from the noise, she was very happy to sit and poo on the toilet.

Difficulty understanding social rules

If Anton does not understand why he needs to sit on a toilet, explaining with words is not likely to be helpful. Explaining it through pictures or actions is more likely to be successful. This can be done using a social story (see Chapter 10) with pictures of Anton, perhaps building a favourite activity or reward after the poo into the story.

It is likely that your child opens his bowels at roughly the same time each night. If you watch out for when this is (and keep a diary for a few days) then you will have an idea of his bowel habit. This will help because you can then either:

- sit him on the toilet at a regular time each day as part of a routine, or

- keep an eye on him, and when he begins to strain, take him to the toilet, remove his nappy, sit him on the toilet and give a small reward when he has succeeded (e.g. a chocolate button).

WHAT is the problem?

Smears faeces on the walls or elsewhere or plays with the poo

Jim is a fifteen-year-old boy who lives with his single-parent mother and his sister. He has severe autism, has very little speech and dislikes change. He likes to do things certain ways and in certain orders and becomes very distressed if this does not happen. He also likes collecting certain things, such as bottles and labels, and likes to stroke objects and surfaces, apparently interested in the texture. He attends a special school with a small number of young people some of whom also have ASD. He can poo on the toilet and will do so at school at a regular time each day with limited help. For most of the time this works well. However, when Jim is distressed, he takes faeces and smears on the walls, on his clothes or on anything around him including other people. This distress appears at times to be caused by an earlier incident that has upset him, such as not being able to complete a routine that he is used to. The commonest example of this is when he has been expecting to go to the toilet at a particular time at school but is unable to do so because another boy is in the toilet.

WHY might it be happening?

There are a number of reasons why Jim's behaviour might be occurring. Here are some of the things to consider.

Liking for routine

Jim likes to do things in a certain order and dislikes his routines being altered.

Language difficulties

Jim has very little language, which means that he cannot always let people know his needs or communicate his frustration.

Things that keep the behaviour going

Jim may like some things that happen after the behaviour and this may make the smearing more likely to happen again. For example, he has learnt that when he smears as he waits for the toilet, then the adults around him rally round and make things happen for him.

Sensory interests

Jim is very interested in textures of objects and some of his smearing may be related to this.

Difficulty understanding others

Jim has mindblindness and so does not know that communication may be helpful in letting others know his needs or asking for help. He has not understood the messages given to him by adults in the past about germs and cleanliness; these might have led him to wanting to avoid smearing. He has no need to be liked by others or seek their approval (mindblindness again), thus he is not motivated by a need to be liked or to avoid upsetting others.

HOW might we deal with it?

As you can see, a number of factors may be conspiring in this situation to provoke it. The first question to ask is which of the above may be affecting your child's smearing. An understanding of the issues involved will help you decide what to do about it. This does not need a specialist or an expert, but does require some thought and discussion with others who know your child.

If we take each of the above issues in turn we can consider what might be done.

Liking for routine
PREVENTION

As discussed elsewhere, (see Chapter 9) prevention is a helpful way of dealing with intense habits. If parents or teachers notice a new fixation is developing that may be unhelpful in the future, they could try to change it gently.

> When Luke was eight he would only go to the toilet only when a certain other child went. Preventing this early on was useful, because Luke was the type of child who developed fixed routines very readily. If it had become fixed it would cause problems when the child left the class or was absent because of illness.

Similarly, if a child always wants to go to the toilet when the school bell goes or at a certain time, then this may become a problem if the bell is broken, there is someone else in the toilet at that time or the child is out of school.

VISUAL TIMETABLE

Another solution to a problem like Jim's is for the child to have a visual timetable that shows the sequence of events placed on the wall in the morning. Doing this every day and introducing the child to it in the morning creates reassuring routines but also offers the flexibility to change things, with a warning to the child that something has been changed. This visual routine could, for example, have a picture of Jim having his lunch, and then going to the toilet, and then a picture of him doing his next expected activities – washing his hands, going into the playground, etc. The picture of the trusted adult around at the time could be varied each day so that there is flexibility about who takes him. The order can be changed as appropriate.

Language difficulties

This visual timetable can help with communication. In addition, there are other sections within this book that discuss ways of helping children to communicate. These include the Picture Exchange Communication System (see Chapter 11), speech and language therapy techniques and social use of language work (see Chapter 10) and social skills work (see Chapter 10).

Things that keep the behaviour going

When a difficult behaviour is occurring it is always worth asking the question: 'Is something happening that is making this behaviour more likely to occur again?' It is surprising what you may find. Things may happen that make the smearing more likely to happen again because of some pleasant experience the child has gained. These may come from unusual or unexpected places, so you have to be a bit of a detective. In this instance some examples might be:

- Jim liking the feel of the faeces (no matter how unpleasant we may find this idea). The texture may be interesting and he may not be constrained by socially mediated ideas about poo being unclean.

- Jim liking noise, for example the adult shouting.

- The smearing may mean that two adults come and deal with the problem, and Jim may like this.

- It may be that smearing his trousers means that Jim has to put on the standard school pair from the cupboard, which happens to be tracksuit bottoms made of a soft material that Jim likes.

- It may be that Jim smearing outside the toilet means that he gets taken in quickly which is what he wants.

There may be other possibilities in the case of your child. You may be able to brainstorm other important factors relevant to your child's situation. Once you know what they are, you can begin to plan how to deal with them. There may be two main ways to deal with Jim's smearing:

1. Taking away the factor that is making smearing more likely.
   If Jim enjoys the shouting of an adult that his behaviour
   provokes, you should stop shouting in that situation. This may

make the behaviour get temporarily worse, because Jim will redouble his efforts to get the outcome he is after and, because smearing has worked before, he may try it all the more. This can be very difficult, particularly for a busy teacher or exhausted parents (often the case with very challenging young people). After a while, if the adult has stuck with the new strategy despite the difficulties, the behaviour will disappear.

Jim may be smearing his trousers so that he can wear a different pair of trousers that he likes. As you read this you may be thinking how much easier life would be for him if he could communicate the fact that he likes the material on the other trousers better. A simple solution might be to buy him trousers that he likes.

2. Distracting Jim or finding something else that he likes to do instead of smearing may help

If his parents choose a distraction that means Jim cannot smear at the same time, then the smearing will disappear. An example of this might be that if he usually smears after going to the toilet, the parents find something else for him to do at this time, perhaps quickly coming in when he is finished and encouraging him to wash his hands. They have then encouraged an alternative healthier habit. Jim liked the texture of water and this worked well, but the assistants soon learnt that they needed to be on hand to move him swiftly from the toilet to the hand-washing to avoid him becoming restless.

Sensory interests

If Jim is interested in the textures of objects then some of his smearing may be related to this and some of the strategies above may help. For example, after pooing appropriately in the toilet, Jim could play with something he likes. If he likes the texture of play dough or plasticine then it may be appropriate to let him play with this after using the toilet (and washing his hands). Again, the visual timetable can be used to let him know that this is what will happen and if he is looking forward to the play dough this may be enough to stop him smearing. We know of one child who used to have a small sandbox on his lap when he was on the toilet and he liked running his fingers through it so much that his smearing stopped. We would not necessarily recommend this – it may lead to a child spreading the sand around – but this gives an example of how innovative parents can be with their child's difficulties.

Difficulty understanding others

If Jim has not understood the messages given to him by adults in the past about germs and cleanliness, there may be little that anyone can do about this. It may be a case of waiting until he is older when he may be able to understand these things better.

There are other sections within this book that discuss ways of improving a child's skills in understanding others' emotions or points of view. These include teaching mind-guessing skills, social skills work and work on understanding feelings (see Chapter 10, 'Developing Social Skills').

Children who have no concept of wanting to be liked by others or do not seek the approval of others because of their mindblindness are not likely to respond to interventions that work on guilt ('Now you're making lots of work for me by doing that'), personal appeal ('Please, for *my* sake, don't do that') or potential praise ('Now if you're good I'll be very pleased'). These are strategies that are unlikely to succeed.

Children with ASD are unlikely to be soiling deliberately to hurt your feelings. They may be trying to get the environment to respond (something to happen) without knowing whom or how to ask.

The key message here is not to be too upset by lack of the child's understanding of your needs, or to be too upset by lack of emotional response, but to use different ways of trying to help children change behaviour.

WHAT is the problem?

Only going to the toilet in one place or particular places

Jessica, aged ten, would only go to the toilet in her own home. This was a problem because it meant that she had accidents at school. The family also found it very difficult to go on holiday because Jessica would invariably become constipated and distressed.

WHY might it be happening?
Liking for routine

Jessica had a routine and went to the toilet at home every day at the same time in the same place.

Sensory interests and fears

Jessica felt very comfortable in her own bathroom. It was familiar to her and there may have been things she liked to do while in the toilet connected with her sensory interests: for example, counting the stripes on the wallpaper.

Language and communication difficulties

Jessica's speech and communication difficulties may make it difficult for her to express her needs in other places.

Things that keep the behaviour going

There may have been rewarding experiences for Jessica that happened after going to the toilet at home and did not happen elsewhere.

HOW might you deal with it?
Liking for routine

It may be possible for her parents to create new routines for Jessica that include toilets in other places. It would be sensible to make this somewhere that Jessica feels safe and secure (e.g. her grandparents' house) in the first instance. It may be helpful to make a visual timetable of the day and build going to the toilet in certain places into this. This will give Jessica warning and prepare her. Some families have used social stories (Chapter 10) to help their children understand that going to the toilet in different places is OK.

Sensory interests and fears

It may be worth exploring whether some of the things that make the toilet at home feel safe to Jessica could be used elsewhere (e.g. at Grandma's house). For example, one family realised that their son hated sitting on plastic seats, but seemed to be happy with wooden ones. They bought a new wooden seat for the house of his respite carer where he would not go to the toilet, and within two days he was going quite happily.

Language and communication difficulties

If Jessica finds communicating her needs difficult, then the Picture Exchange Communication System (PECS) may help. It will allow her to learn how to ask for what she wants.

Things that keep the behaviour going

If Jessica is only getting certain rewards at home then it may be worth looking at introducing them in other places. For example, if there are things that happen after using the toilet that she likes, her parents might think about introducing them in other places.

WHAT is the problem?

> Seems frightened to 'let go' and becomes constipated

Ian is a five-year-old boy with ASD. His parents had made many attempts to toilet train him. Although he would wee happily in the toilet he would not sit on the toilet or use the toilet to open his bowels. Over the last year he had become increasingly distressed about opening his bowels, crying in pain when he needed to go and when he filled his nappy. He had become very constipated on several occasions to the extent that he needed to go into hospital for an enema. The problem gradually became worse as he tried not to let go of his poo and small amounts leaked into his nappy causing him discomfort and unpleasant smells. His parents were becoming very stressed and concerned about his health. They tried coaxing and getting cross but nothing worked. He was prescribed medication by his doctor but refused to take it after a few days saying, 'Yuk', and spitting it out.

WHY might it be happening?
Things that make the behaviour worse

Due to their own concerns about Ian, his parents found themselves becoming very cross with him. On one occasion they had taken him to the toilet and insisted he sat on it in the hope that he would go after seven days of constipation. They recognised that this had made matters worse and that he had become even more fearful. Having enemas was also very upsetting, reminding Ian that things associated with his bottom were painful and scary.

Liking for routine

Although Ian liked routine in the rest of his life, there was no routine around visiting the toilet. The unpredictability of his bowel movements seemed to be distressing for him, because it had not become part of a routine and happened when he was not expecting it.

Sensory interests and fears

Ian's parents thought that he had developed a fear of letting go because he did not like the sensation. This had possibly become worse when he had been in the toilet on very rare occasions and he had been distressed by the noise and splash. He disliked these noises. Additionally, the more he held on, the more constipated he became and the more painful it was for him to pass anything. He also disliked intensely the smell of his dirty nappy and hated sitting on the toilet, which may have been to do with the feel or colour of the toilet.

HOW might we deal with it?
Things that make the behaviour worse

Ian did not understand why his parents became cross with him. They were understandably very anxious for his well-being but he did not appreciate this, as difficulties with 'mindblindness' and comprehension made this impossible for him. His mum and dad recognised this and resolved to keep as calm as possible, taking it in turns to help him as each of them became tired.

Liking for routine

Ian's parents decided to start a new routine for toilet time. They knew that he didn't like to sit on the toilet but tried to find ways to make it more acceptable. They put the toilet seat lid down with a cushion on it and sat him on top with his nappy on and read him his favourite books. They did this each day 20 minutes after each of his meals. Soon he came to look forward to this. After a while they persuaded him to sit on the toilet seat – which was adapted with a child seat to make him feel safe. There was never any mention of his having to poo at this point.

Sensory interests and fears

As Ian had become constipated it was important to try to find some medication that he would take. However, he often found the taste of medicines unpleasant. The first medicine had a strong flavour and had to be taken in large quantities. His mother had tried to disguise the taste by adding it to drinks, ice cream and puddings but he spat it out immediately. Having explained this to the doctor they experimented with different types of medicine eventually finding one which he could take in syrup form and only required a half teaspoonful every three days. This tended to give him a tummy ache but prevented constipation and he often went about 30 minutes after taking it. He also ate more fruit with lots of roughage. He liked bananas.

When Ian started to become distressed with tummy ache or going to the toilet, his parents comforted him gently. They left his nappy on which seemed to help him to feel secure. When he was straining they chatted and joked with him and reassured him with cuddles. They also started to talk about the poo as something separate from him: they would say, 'Tell that poo to get out now!' 'Silly poo!' 'Now I've got you out! Hooray!'.

Summary

Helping a child learn to go for a poo on the toilet involves

- making sure they are ready developmentally
- helping them learn a new routine
- minimising any fears the child has
- a patient and calm approach.

Chapter 16

Sleeping

Sleeping problems are common in children and even more common in children with ASD. These are usually difficulties in settling children to sleep and children waking during the night. When children sleep poorly they are more likely to be bad-tempered during the day and to have more difficulty concentrating. Their parents or carers are also affected by lack of sleep and often become irritable and feel more stressed. Not surprisingly then, poor sleep patterns can lead to parents finding it difficult to cope during the day and can cause problems in relationships between each other and with the child. Finding ways to manage sleep problems are not easy but essential to everyone's well-being.

Many of the parents with whom we work tell us that tackling sleeping problems with their children is very, very difficult. It is usually much longer before the ideas described here achieve success than when they are tried with children who are not on the autism spectrum. Children on the autism spectrum appear to have much more stamina and seem able to shout for longer than others! Some of the ideas here depend on parents being persistent, consistent and determined. We believe, however, that for both you and your child, it is worth the effort. Before you begin to make any changes to help your child to sleep better try to be clear about the following:

- what the problem is exactly

- why it might be happening

- what you plan to do

- that you have the energy and determination to carry any plan through.

TYPES OF PROBLEM

- Difficulty settling to sleep

- Won't go to bed and has tantrums

- Will not go to sleep without parents in the room

- Resists sleep and fears being alone

WHAT is the problem?

Difficulty settling to sleep.

Moses, aged 20 months, had been difficult to settle to sleep when he was around a year old. This seemed to get worse as he got older. At first his parents would get him up and let him sit in the sitting room with them at various points in the evening. In the night if he woke they would give him a drink of milk from his cup. It seemed after a while that whenever he woke he wanted their company and a drink of milk. It got to the point that he would scream frequently when left at night. They found it easier to meet his demands and never really sat down to talk through what they might be able to do. Both parents were getting frazzled. Moses was catching up with sleep with naps during the day.

WHY might this be happening?
Mindblindness and getting the gist

Most children Moses' age won't be thinking or worrying about whether their parents are getting any sleep. Children at this age just don't think like this, whether they have autism spectrum difficulties or not.

Like most children his age, Moses was still getting used to the concept of night and day. But Moses' daytime naps and long wakeful periods in the night were not really teaching him the difference between night and day.

Parents' response

Moses liked to be with his parents and they saw no problem with this at first, but getting him up regularly through the night taught him that crying led to getting a drink and the warmth of his parents' arms. He liked this.

Routines and change

Moses soon formed a habit where waking up meant getting a drink and getting up. He liked this routine and did not want to change it.

HOW might we deal with it?
Mindblindness and getting the gist

Even though Moses had no understanding of his parents' needs, *they* did! They were motivated to change things by a need for sleep and space. Moses would need to get the hang of what night and day were and this would have to be built into any plan.

Parents' response

Julia and Simon, Moses' parents, knew that some of the things that they had been doing inadvertently reinforced some of Moses' sleep problems.

Routines and change

Moses' parents hoped that, if a new routine could be established, Moses would settle to it; but they knew that he would not be pleased at first and would resist change. His parents were ready for some serious distress along the way. They decided to try a technique called 'controlled crying'.

Controlled crying

The technique 'controlled crying' is useful when children want their parents to stay with them to get to sleep or when they are protesting about going to bed even though they are clearly very tired. It is also a good strategy to use if they persistently wake during the night and want to get into bed with you. Before beginning something like this, parents need to be sure that the child is not unwell or frightened. They need to be very determined, as Simon and Julia were, that they can carry through the recommendations and that both are in full agreement with the plan. It involves making sure that the child is safe, but not getting him up and avoiding any responses that teach him that he should be up. It means temporarily switching off emotionally and ignoring the child's crying but checking on him at pre-determined regular intervals.

When the child cries after you have put him to bed or during the night, you choose not to respond immediately. Instead, having decided how long you can cope with the crying in advance, you wait for the appointed number of minutes (e.g. two minutes) and then go in to the child saying in a calm and clear way, 'Bedtime. Go back to sleep'. Then you leave *without fuss or distraction.*

If the child is still crying two minutes later, you go back in and do the same. You keep doing this until the child settles. The next night add a minute or two before going in each time. The first night this took Julia and Simon several hours and they took it in turns. Julia could not just leave Moses, so when she went in, she briefly picked him up and cuddled him as she was talking but quickly put him down again. The number of times they went in reduced after three days and reduced each day after this.

Julia found this very hard initially. It is very distressing for most parents to hear their children crying themselves to sleep. It is, however, a very successful strategy and worked for Moses. After eight days they only needed to go in once or twice and after one month he was sleeping through. Julia and Simon were good at sticking rigidly to the time agreed before going in and then leaving without any fuss. Remember that you are teaching your child to be able to go to sleep or back to sleep on their own and in the end, you will all be grateful for the sleep. If the child wakes during the night and comes into your room, take her by the hand and lead her back to bed straight away, without any fuss saying, 'It's still night time. Back to bed'.

This strategy worked well for Moses until he was six years old and his parents were faced with another sleeping problem!

WHAT is the problem?

Won't go to bed and has tantrums

Moses, now aged six, had been difficult to settle to sleep when he was around 20 months old, as we have just discussed. His parents had overcome this difficulty and since then Moses had been a good sleeper. He had a clear routine and settled well. Unfortunately, this all changed quite dramatically.

One day, after he had been at school for a few months, he came home looking very unwell. He had caught chicken pox. He was sick a few times and was very unsettled. His mother brought him downstairs to comfort him while his father changed his bed. After he had recovered from the chicken pox, he had great difficulty settling to his bedtime routine again. He kept coming downstairs on his own and protesting loudly when his mother insisted that he stayed in bed. His parents tried the controlled crying strategy again but he started having temper tantrums, throwing toys around the room and banging his head on the floor in rage. Initially they tried to ignore this as best they could but they found that he was waking his baby brother and they were worried that he might hurt himself. Bedtime became a battleground.

Julia and Simon were at a loss as to how best to help him. They were also exhausted as they spent most of their evening taking him back to bed. Their usual strategies just weren't working. In fact, the more they ignored him, the more he banged his head and the crosser they became, the angrier he became too.

WHY might this be happening?

Change in routine

The change in Moses' behaviour after his illness was remarkable. His routine had been disrupted and he had enjoyed the extra care he received from his parents when he was ill. Being downstairs had been comforting for him at a time when he was confused and distressed. Not surprisingly, he wanted this to continue. He had established a new routine that he was loath to break.

Parents' response

Moses' parents found it very difficult to keep him in his room and tried to ignore the tantrum that was going on inside. They worried about him disturbing the neighbours or his brother. They worried about him causing damage to the room and possibly to himself. They were particularly concerned about his head-banging. When Moses' parents went in to check on him, he either ran out of the room or went to them for a cuddle. Either way, they were inadvertently reinforcing his behaviour. He had learnt that his rage and tantrum brought his parents to him for a cuddle or for a 'game' as he ran out of the room!

Mindblindness

Moses was not aware of his parents' concern for his well-being nor of their distress. He had no understanding that he was waking his brother or that everyone was exhausted by his bedtime tantrums. All that he knew about were his own needs.

Bad associations

Moses had been very sick with the chicken pox. It is quite possible that he had learnt to associate his bed with unpleasant times. With time his room also became associated with his rages, which may have been unpleasant or frightening for him.

Fear

Moses' parents wondered if he was frightened about being left in his room.

Communication

Moses was not able to tell his parents what was wrong or what he wanted. They had to try to work this out from his behaviour. Meanwhile, he was very frustrated, angry and upset at bedtime. His parents could not reason with him as he was unable to understand.

HOW might we deal with it?

All of the strategies Simon and Julia had found helpful in the past did not seem to be working with Moses' bedtime tantrums. They felt that the strategy they had used when he was a baby was not practical or safe. Bedtime had become a very stressful time and Moses was not getting enough sleep. He had been bad-tempered at school and had been in trouble for hitting some of the other children. This was very much out of character for Moses and seemed to be related to his being very tired.

Liking for routine

Julia and Simon felt that whatever they tried to do needed to have a clear routine with which Moses was comfortable.

Parents' response

Moses' parents realised that some of their responses might inadvertently be keeping things as they were. They began to think how to combat this. They did not want weeks of battling as they found this exhausting and felt bad about it.

Mindblindness

Moses' parents accepted that he could not understand their distress and exhaustion and that getting frustrated with him about this probably made things worse.

Bad associations

Julia and Simon recognised that Moses' room had some bad associations and had once more to become a place where he was comfortable to settle. This might mean making sure he was in the right frame of mind and tired before putting him to bed.

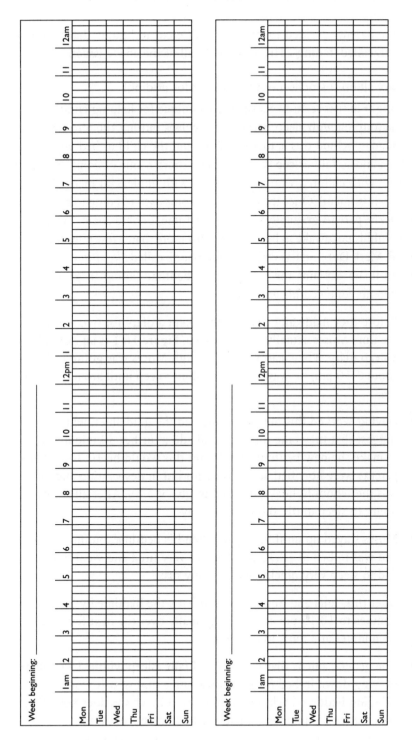

Figure 16.1: Sample sleep diary A. Each box is a 15-minute period. Block these out in black when your child is asleep. Mark in blue when your sleep routine starts. Mark in red when your child gets into bed.

Moses' parents decided to try a very different technique that they had read about, called 'fading'. This fitted with all of the above issues.

Temporary sleep restriction – staying up later (fading)

Fading might at first seem like a strange technique for helping children who are not getting enough sleep because it involves putting them to bed *much* later! The idea behind this is that you don't put the child to bed until she is really tired and so falls asleep within a much shorter time of going to bed. It works well with children who associate bed with unpleasant memories (e.g. illness or punishment). Once the child has become used to going to bed and to sleep quickly, parents gradually bring the bedtime forward again. The plan is that the child is not awake in her bedroom for more than a few minutes as she is so tired. Mark Durrand has written a good book called *Sleep Better!* (Durrand 1998). In it, he explains the technique of bedtime fading in great detail. Moses' parents followed his guidelines.

- Before they made any changes they kept a diary for two weeks of the time Moses actually went to sleep. Figure 16.1 is an example of a sleep diary. They learnt that, although Moses was going to bed at about 7.30 pm, he wasn't finally falling asleep until around 10.00 pm.

- Having worked this out, they followed the guidelines, which suggest that they take this time and add a further 30 minutes to it to make the new bedtime. For Moses this would be 10.30 pm! His parents were horrified at this thought but in desperation and as it was the school holidays, decided to give it a try. After all he wasn't going to sleep until 10.00 pm anyway.

- Moses stayed up until 9.30 pm, when his bedtime routine began, and was in bed at 10.30 pm. He was very tired and went to bed and to sleep very quickly without any fuss.

- After this, Julia and Simon brought back the bedtime by 15 minutes to 10.15 pm and then gradually over the next few weeks, 15 minutes at a time, to 8.30 pm.

- The general rule is that if your child falls asleep within 15 minutes of lying down in bed for two consecutive nights, it is worth bringing bedtime back by 15 minutes. If he or she does not fall asleep after 15 minutes, extend the bedtime by an hour.

- One of the hardest things was keeping Moses awake until the appointed bedtime. His parents tried to keep him busy with puzzles and drawings. They did not allow him to play with his computer as they wanted to keep this time fairly boring and quiet. They also explained the process to his teachers when he returned to school and asked them to try to discourage him from napping at school as this would have meant the plan would suffer considerably since Moses would not be tired at bedtime.

Moses' parents were surprised at how well this worked for him and how quickly their lives were restored again!

Temporary sleep restriction (waking children earlier in the morning)

Putting Moses to bed later in order to restrict his sleep temporarily was a successful strategy. However, sleep restriction can be just as successful at the other end of the day.

> Rose, aged eight, was already going to sleep late, usually at about 10.00 pm. She also woke during the night for several hours. She was very tired during the day and often had a nap at school. Her mother, Sofia, completed a sleep diary for Rose for a week. She discovered that Rose slept for about ten hours a day including naps – but not at the right times!
>
> Sofia worked out a new sleeping plan so that Rose would sleep for *less* time – about nine hours in total. Rather than putting her to bed later, she woke her an hour earlier in the mornings. This was very difficult because at first Rose was still waking in the night and was very grumpy! Rose's teacher was very helpful in helping to change her sleeping patterns by trying hard to keep her awake during the day. Rose was very tired by 10.00 pm, but her mother persisted with the sleep restriction plan and continued to wake Rose early, ensuring that she had no more than nine hours' sleep initially. Over the following weeks, Rose's sleeping patterns were gradually adjusted. She started sleeping through the night, which was a huge relief for Sofia. Soon after this, Sofia gradually started allowing Rose to sleep for an extra 15 minutes in the mornings until she was getting her required 10 hours again.

One of the advantages of this technique is that, generally, it is much easier to extend the length of time children sleep in the mornings than it is to persuade them to go to sleep earlier at night.

WHAT is the problem

Not going to sleep without parents in the room

Alex, aged seven, was usually put to bed at night by her mum. Alex's mum had established a clear routine over the years which included supper, TV time, bath time, pyjamas on, a drink of milk, toilet, wash hands and clean teeth, into bed, story time and lights out – time to sleep. The only problem was that Alex insisted that her mum, Sally, stayed with her until she fell asleep and, in fact, that Sally lay down next to her in bed. When she thought Alex was asleep, Sally gently tried to move away from her and creep out of the room. Unfortunately Alex was easily disturbed and often sat up and shouted 'Mummy stay!' as she was crawling out of the room on her hands and knees! It sometimes took up to three hours for her to fall asleep and often her mum fell asleep too!

WHY might it be happening?

Need for routine or sameness

Alex had always been a difficult baby to settle asleep. Her parents had rocked her to sleep in their arms at first and as she grew older had allowed her to fall asleep downstairs on the sofa before carrying her upstairs to bed. She was often disturbed as they moved her and her parents had to lie with her to encourage her back to sleep again as quickly as possible. As she grew older they established the *habit* of staying with her until she fell asleep. Her mother thought that Alex would grow out of it, but she was showing no signs of this yet.

Sensory sensitivity

Alex had very acute hearing and the slightest noise alerted her to her mother's departure. She was also very sensitive to the light and during the summer months took a great deal longer to get to sleep.

Communication

Alex was able to use a few words including 'No. Mummy stay!' but she was unable to communicate why she needed her to stay.

Her mother's response

Alex's mum had always worried about her. Alex had been a very fractious baby who was difficult to feed and get off to sleep. She had failed to gain weight as expected and was admitted to hospital on two occasions with asthma attacks. Sally had always felt that there was something else that was different about Alex as she did not respond in the same way as her elder brother had done. She was distraught when Alex was diagnosed with ASD at the age of three. Sally felt very protective towards Alex and worried about leaving her alone. For various reasons, it was Mum rather than Dad who usually took Alex to bed. Sally had tried many times to leave Alex to go to sleep alone, sometimes – not surprisingly – becoming cross with her. Sometimes Alex's dad tried to take her to bed suggesting that they leave her to cry for a while to see if she would settle alone but her screams were too distressing for her mother (and the neighbours!) and they reverted back to Mum lying with her again.

HOW might we deal with it?
Need for routine or sameness

Alex's parents had established a routine very early on in her life of staying with her until she fell asleep. This had not given her the opportunity to recognise that she could fall asleep on her own. They knew that routine was essential for Alex but had been reluctant to change it out of the fear that it might get worse! They decided, however, that their whole evening was ruled by Alex and wanted to claim back some time for themselves. They resolved that a new routine would have to be established but this time they wanted to think it through carefully to make sure that their needs, as well as Alex's and her brother's, would be met.

Sensory sensitivity

Alex was very sensitive to noise and light. Her parents bought new blackout curtains to keep out the daylight from outside as it was summer. They also put a very dim night light in the room. Alex had always liked music so they decided to try a soothing musical tape.

Communication

Alex's communication skills were very limited. Her parents wanted to try to help her to understand that the bedtime routine would change. They had used photographs and picture sequences in the past and planned to use these to help her. They had also heard about social stories and asked us for help writing one for her.

Mother's response

Alex's parents spent a great deal of time talking about the old bedtime routine and why it had become so difficult. They agreed that her mum found it almost unbearable to hear her crying. Mum had tried many times to leave Alex to cry but had always ended up in bed with her again. She was also very embarrassed about what their neighbours might think. Eventually, Sally reluctantly agreed that perhaps she wasn't the best person to put Alex to bed initially and that Alex's dad should take charge as he felt better able to cope with the inevitable screams. Sally also decided that it would be best if she was not in the house for the first few nights of the new routine as she would be tempted to go in to comfort her. Alex's parents went to explain to their neighbours that they were trying a new bedtime routine and apologised in advance for any disturbance in the early evening.

They devised a plan as follows:

	Mon	Tue	Wed	Thurs	Fri	Sat	Sun
Time to bed at night	7.30	7.45	7.15	7.30	7.15	7.30	7.15
Time to sleep at night	8.15	10.00	8.15	9.30	8.00	9.30	10.00
Time awake in night	2.15 to 3.30		3.00 to 3.30			4.00 to 4.30	
Time woke up in morning	6.30	7.00	6.15	6.00	5.30	6.00	7.30
Time went to sleep in day for nap						4.00	
Time woke up in day after nap						4.45	
Total hours asleep	9	9	9½	9½	9½	8¾	9½

Figure 16.2: Alex's sleep diary sample B

It is a good idea for parents to keep a diary for a week or two before they make any changes. This sleep diary was to help Alex's parents to find out her natural sleep time. They needed to be sure that she was tired before putting her to bed. Figure 16.2 opposite shows a copy of this simple sleep diary (there is a blank version in the Appendix).

Alex was falling asleep between 8.00 pm and 10.00 pm when her mum stayed with her. Her parents decided that they would put her to bed at around 8.45 pm in the first instance. They thought that they could adjust this with time depending on what happened. When they changed the routine, they also kept a similar diary.

2. *Routine*

Alex already had a clear routine that her parents decided to keep. The only changes were that they would start the routine later and that Dad would take her to bed. Then, after 'lights out', he would say, 'Goodnight Alex', put on the music tape and leave the room. They prepared Alex for these changes by reading her social story several times during the day and by making a picture board showing her that Daddy would take her to bed. Alex's bedtime social story follows.

> Alex has a nice bedroom. It has a bed to sleep in and a wardrobe for her clothes. Dad will help Alex to have her bath, put her pyjamas on, get her drink of milk, go to the toilet, wash her hands and clean her teeth. Alex's dad will take her to bed and she will get into bed. Alex takes La La to bed with her. Dad will read a story. Then he will close the curtains, switch out the big light and kiss Alex goodnight. He will switch on the music and say, 'Goodnight Alex'. Then he will go out of the bedroom. Alex will stay in bed and listen to the music. She will try to go sleep. In the morning Alex will get up when it gets light outside or when Mum or Dad turns on the light.

3. *Bedroom changes*

New blackout curtains, a night light and a tape recorder for music were introduced to Alex's bedroom.

4. *Stick with it!*

Alex's parents knew this would be hard! As expected, Alex protested greatly when her father left the room. She got out of bed and screamed loudly: 'Mummy stay!' Her dad took her back without making any fuss, calmly saying, 'Bedtime Alex', and waited outside the closed bedroom door. Each time she came out, Alex's dad took her back again. After about an hour the sobs stopped. The next two nights were just the same. Alex's dad was tired and both parents questioned whether or not this was the right approach. Her mum had not been able to go out as planned. Finally, however, they decided together to stick with it and helped each other through the next few difficult nights. Gradually, Alex's protests lasted for shorter periods and within 10 days she was settling down to sleep for her father without any fuss. Several weeks later, her mum and dad took her through her bedtime routine together and then her mother tried it successfully on her own.

This technique is very difficult for parents but very worthwhile if you can do it. Settling to sleep patterns can improve very quickly. In the long run most parents are very pleased when sleeping patterns are good. This desensitisation approach is discussed again later.

WHAT is the problem?

Resists sleep and fears being alone

George, aged 11, has a diagnosis of Asperger syndrome. He had great difficulty getting off to sleep even though he was very tired. When he was younger, his mother Maureen used to stay in the bedroom with him until he dropped off to sleep. When his sister Sian was born, it became increasingly difficult for her to stay with him all of the time because often Sian needed her attention. Eventually, George learned to cope without Maureen being in the same room with him, but he had never learnt to tolerate being upstairs in his room unless she was also upstairs. George often came out of his room to check that Maureen was still upstairs. She had established a habit of working or doing the ironing upstairs waiting for him to settle.

George became very frightened, angry and upset if Maureen went downstairs even for a few moments. On one occasion, he dragged Sian out of bed because she wouldn't wake up and then tried to wreck her bedroom. Another time he tried to set fire to one of his model aeroplanes. George's father, Tom, worked long hours and often didn't get home until after 9.00 pm. When he got home he used to stay upstairs with George while Maureen prepared them both a meal. George was still quite often awake when the meal was ready and as everyone was so tired, his parents ate their meal upstairs in the bedroom and then went to bed themselves. They both agreed that this was ridiculous but couldn't cope with George's distress if they tried to go downstairs. The situation was growing increasingly worse because Sian had started getting upset too and George was not getting off to sleep until after midnight, leaving him tired and unable to concentrate at school.

WHY might it be happening?
Routine and time
The routine in the house was that the children had their evening meal at around 6.30 pm and started getting ready for bed at around 7.30 pm. As George disliked change and this had been a routine for so long, Maureen and Tom had not considered changing it. Maureen noticed that George's anxiety about being upstairs alone seemed to begin after he had put on his pyjamas. After some consideration, she began to wonder if putting on his pyjamas was a trigger point. She also considered that getting ready for bed at 7.30 pm might be somewhat early for an 11-year-old. Most children and young people fall asleep within about 30 minutes of lying down. If not, it is possible that they are not ready for sleep and have more time to worry. It is generally better to encourage children to go to bed when they can fall asleep easily. It seemed that George's anxiety was keeping him awake.

Anxiety
George had always worried about being on his own. He could cope with being alone for five or ten minutes in daylight if he was warned in advance but he couldn't be left alone after dark. Having his parents within very easy reach made him feel safe.

Mindblindness
George could not understand that his behaviour had a significant effect on his parents. He did not understand that his parents had to prepare meals, do household jobs or needed to have time on their own to relax. Nor was he able to recognise his sister's needs. He was only aware of his own needs.

Benefits to him

If George could keep one of his parents upstairs with him, he felt safe and did not worry as much.

Parents' response

Maureen and Tom had been very worried about George. Since he started high school, his anxiety had increased greatly and his behaviour had deteriorated. He became upset very easily and had started hurting himself and his sister. Not surprisingly, his parents were anxious to keep everyone safe and felt that staying close by was a good way of doing this. When his parents were close by they knew that George, Sian and the house were all safe.

Maureen also recognised that in some respects there were other benefits for her in that she was using some of the time that she was upstairs to relax and avoid some household jobs. Both parents realised that they had developed the habit of complying with George's wishes as a way of reducing his anxiety, trying to keep him happy and hence avoiding situations where he might get distressed and hurt himself and someone else.

Control

George liked to control everything he could in order to feel that his world was safe and predictable. He had a clear view of how the world should be and if this did not fit in his mind, he went into a rage.

George felt safe when his parents were with him. He felt unsafe when they were not there. He became frightened and went into a rage when they didn't comply. As his rage was often so severe, they ended up doing as he wanted. This made him feel safe and in control again but reinforced his belief that he was unsafe on his own.

Getting the gist

George had a poor understanding of what was going on. He didn't under-stand the purpose of bedtime routines or sleep.

Sensory experiences

George disliked the dark and was very sensitive to noise.

Communication

Although George used language very well, he had great difficulty expressing his feelings, needs and problems.

Dreams

George did not always recognise the difference between real and pretend. Dreams often prevented him from sleeping and increased his fears. It seemed that sometimes he went to see his parents to seek reassurance.

HOW might we deal with it?

Routine and time

George's parents realised that the bedtime they had established many years ago was probably no longer suitable for George now that he was nearly 12. He seemed to worry more when he was in bed lying awake and he was not getting the amount of sleep they felt he needed. However, George relied heavily on routine and they knew changing it was bound to cause some upset.

After a great deal of thought, they decided that they could no longer go on in this way and that, in the long term, it would be worth the temporary distress involved in changing the situation. As Maureen was spending most of her evening upstairs with George from around 7.30 pm onwards, she had little chance to do anything else until Tom came home. They decided to move bedtime to 8.30 pm. They hoped that this meant George would be a little more tired and that Maureen would not have to spend so much time upstairs and could do other things.

Anxiety

George's parents believed that his anxiety played a large part in his difficulty with being alone at night. Their aim was to help him to feel safe when they were not in such close proximity. They realised that their distance away from him was particularly important. They wanted him to feel safe but wanted him to learn that he could be safe even when they were further away from him. Part of the plan that Maureen and Tom decided to put into place was a desensitisation programme. This involved them starting from a point where he felt safe and in small steps moving a little further away.

Mindblindness and control

George could not understand why his parents could not simply stay upstairs as before. His parents had to explain to him that they had jobs to do and that they needed some time to watch television or talk to each other. George found this hard to understand but began to accept it slowly. It helped when they explained to him that other people had routines that were different from his and that these routines might mean that his parents couldn't always be with him if they were doing something else. This was easier for him to follow than information about feelings, although they continued to give this.

The idea of others having a different routine and schedule also helped with respect to control issues. George knew that his father came home at a certain time, so there was no reason why he couldn't also 'know' what his sister's and mother's routines might be in such a way as to give some control back to him. Like most young people with Asperger syndrome, George needed help to understand the thoughts, feelings and motives of other people. None of these things came intuitively to him.

Parents' response

George's parents had established a habit of staying with him when he was going to sleep since he was a baby. They had inadvertently been teaching him that he needed them to go to sleep. Sleep was frightening for him as he had experienced many bad dreams and nightmares and found it hard to distinguish between them and reality. Although dreams seemed less of a problem now, getting off to sleep remained a scary experience. Whenever his parents had tried to change their own behaviour in the past, George had reacted with fear and then rage. As his rage was extreme at times, Maureen and Tom responded by complying with his demands to stay close by. This had the effect of teaching him that certain behaviours resulted in his parents responding to his demands – that getting angry, hitting his sister, hurting himself or lighting a fire made his parents stay with him. When his parents realised this, they knew that they had to change their own behaviour, particularly as George's behaviour was becoming increasingly dangerous. As they began to put some firmer boundaries around him, making rules with very clear consequences, his behaviour gradually began to improve.

Desensitisation or graded change programme

The plan was that George's parents would sit outside his bedroom in the first instance and gradually move down the stairs towards the sitting room. The objective was to help George to understand that he could get off to sleep and feel safe at night if his parents were not upstairs with him but close by. As this bedtime problem had been going on for so long, Maureen and Tom knew that dealing with it would not be quick or simple! George was able to understand well and so his parents explained the plan to him and to Sian in detail. They were very clear and strict about the rules. The children had a drink and a biscuit before going upstairs and getting ready for bed at 8.30 pm. (This included: going to the toilet, getting washed and putting on their pyjamas. Maureen and Tom were keen to ensure that they had no reason to get out of bed after they had settled down.) Once in bed, they could read until 9.00 pm and then switch out their lights and settle down. They could leave their bedroom doors open and the landing light would be left on. Maureen and Tom told the children that one of them would sit on a chair at the top of the stairs reading after George and Sian had gone to bed. George and Sian were told to stay in their beds after 9.00 pm. In order to encourage them to do so, a reward system was used.

Rewards

Both children could see their parents sitting on the landing from their beds, so at this stage there was no need for George to seek out his mother or father for reassurance to reduce his anxiety. It was important to help him to establish a habit of staying in bed, however, as he had been used to getting up several times an hour to check his parents' whereabouts. The family made some charts together to complete the following morning (see Figure 16.3.)

Time (pm)	Mon	Tue	Wed	Thurs	Fri	Sat	Sun
9.30							
10.00							
10.30							
11.00							
11.30							
12.00							

Figure 16.3: George's reward chart

For every half hour George stayed in bed between 9.00 pm and midnight, he could tick the corresponding box. His parents set him a target that they thought was achievable: 28 ticks a week in the first instance. If he reached the target by the end of the week he was given £2 extra pocket money. (This was the reward he had chosen.) A similar chart was also used for Sian.

At first, George found the new routine very difficult. He started calling out to his mum, but she had to explain clearly that it was now time to go to sleep and there was to be no talking. Sometimes George got out of bed and there were tantrums the next morning when he didn't get a tick in some boxes. However, after three weeks, things settled and although his parents were very tired and bored, they thought that the plan might work!

The next stage was to move the chair just out of George's sight. Again, he was told about the plan and the reward charts. As time went on, his parents began to move down the stairs in a very planned way. After several weeks, they were able to sit downstairs together and the children learnt to get to sleep without their parents being present upstairs. There were still times when George became very angry, insisting that his parents stayed with him, or came downstairs. His parents were equally determined, however, recognising the importance of being consistent in their approach.

A map of parents' whereabouts

George was anxious to know where his parents were in the evening. A small map of the house with velcro stickers helped him to visualise where they were and feel more confident that they were not too far away. This was really useful when his parents were working on the desensitisation plan in the evenings.

Nightmares and night terrors

Nightmares

Most people and children have nightmares. Children often wake up when they are having a nightmare feeling distressed and confused. They can usually remember their dream and can be comforted by their parents before falling back to sleep again. Gentle reassurance from parents usually helps them to return to sleep. Children with autism often take longer to settle back to sleep, due to their difficulties understanding the difference between what is real and what may have occurred in a dream.

Night terrors

Although there are many similarities between nightmares and night terrors they are quite different. They start in much the same way with the child crying or screaming out loud. However, in night terrors, although children may appear to be awake, sometimes with their eyes wide open, they are in fact still in a deep sleep. Often they are very hot and sweaty. They appear to be terrified and very distressed. They will often push their parents away and refuse to be consoled. Parents are usually very distressed by their children's night terrors particularly when they don't know what is happening. The children go back to sleep without waking after a while and unlike children who experience nightmares have no recollection of the event the following day.

Often, a pattern of night terrors occurs, in that they happen at around the same time, several times a week, for some time. When they are troublesome in this way, it is probably sensible for parents to intervene. Luckily, in many cases the problem is fairly easily resolved.

Parents need to keep a sleep diary, charting the times when the child has night terrors. Once they have a clear idea of the time it usually happens, they will need to wake the child up 30 minutes earlier. So if the child has a night terror at 11.30 pm, she should be gently woken at 11.00 pm. There is no need to wake the child fully but just enough that she opens her eyes. After doing this for about a week, and if there are no further episodes during this time, parents can experiment with not waking the child one night. If the child doesn't have a night terror parents should try waking the child every second night and gradually reducing the times they wake her until there are no more night terrors.

Other interventions to try

Start good habits young

Try to establish good sleeping practices when the child is younger. Changing habits later is much more difficult.

Use of a sleep diary

Whenever you are trying to change your child's sleep habits, keep a sleep diary for about a week first (see Figures 16.1, 16.2, 16.3 and Appendix 2). This will give you lots of information about your child's sleeping habits, which will help you to decide which interventions will be best. Keeping a diary during the time of trying new strategies also helps you track progress.

Sleep hygiene

Establishing good sleep hygiene practices is important. 'Sleep hygiene' is a phrase that some professionals use to talk about good practices that encourage healthy daily sleep patterns.

The bedroom

The bedroom should be quiet, dark and warm. It should have pleasant associations and not be a place of punishment.

Bedtime routine

There should be a clear evening bedtime routine. An example is:

- bath time
- pyjamas on
- drink and biscuit
- toilet
- wash hands and clean teeth
- into bed
- one short story
- kiss parent goodnight
- lights out
- parent says 'Goodnight' and leaves.

Bedtime

Bedtime should be when your child is tired. A sleep diary can help you work out when this is. Try to keep to the same time each night when you are trying to establish a new routine.

Sleep

- Children need to learn to fall asleep on their own.
- Avoid daytime naps after about the age of three or four.

Food and drink

- A light snack of milk and biscuits before bed can help avoid children's need to ask for food and drink after they have gone to bed.

- Avoid drinks like cola, coffee, chocolate or tea as these contain stimulants and may keep children awake.

Desensitisation

Sometimes it is to a parent's advantage to make changes to a child's routine in one sudden move. If children have large problems with change and you need to make changes then doing lots of small changes may create a protracted period of discontent and distress for the child. This is why many parents find 'controlled crying' (above) helpful. However, if this is not possible because of disruption to other members of the family or neighbours, or because very high levels of anxiety are prompted in the child, then sometimes an approach called 'desensitisation' may work. This is particularly helpful for some situations such as profound anxiety.

The theory is to help the child change gradually and to get used to each change as a way of dropping anxiety, before moving on to the next change.

Seth, who had a diagnosis of autism, was five and for two years he had slept in the same bed as his eight-year-old sister, Margaret. Margaret was getting older and wanted to have a bed of her own. The family had had an extra bedroom since moving house six months before, but Seth was so distraught whenever Margaret was not with him at night that the family were complying with his wishes. However, they realised that this could not go on for ever and with advice came up with a desensitisation plan.

First, Margaret slept on a camp bed by Seth's bed for a week or so. He was initially a little troubled by this but soon came round (he learnt to cope with the anxiety that this small change created). Then Margaret's camp bed was slowly moved as the weeks progressed across the room (some furniture was moved at points). Then the camp bed was put into the room next door with both doors open. Again Seth had some difficulties with this but coped. Finally Margaret slept in her own bed.

This strategy can also be useful for children who sleep in the parental bed.

Medication

Some children sleep so poorly that parents or carers seek advice from their doctor. Doctors sometimes prescribe sedatives of some kind. This may be helpful but is usually only a short-term solution. Some people suggest that medication may help when trying to get a child back into a pattern. Our experience is that many sleep problems recur when medication is stopped. We usually advise that medication is only used when absolutely necessary and always in conjunction with other plans and interventions such as the ones described in this chapter.

The sleep hormone melatonin is increasingly being used for sleep problems. In the US it is used for jet lag and a range of sleep disorders. It is not currently licensed for children's sleep disorders in the UK but can be used on a named patient basis and can be effective if sleep–wake cycles are very disrupted. Again it is probably not a long-term solution because it affects natural sleep hormone release, but can be used alongside other measures such as those in this chapter with a view to stopping it after a few months.

Summary

- Helping children to change their sleeping habits is hard work for parents but definitely worth the effort in the long term!

- Keep a sleep diary before you begin.

- Try to be clear about what the problem is and why it might be happening.

- Think carefully about the techniques described in this chapter and decide which ones are best suited to you and your child.

- Choose a time to put the plan into action when you have the stamina and determination to carry it through.

Chapter 17

Preoccupations

Many children with ASD develop preoccupations with objects that go well beyond simple interests. These preoccupations tend to be very narrow in range, are pursued with great enthusiasm and can be extremely absorbing. Preoccupations may be based around:

- very unusual interests (unusual preoccupations)
- unusually intense interests in normal things (preoccupations with abnormal intensity)
- sensory interests (see Chapter 6).

Unusual preoccupations

These are things with which a child may become preoccupied that children are not normally particularly interested by. The list is of course endless, but some examples are as follows:

Objects

- collecting unusual objects (e.g. dead batteries, old keys)
- collecting objects such as sticks, stones or bits of fluff
- collecting objects but not using them for the purpose they were designed for: for example, just keeping them in piles but never using them (e.g. rubber bands, Blu-tack, curtain hooks, paper clips, bits of string, straws).

Activities

One example is rewinding videotapes over and over to watch very specific sections.

Pursuit of knowledge

As children and young people grow older, they often begin to collect knowledge. The more able people with ASD become avid surfers of the Internet or ardent readers of books about their special topics, such as:

- statistical knowledge of things (e.g. seating capacities of football stadiums)

- a fascination for logos

- serial numbers on water hydrants, manhole covers or other public objects.

Environment

This could be a fascination with things in the environment that would not usually be the subject of intense interest (e.g. the whereabouts and details of every car wash, pylon or lamp post in the area).

Preoccupations with abnormal intensity

Sometimes children with ASD become preoccupied with things that are normal things to be interested in but in which the child has a very intense interest indeed, much more so than other children. Most people think 'computers' at this point, but this is a bad example because most children will become preoccupied with computer games (they have been designed specially to get children's interest). Better examples are as follows:

Objects

Children with ASD may develop a fascination for objects that are not necessarily unusual in themselves but the intensity of the interest in them is (e.g. postage stamps, electrical goods).

Activities

Examples of a preoccupation with activities include a liking for certain games or toys (e.g. marble runs) or a profound liking for particular children's television shows or videos (e.g. *Toy Story, Thunderbirds, Wallace and Grommit, Thomas the Tank Engine, Teletubbies*).

Pursuit of knowledge

This could include:

- an intimate knowledge of the bus timetable for a whole area
- an in-depth knowledge of cars, their makes and manufacturer's details
- a fascination with aspects of science (e.g. UFOs, aliens)
- a fascination with aspects of history (e.g. Egypt, war)
- a fascination with people's personal details (e.g. ages, heights, shoes sizes, jobs)
- a fascination with football league tables or stadium capacity sizes
- an in-depth knowledge of collectors' cards (e.g. football cards or Pokémon cards).

Environment

Examples may include:

- a fascination with time
- a fascination with changes in the environment
- a fascination with who is or is not in the building (e.g. at school)
- a fascination with directions to and from a place.

Preoccupations with sensory interest or parts of objects

Sensory interests are discussed in Chapter 6. A preoccupation in sensory interests might occur when some children become preoccupied with parts of objects: a toy car is not used as a car, but the wheels or the doors of it become the focus of interest and are repetitively flicked.

Principles for intervention

When considering what interventions would be useful it is worth first considering a number of factors that may influence your decision about how or whether to try to do something about the problem. Consider:

- the impact on family life
- your energy levels!
- the likely resistance to any change.

These important issues apart there is one particular way to focus on the child's difficulties that sometimes helps families to clarify whether or not to try to do something about the problem.

	My child now	My child in the future
Is the problem behaviour likely to impair my child's social or intellectual development?		

Figure 17.1: Should I seek to change the behaviour?

If the answer to either of these questions is yes then it is usually worth thinking about ways to improve the situation. For example, if a child has a preoccupation for wiping the wall with a cloth and will do so for several hours per day, it is likely that this will adversely impact on that child's intellectual and social development because it is an all-encompassing activity that stops the child doing anything else. It may have its place in relaxing the child at times but if it becomes prolonged and entrenched it is likely that you will want to do something to limit it.

If a child has a preoccupation for kissing people (regardless of who they are) parents and carers may consider this harmless enough in infancy but if it becomes an entrenched behaviour it may go on into teenage years and adulthood and may markedly impact upon a young person's acceptance into social circles. It may even get him or her into trouble. It will be worth looking at ways of limiting this behaviour: for example, establishing a rule that the child should only kiss his brothers and sisters, aunts and uncles, parents and grandparents.

It is important to remember that our aim in helping children with preoc-cupations may be to limit their behaviour so that it no longer intrudes exces-sively, not necessarily to prevent it completely. Children usually get a great deal of enjoyment out of these activities and preventing them can be coun-ter-productive. If they only have a few interests, removing one of them is likely to cause distress. Also, we know that new, different preoccupations are likely to take their place.

Preoccupations are not all bad. They can be used to encourage social interaction with less anxiety and facilitate some aspects of communication.

Preoccupations are largely things that the children enjoy, but some may be centred on fear. Children are more likely to need help addressing these. We describe three examples in this chapter. There are numerous others. We describe two preoccupations that were enjoyed but very repetitive and stuck, and another that caused distress.

TYPES OF PROBLEM

- Preoccupation with lining things up

- Preoccupation with rollercoasters

- Intense fear of glitter

WHAT is the problem?

Preoccupation with lining things up

Justin was a six-year-old boy with autism who spent long periods of time lining things up. He would line up cars several times a day. In the bath, he would line up sponges and soaps around the edge of the bath. He lined up plastic construction bricks in the lounge as soon as he got home after school. He would want to do this on his own, did not like others to move anything he had arranged and would invariably know if someone had moved something while he was out of the room. For a period of time he would get towels out of the linen cupboard and line these up all over the floor of the living room. He particularly liked lining up yellow things.

We used the behaviour management template described earlier in the book (see Chapter 9).

1. What is the problem?

Lining things up in play. Justin's parents would like his play to progress from only lining things up.

2. Why does your child behave in this way?

Situations and settings: Where does the behaviour happen? Where does it not happen? Is it to do with something in the environment (smells, noises, what other people do, etc.)? Who is around when it happens?	Usually in the lounge. Seems to like others to be around, but doesn't want them to join in.
Triggers and timings: When does it happen? Is it to do with anything pleasant or unpleasant)? What are the timings in relation to other things? When does it not happen?	When he has free time. More when bored or happy.
Mindblindness: Is it to do with mindblindness? Does your child realise he/she needs to communicate his/her needs to someone? Can your child see others' points of view or understand feelings and needs of others in this situation?	Doesn't realise when he builds things that he might be in the way of other people. Not tuned in to the stress it can cause in the family.
Getting the gist: Is the problem associated with not understanding what is going on and why? Does your child understand the meaning of events and that things have a certain order?	Doesn't seem to have got the gist of play with toys or with his sister.
Imagination: Does your child think imaginatively and does this affect the behaviour?	Has no imaginative play. This seems important because his play has little imagination in it and so never progresses from lining things up and patterns.
Preoccupations and sensory experiences: Is the problem associated with sensory experiences and/or preoccupations? Is the environment too complicated or interesting?	Interested in patterns and the colour yellow.
Social interaction: Does your child do this alone or with others? How does this affect the behaviour?	Never seeks social interaction. Tolerates it when it is given. Plays alone but likes to be in the vicinity of family members.
Communication: Is the problem associated with language or communication difficulties?	Has difficulty communicating his needs.

Emotions: Is the problematic behaviour related to anxiety or mood? Is it to do with your child's temperament? Is there anything else that might be affecting or upsetting your child (e.g. memories, dreams, illness, tiredness, boredom)?	Does not do it when tired, ill or upset. Does it when happy or bored.
Sameness: Is it to do with a need for routine or habits? Is there a problem associated with being in control? Has there been a change of routine at home or at school?	Likes routine. Seems to want to do it when he comes in from school.
Responses: How have others responded to the behaviour? Does something happen after the behaviour that is important? How does it affect the behaviour in the future?	We [his parents] don't get cross, but don't get involved. His two siblings are not interested in what he is doing and so don't play with him.
Benefits: What positive outcomes happen for anyone (e.g. you, your child or your child's sibling) as a result of the behaviour? (Rack your brains: there usually *are* some!)	He feels calm and secure when playing in this way. It keeps him occupied when we are doing other things

3. What is the goal?

Justin's parents spent some time discussing what the goal should be. At first they thought it should be to help him to play imaginatively but when they applied the SMART principles (specific, measurable, achievable, realistic and time limited) they decided this was not specific enough and probably not achievable in the short term. Instead, they tried to break the long-term goal of helping him to play imaginatively into much smaller parts. They decided a good starting point was *helping him tolerate a parent playing with him for five minutes in his lining-up games.* Once he could tolerate this it would be possible to build on it, introduce flexibility to his play and eventually introduce some simple imaginative ideas.

4. Plan strategies

Justin's family suggested a variety of strategies. His parents realised that they would have to plan carefully. They would have to choose a time when both parents were available as one of them would have to look after his active younger brother at the same time so that he did not intrude. They decided that one parent (usually Dad) would offer to get the bricks out, and if Justin got them out himself Dad would get down on the floor with

Justin, and initially just sit near him. He would then handle the bricks but would let Justin move them where he wanted. On each occasion Dad would get a little more involved.

5. Checking

This plan would benefit both Justin and his parents. It might be tiring but his parents thought it worthwhile, and Justin's older sister was also enthusiastic once it had been explained to her.

The outcome

The plan worked well. Justin was able to tolerate his parents playing with him and after about ten days he began to tolerate his sister playing with him too. The family went through the process again and generated further incremental goals to do with his play. Over time Justin's play became more flexible and he began to build towers with his parents.

WHAT is the problem?

Preoccupation with rollercoasters

Jonathan was a 15-year-old boy who was preoccupied with rollercoasters. He knew information about every rollercoaster in Britain, the US and Europe. Whenever he met new people he would discuss rollercoasters very soon after meeting them, asking lots of questions (often not waiting for the reply before answering himself) and quoting lots of facts. His wall was covered in pictures of rollercoasters and he liked to go on the Internet to look up rollercoaster sites.

WHY might this be happening?

Sensory interests

Some of Jonathan's preoccupations seemed to be to do with his interest in movement and patterns. From a young age he was fascinated by his fingers when he held them in front of his eyes. As he got older he would wave his fork backwards and forwards in front of his eyes apparently fascinated by the patterns. When older still he developed an interest in pylons, and would want to stop and look at them and sometimes rock from side to side watching the patterns that this made. He also liked scaffolding and would want to go and see the scaffolding outside a local church which was being repaired.

Anxiety

Jonathan appeared to use talking about rollercoasters as a way of calming himself. It was a topic he knew a lot about and was interested in. In social settings where Jonathan was anxious he would fall back on the topic of rollercoasters to get him through.

Getting the gist

Jonathan was not as interested in going *on* the rollercoaster, and the exhilaration of this, as he was in facts *about* the rollercoaster. When he was taken to see one he would walk around it, studying the structure and watching, but he rarely went on it. He hadn't really got the hang of the social aspect of rollercoasters.

Mindblindness

Jonathan did not understand that other people were not all interested in rollercoasters. He could not discriminate between interested people and those who were not interested. He could also not tell when he was boring someone when talking about rollercoasters. In addition, he would jump into talking about rollercoasters before the pleasantries of getting to know someone were over. He often didn't even bother saying 'hello'. This showed a lack of understanding of the needs of others in conversation and a lack of understanding of social cues.

HOW might we deal with it?
Sensory interests

Rollercoasters seemed a natural extension to Jonathan's interests in patterns and pylons. He seemed interested in the metal structures that held them up as well as the wheels and the rushing cars. His parents were relieved that this was a more socially acceptable interest than his previous interests in pylons and scaffolding. In fact they had encouraged it as a way of moving him away from less socially acceptable interests. Some professionals call this 'shaping' an interest and his parents very successfully did this.

Anxiety

In many ways it was appropriate for Jonathan to use rollercoasters to get him through social situations. It calmed him down and allowed him to interact with others. It would not be appropriate to stop Jonathan altogether.

Getting the gist

There is always a trade-off between wanting young people with ASD to improve their social skills and allowing them to do things that help them to be in social situations even if they are at times socially awkward. Jonathan did not have the same understanding and motivation for his interest in rollercoasters as other young people do. His was more technical and to do with patterns and shapes and so he did not really get the gist. However, this particular interest allowed him to enter social situations with more confidence and this was a good thing.

Mindblindness

Jonathan struggled to understand what others' interests were, when they were bored with him talking or what their needs in a conversation were. These were things his family set about helping him with. At home the family set time limits for when and how long he could talk about rollercoasters. They also taught him very clear rules for what to say and do with someone you meet before being allowed to talk about rollercoasters. The school staff met with his parents and an educational psychologist to reinforce these rules in school. They also had some good ideas.

Jonathan liked these rules and stuck to them. They included how to introduce himself and what the verbal rituals of this were (e.g. 'How do you do, my name is Jonathan.' [pause] 'What is your name?'). If talking with a child he learnt to ask how old they were. If talking to an adult, he learnt to ask where they lived instead. (One child we know who was taught to ask new acquaintances their age, used to ask everyone he met without realising that this is a question that is more acceptable to children than to some adults.) He would then ask what their hobbies were before proceeding to tell them all about rollercoasters. The family were happy with this and thought that it worked well.

WHAT is the problem?

Intense fear of glitter

Nathan is an 11-year-old boy with Asperger syndrome. He worries when he sees glitter. His fear increases the nearer he gets to it. It is not clear why he has such an intense fear of glitter. His mother believes that he was born with it. On talking with him it is clear he has an instantaneous fear but also seems to fear that it may get into his mouth and cause problems. This may have been made worse when he was younger and another boy used to taunt him by putting glitter in his own mouth. He can spot glitter in small amounts even when others have not seen it. When he is concerned that there may be glitter around he becomes distracted, loses concentration and can shout out that he has seen glitter. He refuses to enter situations where the glitter is (or might be) and this has led to conflict (e.g. in school).

WHY might this be happening?

Sensory interests and fears

Nathan may be interested by the sight or texture of the glitter. However, he does not mind sand or tin foil. It was clear that he had an intense fear brought on by sight of glitter. He went pale and clammy and looked very frightened.

Things that keep the behaviour going

It is worth thinking about whether Nathan gets any benefits from his fear of glitter. The situations in which Nathan has complained about seeing glitter are in shops, at parties and in school situations. It is possible that all of these are difficult social situations for him and that by showing that he is afraid, he gets to leave the situation. Getting away from the social situation may be a desired outcome for Nathan that reinforces the fear of glitter.

At home Nathan shouts for his mother, who is very well aware of the problem. She sorts it out for him, usually by changing the course of events (taking him out of the shop, or picking up the glitter and disposing of it).

Nathan's teenage sister, Sophie, has learnt that he hates glitter. She is frustrated that he is poor at understanding boundaries. She frequently found him wandering in and out of her bedroom when she did not want him to. She found this intrusive until she discovered that if she laid a line of glitter across the doorway he would not come in to her room!

Teachers have sent him home because of conflicts (e.g. when he refused to go into the hall because he had seen glitter, and he refused even when the head teacher was called). He likes being at home and so this did not help.

Difficulty getting the gist

Nathan may never have fully understood the purpose of glitter. Like children who fear laughter or clapping (both of which we have come across) glitter represents a social signal for celebration, and Nathan may have difficulty with the social nuances associated with celebration. In just the same way that certain foods may be associated with unpleasant events (e.g. a school meal we were forced to eat in childhood may lead us to develop a revulsion to it) glitter may be associated in Nathan's early life experiences with unpleasant social situations.

Mindblindness

Nathan does not understand the teacher's standpoint when the teacher tries to force him into situations where there is glitter. The teacher has been known to say things like 'Come along, it's only a bit of glitter – it won't hurt you' and then physically shepherd him into the situation saying 'You'll get used to it'. Nathan does not understand the teacher's need to be in control and have all her children in one place doing the same thing. Similarly, the teacher appears not to understand Nathan's powerful fear.

Communication

Nathan will often not see the need to explain to adults what he is upset about or why.

Temperament

When Nathan is tired or unwell or upset, his reaction to glitter seems amplified.

HOW might we deal with it?

Nathan and the family set themselves the goal of being able to be in the same room as glitter without fear that prevented everyday activities. This was a specific, measurable, achievable, realistic goal (SMART). The family brainstormed possible solutions by using the list of headings under 'WHY might this be happening?' to consider the problem in more depth.

Sensory interests and fears

A desensitisation process was considered (see Chapter 9 'Managing Behaviour'). Mum wrote a long list of potentially fearful situations for Nathan and he gave them scores. She discovered that his fear of glitter in a paperweight was 0 because he felt it could not get out. They drew up a hierarchy using Nathan's list of fear scores. They set targets and rewards. He started by making glitter by cutting up tin foil and gradually worked his way up the list with family and school support.

Things that keep the behaviour going

Mum began to consider when it was appropriate to rescue Nathan and when it was better to support him to find his own solutions. This was considered both for situations where glitter was present but also in social situations. The family liaised with school about Nathan's difficulties to help them gain better understanding both about the problem and how to help him with it.

Clear rules about bedrooms were established so that Sophie would not have to revert to using glitter to keep Nathan out of her room. Nathan likes rules and so this was thought to be useful.

There were difficulties helping the teachers understand how much of a problem this was for Nathan. The education autism adviser was asked to give advice to teachers.

Difficulty getting the gist

The family had already begun to help Nathan understand the context of glitter (e.g. at parties and Christmas) although Nathan still struggled to cope with it being around outside these contexts.

Mindblindness

Some attempts were made to help Nathan understand the teacher's perspective. The strength of Nathan's fear and his mindblindness made this difficult.

Communication

Teachers and family decided to be more proactive in finding out from Nathan the cause of any distress that he showed.

Summary

There are too many preoccupations to consider all of them in detail in this chapter, but the principles remain the same. Is the preoccupation a help or a hindrance to development? Can the preoccupation be shaped in such a way as to help the child's development? If it looks to be a damaging preoccupation (either now or potentially in the future) what strategies can be used to help the child learn alternatives?

- Do not try to prevent preoccupations entirely (unless they are dangerous) – just put limits on them (e.g. where, when, how long, with whom, etc.).

- Only try to change preoccupations:
  - if they are causing impairment of social or intellectual development
  - if they will be unacceptable later in life (e.g. stroking women's legs)
  - if they start to control family life (e.g. dictating what colour clothes people must wear!).

- Try to think of ways of using preoccupation to help the child's development.

Chapter 18

Compulsions, Routines and Rituals

Children with ASD are more likely to develop compulsions, obsessions, routines and habits or rituals than other children. It may be worth clarifying what we mean by some of these words.

- *Obsessional thoughts* are repetitive, troubling thoughts or images. An example would be a thought that repeatedly and intrusively enters your mind even when you don't want it there. A feature of the obsession is that the individual feels some dislike of or resistance to the thought, but still cannot get it out of his or her mind. This creates a distinction from:

- *Preoccupations,* which are intensely held likings for things. These preoccupations (unlike obsessions) are not unwanted intrusions that are resisted or disliked by the individual. Quite the reverse, they are pursued with vigour. Preoccupations may be based around normal interests but are very intense or may be based around very unusual interests. Preoccupations are common in ASD and are covered in Chapter 17.

- *Compulsions* are more like obsessions but involve actions and they are discussed in this chapter. A compulsion is a repeated, powerfully felt need to do something. A compulsive *routine* or *ritual* (not the same as a religious ritual) is a series of actions, usually performed in the same order and springing from an intense need to repeat them. This might involve always walking the same way around furniture, getting dressed in a particular way or requiring members of the family to be in particular places when you are eating certain breakfast foods in the same order every day. It might involve touching all the radiators on a route from one place to another in the house or treading on all the manhole covers up the street. Some children have a compulsive desire to visit the same shops every time they go into town, or a need to go by exactly the same route. Going wrong or missing out part of the routine or ritual may lead to distress or a need to repeat part or the whole of it again.

Most children will have routines around getting ready for school and bedtimes. These are normal. They form part of the structure of everyday healthy life. The compulsive routines and rituals in ASD are very unusual in either content (see below) or intensity (very extreme or lasting for long periods of time). Some compulsive routines and rituals have a negative effect on everyday life, both for the young person and his or her family. Many of them start as something small and gradually build with the child regularly adding new parts to the routine. Peter was five when he began to insist that the door to the sitting room always had to be closed when he was in the room. As time went by this extended to other doors and, when he was six, he would come home from school and close all the doors in the house as soon as he got home. By the age of seven he was having tantrums if anybody insisted on having any door or window open when he was around. This was dealt with using a reward-based system that helped him to tolerate doors and windows being open.

Most routines are helpful

In general routines that give structure and are harmless are good. They make children with ASD feel safe.

Some routines are unhelpful

Unhelpful routines include those that are:

- impossible to complete
- difficult to maintain consistently
- very time consuming
- likely to increase in complexity with time

- interfering with contentment or daily living.

TYPES OF PROBLEM

Two examples are given below as illustrations. A ritual or abnormal routine can develop around almost any activity.

- He can't leave the house until a lengthy compulsive routine is completed

- She hovers in doorsteps unable to move

We will take each of these in turn considering WHAT the problem is, WHY it might be happening and HOW we deal with it.

WHAT is the problem?

He can't leave the house until a lengthy compulsive routine is completed

Jacob, aged seven, has a morning routine that lasts over half an hour each morning. It involves family members having to stand in certain places while a range of activities have to occur; these are not directly related to getting ready. Jacob starts in his bedroom, requiring all family members except his mother to be downstairs. Everything has to be off the floor. He will move to his parents' bedroom where a complex set of actions involving the mirror and antiperspirant spray takes place. He dresses in a certain order and then has to walk down the stairs grimacing and doing a small jig on the landing and then having to place his Teletubby soft toys in very particular places in the sitting room where no-one is allowed to disturb them. This may all take half an hour and only then can he have his breakfast. If anything does not go to plan then Jacob has to go back and start again.

Why might it be happening?
Mindblindness

Jacob has no idea of the needs of others in the house. He does not understand the frustration of his parents who also have to get him, his siblings and themselves all ready to get out of the house.

Getting the gist and time perception

Jacob does not understand the importance of getting out of the house in time for school. He doesn't really care what time it is. All he has in his head is what he needs to do in the here-and-now. Most children will do things for a purpose over and above the action itself. This is because they get the gist. For example, Jenny (Jacob's older sister) helps her mum bake a cake in the context of preparing a meal for the whole family. Jacob might do it because he likes the patterns of the flour. Jenny uses the antiperspirant because she wants to be like Mummy or because she does not want to sweat too much when with her friends. Jacob likes the sound and the sensation of the spray. Jenny alters her behaviour to fit in with the context and the meaning. Jacob does not.

Liking for routine

Routine makes Jacob feel comfortable. It is far preferable to the social world and its nuances, which he doesn't understand. The routines make his life predictable and make him feel more safe.

Sensory interests

Many of the elements of Jacob's routine are related to his sensory interests or preoccupations. He likes the sound of the spray and he is preoccupied with Teletubbies. These things dominate his thinking and he likes to pursue them.

Anxiety

Jacob has anxieties about social situations. He may be under stress as school time approaches. While he does not understand his parents' stress, the atmosphere in the house with people rushing about and shouting instructions may make him more anxious. He may need more ritual to fall back on to help him cope.

HOW might we deal with it?
Mindblindness, getting the gist and time perception

Jacob benefited from knowing what the morning routine was supposed to be. This involved using a visual timetable with pictures of him and his family doing things as they prepared to leave the house and then a picture of him in the car with his mother and sister. When he is older feedback and discussion about the needs of other members of the family will help him.

A social story also helped Jacob understand the context of some of the events that went on in the morning, and a timer was a useful way of letting him know how long he had before he had to leave the house in the car.

Liking for routine

Routine that helped Jacob feel safe was good but needed to be kept within time constraints, so that it did not affect family functioning. The visual timetable was very powerful for Jacob. Because it was written down in a clear order it seemed to have more power. His mother made flaps that covered each one as they were finished. Jacob enjoyed covering each flap in turn as things progressed.

It is always important to stop children's attempts to add more and more bits to the ritual. Better to have little moans and complaints as you strive to stop additions to the rituals, than larger problems later on. The longer rituals go on, the more difficult they will be to stop. Help your child with short, satisfying routines (especially around bedtime and mornings).

Sensory interests

Jacob's parents considered his sensory interests in this situation. They made some things less readily available and reduced clutter and distractions in the rooms he used. They also minimised potential negative sensory factors. For example, they made sure that the fabric of his school clothes was comfortable for him and liked by him.

Anxiety

Jacob had anxieties about social situations. His parents thought that he might be under stress as school time approached. While Jacob did not understand his parents' stress, the atmosphere in the house with people rushing about and shouting instructions made him more anxious as he had no idea of the needs of others in the house. His parents adopted as calm an approach as possible.

With time Jacob's need for a special routine diminished. This was initially because of the careful planning his parents put into the above. The visual timetable worked particularly well. It initially included aspects of his rituals. With time his parents gradually reduced the elements of the rituals by taking them out of the timetable, item by item, starting with the actions to which he was least attached. Jacob now has a very short and manageable routine.

WHAT is the problem?

> She hovers in doorsteps unable to move

For two years Samantha, aged 15, was encountering increasing difficulty with her ability to change from one activity to another. This was very noticeable when she had to get up and move anywhere new or when she had to go through a doorway. She would stand at the doorway, hovering, swaying and looking anxious and then all of a sudden after a minute or two she would jump through the door. The time she spent standing there was getting longer and longer. The doctors had variously called this 'autistic catatonia', 'ambi-tendence', 'motivational stuckness' and a 'volitional problem'. It didn't really matter to her parents what it was called, but it was affecting Samantha's life in a big way. At school the teachers had to coax her into the classroom. At home she often got stuck with a piece of food on the end of her fork, apparently unable to put it in her mouth. When asked what she was thinking, either she could not explain or she would say that there was a right time for her to go through the door and that she had to go at this precise moment. She wasn't quite sure how she knew when this was but she waited until it felt right.

WHY might it be happening?
Mindblindness

Samantha knew that other children laughed at her but she didn't always tune in to why. She was not good at changing her behaviour in response on how she was perceived.

Getting the gist

Most of us think about events in life in an holistic way. That is, we understand the school routine and have an overview of the place of learning and socialis-ing in school. To Samantha school seemed to be a series of set routines that she had to learn.

To us the door is incidental. We hardly notice it as we go into a classroom. To Samantha it took on a big significance as the gateway from one difficult social situation to another.

Time perception

Samantha has always had problems with time perception. She struggled when she was younger with delays. When she knew something was going to happen she wanted it to happen 'now'. She struggled with concepts like 'next week' or 'later'. As she got older she developed a habit of wanting to delay things. Whenever her parents said they were about to go out with her, she would disappear to the bathroom and hover there. This problem with time perception linked in with her liking for routine and difficulties with change.

Liking for routine/struggle with change

Samantha always had problems changing activities. This could be on a day-to-day basis (changing class, or the activity within class) or over time (moving school). Routines made life predictable and made it feel safer.

Socialisation and anxiety

Samantha's parents felt that much of the delay was due to social anxiety. They felt that she hated thresholds because a new threshold was a new social challenge.

Biology

Research shows us that sometimes genetics or biology (for example, something chemical in the brain) has an influence on how we behave. ASD is more likely to lead to compulsive behaviours or odd movements of the body, and so this may be important here.

HOW might we deal with it?
Mindblindness

Even though Samantha didn't always tune in to the expectations of others intuitively, the teachers found that if they gave very clear messages about what was expected this helped her. Simple structure like 'It is two o'clock now, it is time to come into the classroom' was helpful to her. They found that regular prompts also helped.

Getting the gist

The family and teachers used visual timetables to help Samantha understand the daily routine and how different events followed from each other. A social story about what was going on, the reason for particular activities and expectations may have also helped.

Time perception

Samantha's problems with time perception were addressed by using visual timetables but also, on occasion, using a timer clock to time certain activities.

Samantha found it easier to attend to things when she had a rule to follow (for example, that teatime was at six o clock). While her parents had to be careful that this didn't become too rigid an expectation, they initially found it helpful. When Samantha was getting stuck on the threshold of the doorway, a prompt sometimes helped but parents also used the strategy of Samantha counting down ('three, two, one, go'). Even though this ran the risk of becoming an obsession it dramatically reduced the time it took her to go through doors.

Liking for routine/struggle with change

The school used Samantha's liking for routine. They found she struggled less with things when they established a clear routine that was flagged up well in advance. Any changes were discussed clearly with Samantha and her parents and she was helped to negotiate her way through these.

Socialisation and anxiety

Samantha was helped with her social skills through a range of strategies outlined in Chapter 10. In the short term the school also introduced ways of trying to reduce anxiety. As well as those we have mentioned, Samantha had some aromatherapy with the school nurse and she enjoyed this very much.

Biology

While Samantha didn't need any help other than that discussed above, some young people may need medication to help with obsessions and compulsions.

Other ideas and techniques that might be helpful

Preventing or limiting

Milly, aged nine, wanted to have more and more cuddly toys with her every time she went out of the house. She began by carrying armfuls and then asked her parents to do so too. They then let her fill a pillowcase with them and she also then wanted her parents to carry extra ones. She began to have temper tantrums if she could not. Her parents used a restriction strategy where they limited Milly to five cuddly toys for each trip. At first she had great difficulty choosing and had tantrums saying she wanted more, but her parents stuck to their guns and rode out a week of tantrums. She gradually got used to the new rule. After six months they changed the rule to two cuddly toys and she got used to this successfully within three days.

Milly also loved to play with water. She would regularly tip it from one jug to another anywhere she could. In the past she had played with water from the toilet. She liked to stay in the bath for long periods. Her parents were worried about the length of time she would do this when left. Numerous floors and carpets had been soaked over the months and years. They also worried about her catching bugs when she played in the toilet.

Milly's parents used a successful three-stranded strategy to address this. They made a visual timetable with Milly playing with water in the sink in the kitchen (the kitchen floor could take it!) at certain times in the week. The cat didn't particularly like it as this was where she had her basket and she occasionally got soaked. She took to crawling into a nearby cupboard.

Milly's parents used an egg timer at first to restrict the time and always had a pleasurable activity for Milly afterwards. The egg timer became unnecessary after a while. They made up a socials story (see Chapter 10, 'Developing Social Skills') about where Milly did and did not play with water. These strategies worked well.

Desensitisation

Desensitisation is a very common technique used in managing anxiety, and it can be used for lots of different issues. The idea is that large amounts of anxiety are difficult to tolerate, especially if the child doesn't have good understanding. Small bits of anxiety can be faced and, if the child learns to face them, it empowers her to move on in steps until, before she knows it, she is dealing with the feared situation.

Amy was five and compulsively banged her head on her desk or other surfaces at school. This was so bad that she was fitted with a protective cap. After careful observation it was clear that she head-banged when she was in big groups and a guess was made that this was to do with social anxiety. She never did it in small groups.

A plan was drawn up that took two terms to work through. Amy was taught for a lot of the time in a class adjacent to her normal class in her special school and initially this was with two other children she was happy with. This fitted with teacher availability. She did not head-bang in these sessions and her cap was removed. As time went by more and more people were added until all nine children were in the class. This was done gradually and any interactional problems dealt with as they went along. A year later Amy was not head-banging.

Shaping

Shaping is a technique where the child's compulsions or special interests are steered in a direction that might be helpful to the child. The Options or Son-Rise system uses aspects of this approach (see Chapter 20).

Timothy was 13 and had a compulsion to touch people's shoes and smell them. He was very interested in them and always looked at people's shoes when he saw them. When younger he would often get down on the floor and want to touch them. Some people did not like this, for obvious reasons. Timothy would do it with strangers as well as people he knew.

Timothy's family tried punishments, which did not work and made them feel bad. They tried to reward alternative behaviours but this met with little success. They then decided that if they couldn't stop his interest they would try to shape it or change it so that it was more socially accept-able. They taught Timothy to introduce himself to people and not to go straight to their shoes. They taught him to ask certain socially appropriate questions (such as what their name was) first and then, later, to ask ques-tions about the shoes rather than touch them.

Timothy was happy with this and would regularly ask people what size shoes they had, whether they were made of leather and where they bought them. People found this much more socially acceptable.

Rewarding wanted behaviours

Stella, aged seven, compulsively wanted to visit the same two shops every time the family went to town. She would scream and complain if they went into any other shops. This was a problem because her mother wanted Stella to be able to go out and was getting near the point where she never took Stella anywhere. She thought this was bad for Stella, who needed to experience the world outside their house. At the same time she was exhausted by the screaming, by being under stress for everyday shopping and by the looks and comments of strangers. She explained to Stella that she would receive a sweet for every shop that she went into with Mummy. Stella's mother was surprised that this worked very well. She began by introducing one or two shops but soon extended this to other shops. Stella still wanted to go into her two shops but her mother had no difficulty accepting this since she could now go into other shops.

Rewarding alternative behaviours

Some children who have compulsions to do certain things can be helped to do different things instead.

Dale, aged six, screeched for long periods of the day. He was fascinated, in music therapy, with long, slow, soft, singing noises. After ten sessions much of his loud screeching had been substituted with humming and singing in a soft lilting way. His family were very happy with this. The reward came from his pleasure in the noise. His family also learnt to use music in the house to calm him.

There may be other ideas that you can use to change or cope with compulsions.

Summary

Before the hard work of trying to tackle compulsions ask yourself the questions:

- Is it harming my child's development? (If not, sometimes the compulsion has an important function in reducing anxiety or giving pleasure.)

- If so, can I help my child to change so that his or her development is helped or improved?

- How can I do this in a way that is manageable and acceptable (apply the SMART principles outlined in Chapter 9, 'Managing Behaviour').

Chapter 19

Mannerisms and Repetitive Movements

Children with ASD commonly exhibit mannerisms, odd movements and repetitive movements. Examples of these include spinning around, flapping hands by the sides, running up and down in straight lines, tapping objects repetitively and moving the fingers in front of the eyes.

When is it worth trying to reduce these unusual movements? For the most part children find them comforting. We also know that many of these movements reduce as the child grows. Many of the planned interventions for children on the autism spectrum concentrate on aspects such as communication, social interaction and behaviour. Repetitive movements often improve when these things are targeted; for example, encouraging interaction with parents reduces repetitive behaviours.

> Philip was six and, when given a book to read, would throw it to the floor and dance around it, circling it and humming to himself.

It may be worth specifically targeting repetitive movements if they:

- are excessive and so get in the way of other aspects of life
- attract bullying
- are hurting the child or someone else
- interfere excessively with family life.

TYPES OF PROBLEM

- He flaps his hands and jumps up and down
- He bangs his head repeatedly

We will take each of these in turn considering WHAT the problem is, WHY it might be happening and HOW we deal with it.

WHAT is the problem?

He flaps his hands and jumps up and down

The morning routine of Jacob, aged seven, was long and complex (see Chapter 18). He also had a lot of repetitive movements. When the washing machine was going he would stand in front of it and jump up and down on the spot and flap his arms repetitively. When he watched the television he would hover at the door, approaching and moving away from the television. When exciting parts came on he would jump up and down on tiptoes and shake and flap his hands. He also flapped his hands when he was excited.

WHY might it be happening?
Mindblindness and the social world

Jacob had no idea what other people thought of his movements. He was not able to guess that other people might find them odd and so was not likely to change his behaviour because of the opinions of others. He was also much less likely to want to communicate his pleasure or excitement to others because he was unable to understand that they might wish to share his excitement.

The confusing social world can be frightening. Repeated movements can be a comforting way of experiencing the environment. They may also block out other scary bits.

Getting the gist and sensory interests

Jacob did not understand the function of the washing machine; he was very interested in the vibration, the spinning and the noises. He was more likely to pursue activities that he enjoyed and these were mainly sensory.

Anxiety, boredom and liking for routine

Sometimes Jacob displayed his emotions in the movements. He was more likely to flap or shake his hands when under stress or bored. Jacob was not as good at entertaining himself as some children.

Imagination

Jacob had clear problems with imagination. He was more interested in the concrete aspects of his environment than the abstract aspects of it. He liked to watch and do things that were repeatable. His lack of imagination meant that his interests and play did not naturally evolve by imaginative experimentation or addition as did other children's.

HOW might we deal with it?
Mindblindness and the social world

Getting involved with Jacob would help him understand that two people could be doing the same thing together. He would be able to find alternative ways of displaying his pleasure. When Jacob was younger his movements may have been the only way he could express emotions but, as he gets older, he may find other ways to express them. By the time Jacob was seven he was able to understand several facial expressions on cards. He could use an emotion thermometer (see Chapter 10, 'Developing Social Skills') when he was nine. Helping Jacob to understand the social world and cope within it has been something that his family and teachers have been gently helping him with for years. As he has become older he has used less repetitive movements.

Getting the gist and sensory interests

Jacob's family began to get involved with Jacob in some of his sensory interests. His father learned that Jacob's liking of movement and physical sensations also meant that he liked rough and tumble, and games like 'Row, row, row the boat' when he was younger and other games when he was older. He became fascinated with Dad's golf indoor practice hole and Dad made up a game involving rolling the ball from one hole to another. They used to play together and Jacob's family was pleased that his play became less isolated. His family began to shape his interests into more interactive ones by using his existing interests. While he was doing these things the unusual movements lessened.

Anxiety and boredom and liking for routine

The family realised that leaving Jacob for long periods of time led to more unusual movements. There were times when he needed to relax and watch television but the family made sure that this time was not too long. They had always been tuned in to his distressing times and discussions about his repetitive movements reinforced for them the importance of doing this. Jacob's liking for routine helped because when he knew what he was doing he felt safer and the repetitive movements were less.

The family also began to think of things that Jacob could do when he was bored. The school began to look for strategies to help him learn how to entertain himself. Jacob enjoyed playing on the computer at school. He was making huge progress with his schoolwork through spending time on it. He was allowed to go on the computer for ten minutes when he had finished his other work. His teachers found that this acted as an incentive for him to finish his work but also prevented him from getting bored and flapping excessively.

Jacob's parents invested in a home computer and, within a relatively short time period, he was able to use simple programs with their help. In fact they found sitting alongside him at the computer was one of the best ways to encourage him to engage with them. They were careful to limit the amount of time he spent on the computer from the beginning, as they realised that he needed a variety of different activities to prevent him from becoming preoccupied with any one thing in particular.

Imagination

Given Jacob's problems with imagination, his teachers and family made sure that Jacob always knew what was going on around him and what was expected of him in given situations. They found that giving him factually-based educational tasks was much more likely to engage him than anything abstract. He really enjoyed his work sheets, particularly for maths, and gained a great deal of satisfaction from completing them.

WHAT is the problem?

He bangs his head repeatedly

Head-banging can be:

- an expression of frustration, anger, fear, pain or boredom (emotional expression)
- to elicit liked sensations or reassuring repetition (sensory interests)
- to get the environment to respond (to elicit consequences).

Sometimes what starts as one (e.g. sensory interest) can develop to another (to elicit consequences).

It is always important to try to work out why the child might be head-banging before you begin any intervention.

Amy, whose story is in Chapter 18, used to bang her head at school whenever she was with a large group of children. Her teachers were able to help her by trying to keep the group small where possible and only gradually over time introducing more children to her group.

Sebastian, aged three, started banging his head with his hands and later banging it on the floor or the wall in his bedroom. His head-banging started suddenly and for no apparent reason. He was unable to tell his parents what was wrong. They began to wonder if he was unwell and took him to see their doctor. The doctor examined Sebastian carefully and found that he had a severe infection. Fortunately, this was easily treated with antibiotic medication.

Tony, a six-year-old, used to bang his head on any hard surfaces whenever he was asked to do something he didn't want to do. Mostly he liked to play with his Lego, and any suggestion of change from this usually started a tantrum that led to head-banging. Tony's head-banging was a very effective strategy from his point of view as his parents and other adults were reluctant to cross him in case he hurt himself. He had learnt that if he banged his head, he could continue doing the things he liked best. He had been head-banging since he was two years old.

Tony's parents had tried being firm with him in the past but were horrified when he began to fly into a rage and hurt himself even more. As he was getting older, his parents became very concerned that this behaviour was detrimental to his development. He spent most of his time playing with his Lego. He would not join in any learning or social activities at school. Finally, his parents and teachers agreed that they should work together to try to change his behaviour while at the same time keeping him safe.

WHY might this be happening?
Sensory stimulation

When Tony first started head-banging at the age of two, his parents could see no obvious reason for it. His family thought that, in an odd way, he enjoyed banging his head. He did not appear to feel the pain his parents would have expected even though he sometimes bruised himself. Surprisingly, he rarely cried during head-banging episodes. As Tony grew older, they noticed that most of the time he banged his head when he wasn't getting something he wanted, although he still seemed to feel very little pain.

Tony's head-banging seemed to have begun as a repetitive behaviour from which he gained a sense of enjoyment and satisfaction. Some children with ASD do not seem to feel pain in the same way as other children. It is possible that they may have increased levels of beta-endorphins, which are similar to opiates. It is thought that when some children head-bang, for example, they do not feel the pain but experience exhilaration.

Parents' response

Tony's parents were very alarmed when he banged his head when he was younger. Not surprisingly, they went to him and comforted him. They tried distracting him with his favourite toys like Lego, and at night brought him into their bed. As the months went by, Tony started banging his head when he wanted something or didn't want to do something. His parents had tried to be firm with him but felt that they couldn't leave him to continue to bang his head as he sometimes bruised or cut his head on sharp edges. They found themselves allowing him to control situations in order to protect him. By doing this, they were inadvertently reinforcing his behaviour. Tony had learnt that head-banging resulted in him getting things he wanted. A behaviour that had started out as self-stimulation had been extended to a way of having his needs met.

Getting the gist

Tony did not get the gist about schoolwork or about playing with other children. All he really wanted to do was play with his own toys and, when left to his own devices, was a very happy boy. It was only when he was challenged in some way that his tantrums and head-banging started.

Preoccupations

Tony was preoccupied with Lego. It had been his main source of enjoyment since he was two but unfortunately this was impinging greatly on his development. While he was playing with Lego, he was not learning communication or social skills, or engaging in schoolwork.

Temperament

Tony had always been very strong-willed and determined. When he was a baby he had cried more than most babies.

Communication

Tony had a very limited use of language. His parents had spent a great deal of time trying to work out and meet his needs because he was unable to communicate with them.

HOW might we deal with it?
Sensory stimulation

Tony's parents noticed that head-banging seemed to be pleasurable in some way for him. They thought that, if this were the case, making it less pleasurable might help to reduce it.

Parents' response

After discussions between themselves and his teachers, Tony's parents realised that they had been reinforcing his behaviour with their responses. Mostly this was because they were afraid that he would really hurt himself.

They agreed that while they were trying to help him to stop head-banging, they would have to keep him safe. They knew that the behaviour would get worse at first when they began to change their own responses. They decided that he should wear a protective helmet, they hoped just for a short time, until the situation improved.

Communication

Although Tony's verbal language ability was very limited, he had started using PECS (see Chapter 20, 'Other Interventions'). Tony was very good at requesting his favourite things with them and, in particular, used the symbols for Lego and Playmobil (another of his favourite toys). Other than this, his main form of communication was through his head-banging. Unfortunately, his head-banging was preventing him from developing more communication skills because it was an effective strategy for helping him to get what he wanted anyway! His parents and teachers decided that they needed to help him to develop his communication skills. They started by teaching him about choices.

LEARNING ABOUT CHOICES

The plan was that Tony would be offered choices at first – Playmobil or Lego. Although Lego was his firm favourite, Playmobil could often distract him. His teachers put out Playmobil and Lego and allowed him to choose. Over the next few days, they put out only Playmobil, explaining 'Playmobil first, then Lego', using PECS symbols. The Playmobil was out for a few minutes only before his teachers produced the Lego. The teachers used an egg timer to help Tony to understand when it was Lego time. If Tony started to protest and bang his head, his teachers gently said, 'No banging. Playmobil first, then Lego' and showed him the PECS symbols. If he continued they took away the Lego symbol showing him the symbols for Playmobil or quiet room. (Fortunately, there was a quiet room adjacent to the classroom. This was a comfortable, safe room with soft furnishings and calming music.) This way Tony was given a choice to stay and play as the teacher had requested or to go with her to the quiet room. If he continued protesting she led him to the quiet room and stayed with him until he calmed down. He had his helmet on as agreed with his parents in order to ensure that he didn't hurt himself.

Interestingly, although Tony tried to bang his head at first, he soon stopped. When he calmed down his teacher would repeat his choices – Playmobil or quiet room. Tony quickly learnt that the quiet room was very dull and produced his Playmobil PECS card. He then played with the Playmobil for a while before it was time to play with his Lego.

Encouraged by their success, Tony's teachers began to introduce other activities in the same way. There were many occasions when he protested loudly, particularly at the beginning, but as time went on, he began to realise that his teacher stuck to the new rules regardless of any head-banging. Over the coming months, he even learnt to use the quiet room card as his choice if he wasn't ready to do the activity his teacher had prepared. He sat in the room for a few minutes before agreeing to the new task. Tony only wore his helmet for a few weeks as his head-banging stopped remarkably quickly.

Tony's parents used a similar strategy at home. They knew that it would be difficult at first and whenever possible asked friends and relatives for their support. At school there were several teachers around, but at home his parents were often on their own. It is also much harder for parents to be firm with their children in situations like this because they are emotionally very involved and do not like seeing their children distressed. Tony's parents were lucky to have supportive friends who helped them through the difficult early days. They also wrote themselves a card, which they kept in a prominent place, reminding them that learning to communicate with PECS cards was important for his development and much less harmful than head-banging.

Tony's parents were pleasantly surprised to find that they were able to remove Tony's helmet after only a few weeks and also that this exercise paved the way for his progress with using PECS symbols for a growing number of requests.

Protective helmets

It is important to remember that protective helmets may work in different ways depending on the child and the problem. Amy banged her head more with the helmet on and taking it away dramatically reduced the behaviour; whereas the helmet temporarily reduced Tony's head-banging because it took away the stimulation. There must be careful consideration of the problem and the child before any plan is put into place. This is a good illustration that strategies cannot be used straight off the shelf. They need to be tailored to the child and the situation.

Other ideas and techniques that might be helpful

Working out what the behaviour achieves for the child

If you go back to Chapter 9, 'Managing Behaviour', you will see a template or process for exploring the meaning of any behaviour. This then leads clearly on to what you can do about it. This is particularly important for self-harming behaviours such as biting, head-banging, scratching or poking at the eyes. Similarly it can be used for behaviours that involve harming others. If it is clear that a particular behaviour achieves something for the child (it has a function) then parents and teachers can work out alongside the child ways of achieving the same thing without the harm to self or others. This would usually involve reinforcing and rewarding alternative behaviours (see Chapter 9).

Being a detective and watching out for the flag

Sometimes, repeated behaviours are a flag for something else.

> Jonathan used to regularly rub his ears. This was a new behaviour but Jonathan's parents thought that it was to do with dislike of noise, until his teachers mentioned that they thought he wasn't hearing well in class. When he was taken to the doctor it was found that he had middle ear infections on both sides. The doctor thought that he must be in pain. Jonathan hadn't cried but he had been rubbing his ears a lot.

Sometimes repetitive behaviours are because of physical symptoms or other things such as pain, hunger, thirst or tiredness. They may be because the child is unhappy.

Altering the response

Sometimes it is possible to change a behaviour by altering the response to it. In Chapter 9 we discussed how Zaffar's repetitive biting was stopped when Mum altered her response to it.

Ignoring

Ignoring a behaviour can work if the behaviour is designed to elicit a particular response from an adult. The behaviour will initially get worse if you start ignoring it but usually then gradually disappears (see Chapter 9).

Encouraging an alternative behaviour

Sometimes children can be discouraged from their repetitive behaviours for short periods of time by being encouraged to do something else instead.

> Harry used to flap his hands in assembly at school. His teachers found that telling him not to flap didn't help much. Instead they encouraged him to 'Stand like a soldier' or suggested 'Hands in pockets'. They also gave him toy soldiers to put in his pockets so that he could play with these when he was bored.

Changing the environment

The physical environment may be changed in such a way as to change the behaviour.

> Jessica liked to jump up and down on the wooden floor in the playroom. She didn't do it in any other room and only occasionally at school. The family noticed that she would always do it directly on the wood and would avoid the rug. Sometimes she would move the rug back. They twigged that she liked the sound on the floor. The decided to put a carpet down. Jessica was annoyed and stamped and shouted on occasion in the playroom for about a week after they did this, but settled down after this and the jumping dramatically reduced.

The environment more directly related to the child may also be changed.

> Anya relentlessly chewed her sleeve. Her parents put her in short-sleeved outfits in the summer and this stopped.

Summary

- Mannerisms and repetitive movements are much more common in younger children. They tend to reduce as children get older.

- Children find these movements comforting. For this reason it is better to try to find ways to reduce them rather than to eliminate them altogether.

- Repetitive behaviours usually reduce when children are helped to develop social interaction skills.

- Reducing boredom also helps reduce repetitive behaviours.

- Some mannerisms and repetitive behaviours begin as self-stimulatory behaviours but can easily develop into controlling behaviours e.g. head-banging.

Chapter 20

Other Interventions

How do families know what works?

Parents whose child has been newly diagnosed with autism or ASD will receive many suggestions about treatment. A search of the term 'autism' on the Internet identifies over one million sites. Many of these proffer treatments and even 'cures'. Some of the centres offer good, sound advice. Some are trying to make money and are selling products, assessments, books and treatments. How do parents and carers make sense of all of this? More important, how do they know which are valid and which are not? The answer is that they often don't. There may be thousands of new 'treatments' arriving on a yearly basis and professionals are often asked about them. Imagine that, of 100 new treatments of various types (e.g. diets, massage, homoeopathy, medication, individual therapy, group work), one of them in twenty years' time would be shown to be a very successful treatment. How do we know which of the 100 it will be?

The miracle cure?

Reports of miracle cures regularly appear in the papers but the story of one person may sometimes give a distorted impression. We know two children with ASD:

Sophie and John improved dramatically at a point in time for no reason that we can ascertain. They were on no specific treatment. They probably improved as part of normal development.

After all, children's brains are growing. One of the good things about children on the autism spectrum is that they still develop. As we have pointed out in many chapters of this book, things like mindblindness improve (they are developmental – they improve with time as children grow). If, for the sake of argument, we had given Sophie and John vitamin C tablets just before they improved and told their parents that this was a new trial for autism treatment, then their parents would now be writing articles in the national press saying that vitamin C dramatically improved things for their children. We would then have people all over the country trying it. Some would give up, some would carry on, some children would improve and their parents would then swear by it. They would write notes on the Internet and in the national press. None of the parents who try these things and whose children don't improve would be reported in the national press. There is, therefore, a 'selection bias' in the newspapers that distorts the information we receive. This is not a criticism: it is what happens. Parents feel terribly let down when, years later, they discover from a trial of a large number of children that this treatment makes no difference.

Randomised controlled trials

So, how do we know a treatment really works? If it looks promising then research-funding organisations pay for research often called randomised controlled trials (RCTs). This means that roughly equal numbers of children are divided into two groups; one receives the treatment and the other receives something else. This is usually another treatment but is sometimes a placebo (something that looks like the treatment but isn't, e.g. an identical capsule with inactive substance in it). This is important because it rules out chance and controls for normal development. If we did a study about helping non-walking children who were 12 months old to walk, and we gave them a 'treatment' from the age of 12 to 15 months that showed that 80 per cent of them walked by 15 months, how would we know that it wasn't just a feature of them growing older? We could only know this by comparing to a similar number who did not receive this treatment. For the test to be really fair we would have to toss a coin (randomise) to put children into the two different groups.

Some examples

There are lots of treatments that have been recommended that have no good research studies to back them. For example, *gluten-free diets* and *casein-free diets* have been suggested as treatments for ASD but have no RCTs to show that they work (or that they don't). This does not mean that they don't work, just that good research has not yet been carried out and so good evidence is not yet available. We know many parents who think these diets have made no difference and a small number who are convinced that they have. Is this a real effect or an example of some of the factors mentioned above? As clinicians we really can't say for certain. We need an RCT before we can give good advice to families.

A good example of an apparently effective treatment is *secretin,* a naturally occurring hormone, which was lauded in the papers as a new treatment for autism based on single reports. Some suggested that it was a wonder cure. Several RCTs have since shown no benefit.

Sometimes even the science can be called into question. *Homoeopathic secretin* was for some time being suggested as a cure for autism. However, homoeopathy is based on the principle that extremely minute doses of a substance that causes a symptom should be given to prompt the body into healing responses. For example, the common hedgerow poison Deadly Nightshade (Belladonna) causes thirst and high fever if eaten accidentally. With this in mind it was used in its homoeopathic form using a process that includes dilution down to a very weak solution (sometimes theoretically less than one molecule of substance in a tablet or solution) for children with high fever. Giving homoeopathic secretin would only make sense if secretin itself caused symptoms of autism and since at the time it was being hailed as a cure for autism, homoeopathic secretin made no sense even in homoeopathic terms.

Your child's needs come first

In summary, be careful when assessing evidence before you try something. Some treatments can be harmful as well as helpful. If your child is a very faddy eater then restricting her diet may make her nutritionally deficient and harm her developing brain. Similarly, some behavioural regimes are very strict and intense. Make sure that you are not emotionally or physically harming your child before you agree to try something. You know your children best. Information is there to help you, but just because it is in a newspaper or on the Internet does not automatically make it right.

The rest of this chapter concentrates on approaches, philosophies or programmes that involve a range of interventions not discussed elsewhere in the book.

Treatment programmes

Several intervention philosophies have been developed that pay close attention to the environment of the child to maximise his development. Some of these have very strong proponents and some have strong opponents. We know of some adults with ASD who speak for and some who speak against some of the programmes we are about to describe. Our view would be that to become emotionally too attached to any one approach is probably a mistake. Many of them are similar. They are, by and large, commonsensical approaches and all have good ideas that you can borrow. This book is not intended to cover these in detail, but gives simple information about some of these approaches and details of contacts if you want to find out more.

Some parents in the UK seek funding from education authorities for extra help. While most education authorities provide a range of services for children some of the suggestions below may not be funded because of very high cost and restrictions in education budgets.

Adapted Hanen programme

In 1977 the Hanen Centre was established at the School of Human Communication Disorders in McGill University, in Montreal. In 1995 the Hanen Centre developed a new programme, which it has since called 'More than Words', for parents of children with ASD. In 2000 it held its first training workshop for speech and language professionals on 'More Than Words'. Much of it is down-to-earth, good advice such as keeping language simple in communication, being face-to-face with children and listening carefully to them.

Applied Behavioural Analysis

This phrase has come to describe a certain type of intense programme based on behaviour therapy and has come to be used to describe many of the programmes that have evolved since Lovaas (see below). Keenan, Kerr and Dillenburger (2000) have written a book describing their use.

Auditory integration training

This is different from Sensory Integration Training (mentioned below). It uses sound as a way of exposing the child to a range of auditory experiences. Devices with headphones are used playing music that can be altered and controlled. Dr Guy Berard is an ear, nose and throat specialist in France and a proponent of this type of work.

Another French ear, nose and throat specialist, Dr A. Tomatis, called a listening treatment using sound 'audio-psycho-phonology'. He also used sessions with headphones that could control and filter sounds. The children listen to music such as Mozart and Gregorian chant and listen to themselves by feed-back from a microphone. He believed that it helped listening skills and self-awareness skills in children with autism. It can be used to filter out certain types of disliked sounds. In this way a desensitisation approach can also be used where over sensitivity to noise is a problem. Gradually exposing children to feared or disliked noises helps them to tolerate them better in their environment.

Diets

Numerous diets have been suggested for easing some symptoms of ASD. To date research has not confirmed their effectiveness. Gluten-free and casein-free diets are the most common. (Gluten is in wheat, rye and barley and casein is in dairy products.) The theory is that the proteins in gluten and casein break down in the gut into toxic peptides. These peptides usually go through our system without any problem. Proponents of this theory believe that children with ASD have 'leaky guts' which allow the peptides through the walls of the gut into the bloodstream. They are then said to get into the brain (cross the blood–brain barrier) and cause damage to its functioning. There is, however, no evidence to date from RCTs to show that taking gluten and casein out of children's diet leads to changes in the development of children with autism.

Dolphins

A range of centres offer swimming with dolphins as a therapeutic activity. We have met some families who have taken their families to swim with dolphins. At the very least they have all enjoyed the experience. There has, however, been little independent evaluation of its effectiveness. More information is available through the National Autistic Society (NAS) in the UK or the Autism Society of America (ASA).

EarlyBird

The EarlyBird Project was originally set up by The National Autistic Society (NAS) in 1997 to develop and evaluate a parent training programme. This is now available in most parts of the UK. It is designed for parents of pre-school children on the autism spectrum as an early intervention programme. Parents attend on a weekly basis for three hours. They commit to ongoing work with their child at home. It is a twelve-session programme that trains parents in families of six. It includes three home visits when video feedback is used to help parents reflect on skills that they are learning. It aims:

- to support parents in the period between diagnosis and school placement, particularly in understanding autism

- to empower parents and help them facilitate their child's social communication and appropriate behaviour within the child's natural environment

- to help parents establish good practice in handling their child at an early age so as to pre-empt the development of inappropriate behaviours.

A three-day training course for trainers in the licensed use of the NAS EarlyBird programme and its supporting materials is available at the EarlyBird Centre in West Barnsley, Yorkshire.

Higashi

Daily Life therapy was developed in Japan by Dr Kiyo Kitahara and others. Schools in Tokyo and Boston are well known. It centres its philosophy on the Japanese culture of group performance and belonging. It boasts a 24-hour curriculum that focuses on daily living skills, physical education, music and craftwork. Schools in Japan and America use this approach, and in the UK it is available through the Honormead schools.

Lovaas

Dr Ivor Lovaas from the University of California developed an approach in the 1960s and 1970s based on behaviour therapy. It involves 40 hours of intense

home-based therapy per week with the child. The programme is very structured and requires high levels of compliance from the child and a great deal of
repetition. Several therapists are employed. Trained supervisory therapists are
usually paid to guide the programme and give advice and support to other
therapists. Many parents will join the team of therapists and some train friends
as volunteers.

The programme uses positive reinforcement to encourage learning. Some
have wished to adapt the programme over the years including reducing the
hours and the rigidity of the programme and basing it more in schools. Some
parents are very keen on Lovaas, others less so. The success rates due to this
method are reported to be variable. Some note that social skills learnt by rote
in this way are not easily generalised.

Mifne

The Mifne Center was established in 1987 in Israel. 'Mifne' is the Hebrew
term for 'turning point'. Mifne is an early intervention programme for families
with an affected child under the age of five. In common with other
programmes it centres its approach around reciprocal play with the child. It
does this in a family context. Also like some other programmes it uses a team,
working intensely with the child and the family to generate more communicative opportunities. Goals are set around improving eye contact, the expression
of affection and social awareness.

An intense, residential three- to four-week programme is offered for the
nuclear family, with eight hours' 'therapy' a day for seven days a week. The
affected child, parents and siblings are encouraged to react to any of their
child's responses to build interactions. Therapists employed by the centre have
backgrounds in education, medicine, psychology and special education and
are trained in the Mifne approach (this takes up to a year). With only two
families in treatment at one time there may be long waits and treatment is
costly.

After the family returns home, a therapist from Mifne stays with the
family to help them transfer some of what they have been doing into the
home. Together with the family, the therapist helps integrate the affected
child into school and arranges supplementary therapy as needed. The Mifne
Center tries to maintain longer-term relationships with the family for support
and advice.

PECS: The Picture Exchange Communication System

In PECS, children are taught to exchange pictures for items they want. If they want a biscuit, for example, they give a picture of a biscuit to an adult, who responds immediately. The idea is that the communication is initiated by the child.

The programme starts with single pictures and moves on to choices and later the construction of more complex sentences. The pictures are stored in a portable book and can be attached and removed easily because they have velcro strips on the back. (See Chapter 11 for an example of its use.)

Sensory integration training

Dr Jean Ayres was an occupational therapist and psychologist in Los Angeles. From the 1960s she developed an approach based on the theory that some children's nervous systems would not integrate and understand sensory input (what we see, hear, touch, etc.). The theory suggests that understanding our senses provides us with a composite picture of the world and allows us to plan what to do and how. Furthermore, according to this theory, the integration of sensory input isn't working properly in autism.

While this is true, as we know from theories around getting the gist (see Chapter 5), some have questioned how the theorists get from here to the suggested interventions, which are targeted at individual programmes where sensory stimulation is purported to train up the child's sensory system. This is done primarily by giving children lots of diverse sensory experiences through occupational therapy and physiotherapy and a range of activities. Sensory integration theory seeks to explain over- or under-reaction to stimuli and inappropriate responses. Sensory integrationists also propose that tactile defensiveness (seen in those children on the spectrum who hate to be touched) is to do with this theory, although in our view it is probably explained better by difficulties the child on the autism spectrum has in understanding the social meaning of touch, and problems with unusual sensory experiences and preoccupations (Chapters 6 and 17).

Son-Rise program, the Option Institute and the Autism Treatment Center of America

The Kaufmann family drove the development of the Son-Rise program as a division within the Option Institute and the Autism Treatment Center of America and this has been going now for over 20 years.

The Option Institute is in Sheffield, Massachusetts, USA. Son-Rise is an approach to treatment and education designed to help children with autism and their families and carers. It relies on some key principles that include:

- actively joining in a child's repetitive or unusual behaviours in an attempt to facilitate more social interaction

- focusing on the child's motivations and interests to facilitate learning and the acquisition of skills

- encouraging interactive play and using this for learning

- maintaining a caring, non-judgemental and positive attitude in interactions and expectations

- acknowledging that the parents or carers are the child's most important and lasting resource

- creating a safe, distraction-free work/play area.

This approach exploits the child's interests and the adult interacts with what the child is doing. It very much relies on getting down to the child's level. It suggests that social interactions and learning are best facilitated through the child's own interests. Therapists are specifically asked not to dominate or become directive in play and interactions. Therapy begins in the playroom, set up to specific guidelines and required to be quiet and decorated without intense colours or fuss. The approach recognises that the autistic child's anxiety inhibits interaction and learning, and that environments and activities that minimise anxiety will best facilitate learning. Therapists will often be parents and volunteers who are trained on special courses.

SPELL

The National Autistic Society (NAS) in the UK has used an acronym to put some sort of framework around interventions. It recognises that all interventions should be tailored to the individual but suggests that there are key areas where adults and children with ASD have experiences that lend themselves to intervention.

The acronym for this framework is SPELL, which refers to:

- Structure (to the environment and activities)

- Positive approaches and expectations

- Empathy

- Low arousal

- Links.

TEACCH (Treatment and Education of Autistic and Related Communication Handicapped Children)

The TEACCH approach was developed in the 1970s by Eric Schopler and others at the North Carolina School of Medicine Department of Psychiatry. The approach seeks to help people with ASD pursue life and independence to the best of their potential supported in the community. In 1972 the North Carolina General Assembly passed legislation mandating creation of the division for TEACCH. It was the first American state-wide, comprehensive community-based programme dedicated to improving both the understanding of autism and services for children with autism (and other communication disorders) and their families.

The major priorities include focusing on the individual, understanding autism, and a broadly-based intervention base building on existing skills and interests. TEACCH has as its philosophy the notion that people with autism are part of a distinctive cultural group, not inferior to people without autism. Each programme is tailored to the individual – recognising everyone is different. Organising the physical environment, developing schedules and work systems, making expectations clear and explicit and using visual materials have been effective ways of developing skills and allowing people with autism to use these skills independently of direct adult prompting. Close attention is paid to the learning and social environment and giving a clear structure to all teaching (for example, minimising distractions such as visual stimuli or noise). The importance of parents and of the relationship between home and school are emphasised.

TEACCH suggests structured teaching is important but does not dictate where people with autism should be educated. This is a decision that must be based on the skills and needs of each individual student. While deficits are addressed there is a focus on cultivating strengths and interests and maximising potential. TEACCH is a lifetime approach that recognises changing needs. It suggests the need for periodic assessment and monitoring to keep interventions developmentally appropriate.

TEACCH provides services such as assessment and diagnosis, individualised curriculum development, social skills training, vocational training and parent counselling and training. In addition TEACCH clinic staff provide consultation to a range of professional groups. Parents and teachers can be trained in the TEACCH approach.

Medication

There are no known complete cures for autism, using traditional medicine, herbal medicine or homoeopathy. Drugs and medicines do not treat the core features of autism. To date we don't have any clear evidence to show specific brain biochemical abnormalities. Most treatments for conditions where brain biochemistry is affected (such as Parkinson's disease) have a clear logic and rationale for using particular medicines. We do know that children with autism may be more likely to have higher levels of a chemical called serotonin (5 hydroxy tryptamine) in their blood and, although we know that serotonin is an important chemical in the brain, specific brain abnormalities have not yet been found. We may know more in the future but at the moment there is no logical rationale for any specific medication based on known biochemical brain abnormalities in ASD.

This leaves uncertainty, and also means that many parents and clinicians have tried many different things. The overall message is that educational and behavioural treatments should currently remain the first port of call for dealing with ASD. Sedating children to control behaviour is in our view not ethical. In practice, then, when medication is used it is often on an *ad hoc* basis rather than with the backing of proper research. Very few of the medications used are licensed for use with children or autism. If you have any specific questions about this you need to ask your own family doctor.

Doctors using medication often end up treating symptoms associated with autism rather than the autism itself. Some of the more helpful drugs used are as follows. We have described groups of drugs rather than specifically named medications because, as we write, new advice about restrictions of certain drugs is being given and new research is reporting its findings. For more information go and see your own doctor.

Serotonin reuptake inhibitors (SSRIs)

There are several SSRIs and they are usually used for treating depression and obsessive-compulsive disorder in adults without autism, although professionals are currently advised to avoid using several of them in young people. Doctors sometimes give this type of medication to children who have autism with lots of compulsions, intense preoccupations and repetitive behaviour.

There are some studies of young people with ASD that show that this medication may improve repetitive behaviour and also, on occasion, aggression.

Dopamine blockers

Some clinicians have found that drugs that are used for psychoses (like schizophrenia) may help to reduce challenging behaviour, although most clinicians would want to try a range of other behavioural strategies before considering this. One of the problems with these medications is the side-effects, including potential long-term side effects such as movement disorders. Always discuss these with your doctor when weighing up potential benefits and risks.

Dopamine enhancers

Some clinicians use stimulants (which act in the brain at dopamine and other neurotransmitter sites) to improve severe symptoms of inattention and overactivity. There is very good evidence that these drugs alleviate symptoms of ADHD. So if your child has this as well as ASD this may be suggested by doctors. They probably work less well in young people with moderate to severe learning difficulties and so are more commonly used in Asperger syndrome where ADHD is also a problem.

Adrenaline and noradrenaline systems

Some drugs, such as clonidine, may help with overactivity in autism.

Homoeopathy

There are numerous remedies that are used by many parents to manage stress, anxiety and extreme behaviours. Again, there are not many RCTs to show effectiveness (a deficiency in much of autism research) but we have come across no evidence of any serious harm being caused to children on the autism spectrum, and many parents advocate its use.

Other medication

Some doctors use melatonin, which is the natural sleep hormone, to help with sleep disorders in autism. There are no good research studies to show how well this works and it may suppress naturally produced melatonin, but some case reports have suggested that in some circumstances it works well. It should only be used alongside behavioural treatments similar to those mentioned in the chapter on sleep.

Many other medications have been suggested on some websites or by particular clinicians but research evidence does not support their being recommended by most doctors at the current time. To discuss some of these medications (such as mood-stabilising drugs, beta-blockers, opiate antagonists or anti-fungal agents) it would be important to see a specialist. Even though there are many people requesting them and case reports suggesting they help in some circumstances, there is surprisingly little evidence from proper research studies.

Summary

There are many, varied approaches used to help children with ASD. Only a small number of them have been mentioned here. The National Autistic Society has produced a book covering more approaches in greater detail (NAS 2003). So far, we have not come across any miracle cures, but we have found that several of the approaches described here have been of great benefit to children with ASD and their families.

Early intervention is in our view essential (for example EarlyBird) and TEACCH approaches have revolutionised classroom layout, structure and activities to the benefit of children with autism spectrum disorders. Other strategies such as the Picture Exchange Communication System can make a large contribution to improving communication. Several of the programmes such as Son-Rise also recognise the strengths of creative parenting and the importance of not leaving children to their own devices, but engaging regularly with them from an early age.

Chapter 21

Final Thoughts

We hope that families and professionals find this book useful. We would like to hear from any parent or carer who has found interventions or strategies helpful, and we will try to build them into the next edition. We are learning all the time. We have tried to make the book accessible, and to explain up-to-date theories of autism in an understandable way. We believe that this knowledge will be a source of power for families. The vast majority of parents and carers

we know are loving, caring families seeking to do their best for their children. We hope that this book will help them.

Bringing up children with ASD is much harder work than expected. We see the huge efforts that parents, carers and other professionals such as teachers make to help children develop. We would like this book to be an encouragement to them – recognising that it is at times exhausting, but giving a message that their work is worthwhile and can make a huge difference. We are often in awe of parents and carers and their commitment, and would like to thank so many of them who have taught us so much.

References and Resources

Chaper 2 – Assessment
Autism Diagnostic Interview – Revised (ADI-R)

Lord, C., Rutter, M. and Le Couteur, A. (1994) 'Autism diagnostic interview – revised: A revised version of a diagnostic interview for caregivers of individuals with possible pervasive developmental disorders.' *Journal of Autism and Developmental Disorders 24*, 5, 659–85.

Autism Diagnostic Observation Schedule (ADOS)

Lord, C., Rutter, M., DiLavore, P.C. and Risi, S. (1999) *Autism Diagnostic Observation Schedule – WPS (WPS edition).* Los Angeles, CA: Western Psychological Services.

Diagnostic Interview for Social and Communication Disorders (DISCO)

Wing, L., Leekam, S. R., Libby, S. J., Gould, J. and Larcombe, M. (2002) 'The diagnostic interview for social and communication disorders.' *Journal of Child Psychology and Psychiatry 43*, 3, 307–25.

Children's Autism Rating Scale (CARS)

Schopler, E., Reichler, R. and Renner, B. (1988) *The Childhood Autism Rating Scale (CARS) for Diagnostic Screening and Classification of Autism.* Los Angeles, CA: Western Psychological Services.

Checklist for Autism in Toddlers (CHAT)

Baron-Cohen S., Allen, J. and Gillberg, C. (1992) 'Can autism be detected at 18 months? The needle, the haystack, and the CHAT.' *British Journal of Psychiatry 161*, 839–43.

Wechsler Intelligence Scale for Children – Revised (WISC-R)

Wechsler, D. (2003) *Wechsler Intelligence Scale for Children, version IV.* Oxford: The Psychological Corporation, Harcourt Assessment Inc.

Diagnostic Statistical Manual of Mental Disorders (DSM-IV)

American Psychiatric Association (1994) *Diagnostic and Statistical Manual of Mental Disorders, fourth edition.* Washington, DC: APA.

Classification of Mental and Behavioural Disorders (ICD-10)

World Health Organization (1992) *Classification of Mental and Behavioural Disorders, tenth revision.* Geneva: WHO.

Chapter 3 – The Emotional Impact on the Family

Books that help siblings up to aged seven to understand ASD

Amenta, C. (1993) *Russell is Extra Special: A Booklet about Autism for Children.* New York: Magination Press.

Davies, J. (1993) *Children with Autism: A Booklet for Brothers and Sisters.* Nottingham: University of Nottingham, Child Development Research Unit.

Edwards, B. and Armitage, D. (1999) *My Brother Sammy.* London: Bloomsbury.

Gorrod, L. (1997) *My Brother is Different.* London: The National Autistic Society.

Lears, L. (1998) *Ian's Walk: A Story About Autism.* Morton Grove, IL: Albert Whitman.

Books that help siblings aged 7-13 to understand ASD

Bleach, F. (2001) *Everybody is Different: A Book for Young People who have Brothers or Sisters with Autism.* London: National Autistic Society.

Campbell, K. (2000) *My Brother has Autism.* Hertford: Hertfordshire County Council.

Harris, S.L. (1994) *Topics in Autism. Siblings of Children with Autism: A Guide for Families.* Bethesda, MD, USA: Woodbine House.

Hoopman, K. (2000) *Blue Bottle Mystery: An Asperger Adventure.* London: Jessica Kingsley Publishers.

Spilsbury, L. (2002) *What Does it Mean to have Autism.* Oxford: Heinemann Educational Books.

Sources of information for families

Attwood, T. (1998) *Asperger Syndrome: A Guide for Parents and Professionals.* London: Jessica Kingsley Publishers.

Baron-Cohen, S. and Bolton, P. (1993) *Autism: The Facts.* Oxford: Oxford Paperbacks.

Harris, S.L. (1994) *Topics in Autism. Siblings of Children with Autism: A Guide for Families.* Bethesda, MD, USA: Woodbine House.

Howlin, P. (1998) *Children with Autism and Asperger Syndrome: A guide for practictioners and carers.* New York: Wiley.

Chapter 4 – Mindblindness

Baron-Cohen, S. (1997) *Mindblindness: an essay on Autism and Theory of Mind.* A Bradford book. Massachusettes: MIT Press.

Wimmer, H. and Perner, J. (1983) 'Beliefs about beliefs: Representation and contraining function of wrong beliefs in young children's understanding of deception.' *Cognition 13,* 103–128.

Chapter 6 – Sensory Interests and Sensitivities

Williams, D. (1998) [1992] *Nobody Nowhere.* London: Jessica Kingsley Publishers.

Williams, D. (1998) [1994] *Somebody Somewhere.* London: Jessica Kingsley Publishers.

Chapter 9 – Managing Behaviour

Aarons, M. and Gittens, T. (1999) *The Handbook of Autism: A Guide for Parents and Professionals.* London: Routledge.

Davis, H., Day, C. and Bidmead, C. (2002) *Working in Partnership with Parents.* Oxford: The Psychological Corporation.

Fouse, B. and Wheeler, M.A. (1997) *Treasure Chest of Behavioral Strategies for Individuals with Autism.* Arlington, TX: Future Horizons.

Ives, M. and Munro, N. (2002) *Caring for a Child with Autism.* London: Jessica Kingsley Publishers.

Keenan, M., Kerr, K.P. and Dillenburger, K. (2000) *Parents' Education as Autism Therapists: Applied Behaviour Analysis in Context.* London: Jessica Kingsley Publishers.

Kaufer, F.H. and Saslow, G. (1969) 'Behavioural diagnosis.' In C.M. Franks (ed) *Behaviour Therapy: Appraisal and Status.* New York: McGraw-Hill, pp.417–444.

Schopler, E. (1995) *Parent Survival Manual: A Guide to Crisis Resolution in Autism and Related Disorders.* New York and London: Plenum Press.

Zarkowska, E. and Clements, J. (1994) *Problem Behaviour and People with Severe Learning Disabilities: The STAR Approach.* London: Chapman and Hall.

Zarkowska, E. and Clements, J. (2000) *Behavioural Concerns and Autistic Spectrum Disorders: Explanations and Strategies for Change.* London: Jessica Kingsley Publishers.

Chapter 10 – Developing Social Skills

Aarons, M. and Gittens, T. (1999) *The Handbook of Autism: A guide for parents and professionals,* 2nd. edn. London: Routledge.

Happé, F.G.E. (1994) 'An advanced test of theory of mind: Understanding of story characters, thoughts and feelings by able autistic, mentally handicapped, and normal children and adults.' *Journal of Autism and Developmental Disorders 24,* 129–54.

Holliday Willey, L. (1999) *Pretending to be Normal.* London: Jessica Kingsley Publishers.

Howlin, P., Baron-Cohen, S. and Hadwin, J. (1999) *Teaching Children with Autism to Mind Read: A Practical Guide.* Chichester: John Wiley and Sons.

Rubin, K. (2002) *The Friendship Factor: Helping Our Children Navigate Their Social World – and Why It Matters for Their Success and Happiness.* New York: Viking.

Understanding facial expressions – Software

Gaining Face
Team Asperger
324 East Spring Street
Appleton
WI 54991, USA
www.ccoder.com/GainingFace/

Cambridge University, research led by Simon Baron-Cohen (2004) *Mind Reading: The Interactive Guide to Emotions.* London: Jessica Kingsley Publishers.
Available from:
Jessica Kingsley Publishers
116 Pentonville Road
London N1 9JB
Tel: 0207 833 2307
Fax: 0207 837 2917
www.jkp.com

Understanding facial expressions – Videos

I CAN (1995) *See what I mean* (VHS video) I CAN: London.
Available from:
ICAN
4 Dyers Building
London EC1N 2QP
Tel: 0870 010 4066
Email: info@ican.org.uk
www.ican.org.uk

Stories with emotions and a range of facial expressions for children

Oxford Reading Tree books from Oxford University Press. *www.oup.co.uk/oxed/primary/ort*
Dale, P. (1999) *Big Brother, Little Brother.* London: Walker Books.
The Mr Men and *Little Miss* books by Roger Hargreaves. Manchester: Mr Men World
    International Publishing Ltd.
Hughes, S. (1983)*Alfie Gives a Hand.* New York: Lothrop, Lee & Shepard Books.
Lewis, P. (2001) *I'll Always Love You.* London: Little Tiger Press.
Mckee, D. (1996) *Not now Bernard.* New York: Random House.
Sendak, M. (1988) *Where the Wild Things Are.* New York: Harper Collins.
Wiesner, D. (1991) *Tuesday.* New York: Clarion Books.
Wright, B. and Young, O. *My Grandparents Play Tricks.* (unpublished).

CDs that help children learn empathy and imagination skills

Why do We Have To? and *Safety Scavenger Hunt* are CDs for a PC. (Alphabet Pals Series.) World
    Book Inc. (LRDC), Chicago, Illinois 1994.
Toy Story 2 Activity Centre CD (which links with the film). Disney/Pixar 2002.
Storybook Weaver. CD Deluxe 2004. *www.riverdeep.net*

Websites that explain idioms

The Idiom Connection *www.geocities.com/Athens/Aegean/6720/*
Self-study idiom site *www.a4esl.org/q/h/idioms.html*
A list of idiom websites *www.utexas.edu/student/esl/links/idioms.html*

Social use of language programmes

SULP (The Social Use of Language Programme) SULP was devised by Wendy Rinaldi for
children and adolescents (most recent edition revised in 2001). This is for professionals and takes
them through an initial one-to-one assessment of the child taking approximately 90 minutes
followed by individual teaching sessions lasting 45–60 minutes. Marketing and information from:
NFER Nelson Education
Customer Services
Unit 28, Bramble Road
Techno Trading Centre
Swindon

Wiltshire, SN2 8HB
www.nfer-nelson.co.uk

I CAN is a charity that helps children with speech and language difficulties. It includes courses relevant to ASD. Among other things they run training courses for professionals. These include social use of language programmes and a range of other courses. Information and manuals available from:

I CAN
4 Dyers Buildings
London EC1N 2QP
Tel: 0845 225 4071
www.ican.org.uk

Resources for improving social skills

The InterACT facility is an educational facility for people with ASD. They hold courses on interactional techniques and social skills. *www.theinteractcentre.com/*

TALKABOUT is a social communication skills pack devised by Alex Kelly that includes an assessment procedure. This is not specifically designed for ASD but has some helpful ideas for professionals. *www.alexkelly.co.uk/talkabout.htm*

Clinical Language Intervention Programme (1986) is a series of four worksheets: *Pragmatics, Semantics, Syntax* and *Morphology*. They are written by Semel Wiig and published by The Psychological Corporation (part of Harcourt Brace Jovanovich Inc.), Oxford. Each set costs £31.50 and they are sold only to professionals who register with The Psychological Corporation. UK telephone number for Harcourt Brace: 0207 267 4466.

Improving social skills

Csóti, M. (1999) *People Skills for Young Adults.* London: Jessica Kingsley Publishers.
Csóti, M. (2001) *Social Awareness Skills for Children.* London: Jessica Kingsley Publishers.
Johnson, M. (1998) *Functional Language in the Classroom.* Clinical Communication Materials, The Manchester Metropolitan University. (Available from the MMU Commercial Office on 0161 247 2535.)
Spence, S.H. (1995) *Skills Training: Enhancing Social Competence with Children and Adolescents.* Windsor: NFER-Nelson.

Social stories and social rules

Gray, C. (1994) *Comic Strip Conversations.* Arlington, TX: Future Horizons.
Gray, C. (2000) *Writing Social Stories with Carol Gray.* A video workshop. Arlington, TX: Future Horizons.
Gray, C. (2000) *The New Social Story Book* (illustrated edition). Arlington, TX: Future Horizons.
Gray, C. and Leigh White, A. (2002) *My Social Stories Book.* London: Jessica Kingsley Publishers.

Carol Gray's books and video are available from:
The Gray Center for Social Learning and Understanding
2020 Raybrook SE
Suite 302
Grand Rapids
MI 49546 USA
Tel: 616-954-9747
www.thegraycenter.org

Books for young people with ASD

Bleach, F. (2002) *Everybody is Different.* Kansas: Autism Asperger Publishing Company.
Hall, K. (2001) *Asperger Syndrome, the Universe and Everything.* London: Jessica Kingsley Publishers.
Hoopmann, K. (2001) *Of Mice and Aliens: An Asperger Adventure.* London: Jessica Kingsley Publishers.
Jackson, L. (2002) *Freaks, Geeks and Asperger Syndrome: A User Guide to Adolescence.* London: Jessica Kingsley Publishers.
Romanowski, B., Bashe, P.R., Kirby, B.L. and Attwood, T. (2001) *The OASIS Guide to Asperger Syndrome: Advice, Support, Insight, and Inspiration.* New York: Crown Publishers.

Circle of Friends

Bromfield, C. and Curry, M. (1998) NASEN. In-service Circle Time manual for teachers, Lichfield. *www.nasen.org.uk*
Newton, C., Wilson, D. and Taylor, G. (1996) 'Circle of Friends: An inclusive approach to meeting emotional and behavioural needs.' *Educational Psychology in Practice 11,* 4.
Whitiker, P., Barratt, P., Joy, H., Potter, M. and Thomas, G. (1998) 'Children with autism and peer group support: Using circle of friends.' *British Journal of Special Education 25,* 6–65.

Other helpful websites

The Picture Exchange Communication System. *www.pecs.com/*
Thinking Publications Inc. A US company supplying educational games, books, videos and software for teachers. *www.thinkingpublications.com*
Future Horizons Inc. A US publisher with books on autism, PDD, etc. *www.futurehorizons-autism.com*
LD-Online (US again). Follow the links via LD in-depth then social skills. Gives information about how parents may help young people to enhance their socail skills and how to tolerate annoyances. *www.ldonline.org/*
OASIS (On-line Asperger Syndrome Information and Support) has a large section devoted to social skills, including Circle of Friends and Skillstreaming. *www.udel.edu/bkirby/asperger*
Tony Attwood's site is full of helpful advice and papers, resources and books covering Asperger Syndrome and social skills. *www.tonyattwood.com.au*
EarlyBird site. The National Autistic Society had developed its own training programme for parents of pre-school AD children. This is called EarlyBird and teaches parents the skills they will need to understand and analyse their child's autism, facilitate communication, as well as understand, pre-empt and, if necessary, modify their behaviour. *www.nas.org.uk*
www.autism.net/html/gray.html

www.ccoder.com/GainingFace/Home.html

Mind reading. *www.jkp.com*

www.nfer-nelson.co.uk

Hesley Group website is a website where you will find details of the Hesley Group residential special schools and colleges for young people with special needs. OAASIS (q.v.) can send you their prospectuses. *www.hesleygroup.co.uk*

OAASIS produces a wide range of free information sheets and other publications (for which a charge is made). Send for a list and order form or check the website. *www.oaasis.co.uk*

The InterACT Centre is an education facility for adults and young people with autism and Asperger syndrome. They hold many courses (including social skills and interaction techniques) at:

Westcott Crescent

Hanwell

London W7 1PD

Tel: 0208 575 0046

www.theinteractcentre.com/

Developing communication skills

My First Incredible Amazing Dictionary (CD). London: Dorling Kindersley.

Chapter 11 – Developing Communication Skills

The Hanen programme – it takes two to talk.

This programme provides training to groups of aprents who have young children with delayed language development to help them play a key part in improving their children's language development. Available from:

Winslow Publishers,

Telford Road,

Bicester, Oxon.

OX6 0TS.

Tel: 0845 921 1777

www.hanen.org/

Educational software

www.dotolearn.com/ has pictures you can download for free. You can order a huge selection of others for a small price.

http://dir.yahoo.com/Business_and_Economy/Shopping_and_Services/Children/Software/ lists some of the popular childrens educational computer software.

Chapter 16 – Sleeping

Douglas, J. and Richman, N. (1988) *My Child Won't Sleep*. Harmondsworth: Penguin.

Durrand, M.V. (1998) *Sleep Better! A Guide to Improving Sleep for Children with Special Needs.* Baltimore, MD: Brooks Publishing Company.

Chapter 19 – Mannerisms and Repetitive Behaviours

Attwood, T. (1993) *Why Does Chris Do That? Some Suggestions Regarding the Cause and Management of the Unusual Behaviour of Children and Adults with Autism and Asperger Syndrome.* London: The National Autistic Society.

Chapter 20 – Other Interventions

NAS (2003) *Approaches to Autism.* London: The National Autistic Society.

Adapted Hanen Programme

UK	North America
9 Dungoyne St	The Hanen Centre
Maryhill	Suite 408
Glasgow	1075 Bay St
G20 OBA	Toronto ON
	M5S 2B1
	www.hanen.org/

Applied behavioural analysis

Keenan, M., Kerr, P. and Dillenburger, K. (eds) (1999) *Parents' Education as Autism Therapists: Applied Behaviour Analysis in Context.* London: Jessica Kingsley Publishers.

Institute for Applied Behaviour Analysis
5777 W. Century Boulevard, Suite 675
Los Angeles
CA 90045 USA
www.iaba.com

Auditory integration training

The National Light and Sound Therapy Centre
80 Queen Elizabeths Walk
London NI6 5UQ

The Listening Centre Ltd
16A Station Street
Lewes
East Sussex, BN7 2DB
www.listeningcentre.co.uk

Diets

Autism Research Unit
School of Health Sciences
University of Sunderland
Sunderland SR2 7EE

Dolphin therapy

More information is available through the National Autistic Society (NAS) or the Autism Society of America (ASA)

EarlyBird

NAS Early Bird Centre
3 Victoria Crescent
West Barnsley
South Yorkshire S75 2AE
http://www.nas.org.uk

Higashi

Higashi
800 North Main St
Randolph
MA 02368 USA
www.bostonhigashi.org

Honormead Schools Ltd
The Grange
Hospital Lane
Derby DE3 5DR

Lovaas

The Lovaas Institute for Early Intervention
2566 Overland Avenue, Suite 530
Los Angeles
CA 90064 USA
www.lovaas.com

PEACH (Parents for the Early intervention of Autism in Children)
The Brackens, London Road
Ascot
Berkshire SL5 8BE
www.uk.peach.org.uk

Mifne

Mifne
TMC, Swiss House
PO Box 112
Rosh Piuna 12000
Israel
www.mifne-autism.com

PECS: The Picture Exchange Communication System

UK

Pyramid Education Consultants UK Ltd
17 Prince Albert St., Brighton
East Sussex BN1 1HF
www.pecs.org.uk

USA

Pyramid Education Consultants
226 West Park Place
Suite 1
Newark DE 19711
www.pecs.com

Sensory Integration Training

Sensory Integration International
1514 Corbel Avenue
Torrance
CA 90501 USA
www.sensoryint.com

Son-Rise program, the Option Institute and the Autism Treatment Center of America

The Son-Rise program at the Autism Treatment Centre of America
2080 South Undermountain Rd
Sheffield
Massachusetts 01257 USA
www.option.org
www.son-rise.org

SPELL

The National Autistic Society
Services Division
Church House, Church Rd
Filton
Bristol BS34 7BD
www.nas.org.uk

TEACCH (Treatment and Education of Autistic and Related Communication Handicapped Children)

UK

The Training Services Dept National Autistic Society
Castle Heights, 4th Floor
72 Maid Marion Way
Nottingham NG1 6BJ

www.nas.org.uk

USA

CB7 180
310 Medical School Wing E
The University of North Carolina
Chapel Hill
NC 27599-7180 USA
www.teacch.com

Appendix 1:
A template for making sense of a child's behaviour and planning ways to help

1. What is the problem?

This is not as easy as it seems! Take some time with friends or relatives to explore this in some detail. Ask yourself what your child does (or does not do) that you would like to be different. Try to be very specific and not too general (e.g. 'refuses to put shoes on in the morning' is more specific than 'problems getting dressed').

2. Why does your child behave in this way?

Situations and settings: Where does the behaviour happen? Where does it not happen? Is it to do with something in the environment (smells, noises, what other people do, etc.)? Who is around when it happens?	
Triggers and timings: When does it happen? Is it to do with anything pleasant or unpleasant? What are the timings in relation to other things? When does it not happen?	
Mindblindness: Is it to do with mindblindness? Does your child realise he/she needs to communicate his/her needs to someone? Can the child see others' points of view or understand feelings and needs of others in this situation?	

Getting the gist: Is the problem associated with not understanding what is going on and why? Does your child understand the meaning of events and that things have a certain order?	
Imagination: Does your child think imaginatively and does this affect the behaviour?	
Preoccupations and sensory experiences: Is the problem associated with sensory experiences and/or preoccupations? Is the environment too complicated or interesting?	
Social interaction: Does your child do this alone or with others? How does this affect the behaviour?	
Communication: Is the problem associated with language or communication difficulties?	
Emotions: Is the problematic behaviour related to anxiety or mood? Is it to do with your child's temperament? Is there anything else that might be affecting or upsetting your child (e.g. memories, dreams, illness, tiredness, boredom)?	
Sameness: Is it to do with a need for routine or habits? Is there a problem associated with being in control? Has there been a change of routine at home or at school?	
Responses: How have others responded to the behaviour? Does something happen after the behaviour that is important? How does it affect the behaviour in the future?	
Benefits: What positive outcomes happen for anyone (e.g. you, your child or your child's sibling) as a result of the behaviour? (Rack your brains: there usually *are* some!)	

3. What is the goal?

What is your specific aim (e.g. 'Encourage Moses to interact with us for a few minuites each day')? Is the goal of benefit to you or the child or both? Give a thought to the future. You are trying to prepare your child for the future as well as dealing with the present. Check that it meets the SMART criteria below.

- *Specific.* Be clear and specific (e.g. 'Help Ali to say "hello" to Grandma', rather than 'Help Ali to be more sociable').

- *Measurable.* Have an outcome or something that you can see and count (e.g. 'Say "hello" to Grandma when she comes to visit').

- *Achievable.* Start with something that is possible to achieve, otherwise everyone will feel disheartened.

- *Realistic.* There is little point in trying to achieve something that is unrealistic. If the child has not learnt to speak yet, learning to say 'hello' is unrealistic.

- *Time limited.* Be clear that this is something you would like to achieve in a certain time period. It will help you to focus.

4. Plan strategies

With friends or relatives write down as many ideas as possible that come to mind about how you might deal with the problem, matter how silly they may seem – it's often these ideas that lead to creative solutions!

Choose the strategy (or combination of strategies) that you think is most likely to work and that you are most likely to be able to carry through.

5. Checking

When you have a plan, write it down and check:

- the benefits for everybody concerned

- the costs – it terms of emotions, time and resources

- what might get in the way to stop it working? (Find ways of dealing with these if possible before you begin.)

6. Put the plan into action!

7. Monitor progress

If/when problems occur, don't be disheartened, go through this process again thinking about when, where and why it's not working and plan additional strategies.

Appendix 2: Sample sleep diary B

	Mon	Tue	Wed	Thurs	Fri	Sat	Sun
Time to bed at night							
Time to sleep at night							
Time awake in night							
Time woke up in morning							
Time went to sleep in day for nap							
Time woke up in day after nap							
Total hours asleep							

Index